DISCIPLINE IN THE SCHOOLS
A Guide to Reducing Misbehavior

DISCIPLINE IN THE SCHOOLS
A Guide to Reducing Misbehavior

Samuel M. Deitz
Georgia State University

John H. Hummel
University of Houston Downtown College

Educational Technology Publications
Englewood Cliffs, New Jersey 07632

Library of Congress Cataloging in Publication Data

Deitz, Samuel M
 Discipline in the schools.

 Includes bibliographies and index.
 1. School discipline. I. Hummel, John H.,
joint author. II. Title.
LB3012.D44   371.5   78-18269
ISBN 0-87778-127-3
ISBN 0-87778-128-1 pbk.

Printed in the United States of America.

Library of Congress Catalog Card Number:
78-18269.

International Standard Book Number:
0-87778-127-3
0-87778-128-1 (paperback edition)

First Printing: September, 1978.

TO:

CHRISTOPHER, MARCIA

AND

OUR PARENTS

PREFACE

Teaching is one of the toughest professions in this country and it's getting tougher. The difficulties are primarily the result of a tremendous increase in misbehavior. According to parents and teachers, misbehavior is the number one problem facing today's schools. Teaching becomes, at times, impossible with thirty or more unruly students. Teachers become frustrated, then angry; students do not learn the important academic and social skills so necessary for success in our society. Parents are increasingly aware of the problems currently so evident in our schools and are increasingly unhappy. Eliminating the problems of misbehavior for today's schools would help teachers, students, administrators, and parents.

One barrier that teachers, as well as other practitioners, face when attempting to solve problems of misbehavior is their lack of training in a variety of methods for reducing misbehavior. Colleges of Education do not teach specifics about misbehavior; school systems rarely offer adequate in-service training. Teachers and parents who rely on various forms of punishment often do so because they are frustrated and because they do not know many (or any) other methods. Still, teachers are expected to avoid using punishment even when they have no alternatives.

The main purpose of this book is to teach these alternatives by presenting and explaining a large variety of procedures from which a teacher may choose when faced with problems of misbehavior. All practitioners should find that at least several of the solutions explained in this book are effective for them. This book can therefore be useful to a variety of practitioners, including prospective or practicing teachers, individuals working in day care centers, institutions for the mentally retarded or for the emotionally disturbed, parents, and others. In addition, principals, supervisors, and other administrators can find the book useful both for themselves and for working with their staffs in designing and implementing programs. All of these practitioners face problems of misbehavior and all can use a more thorough understanding of a large number of solutions.

Because we believe that problems of misbehavior should be handled early, and that if they are handled early, there will be fewer criminal acts being committed by young adults, this book is mostly oriented toward solving problems with elementary and middle school aged children. The solutions presented also work with young adults but, often, require different support systems. Occasionally, our examples come from work we've done with young adults, but most often they come from work with children through about the ninth grade. We firmly believe that this book will be useful to *all* teachers, administrators, and parents. Still, to be honest, it is probably most useful for those who work with young and early adolescent children.

In attempting to meet the needs of all those individuals, we have designed and written this book in such a way that it is, above all, useful. The book is divided into three sections. Before each section is a brief discussion introducing the various contents of the section. Section I deals with issues in identifying, defining, and measuring misbehaviors and also with evaluating programs for their reduction. Section II discusses ten procedures which have been found effective for reducing or eliminating misbehavior. The first four either use aversive events, and/or produce some form of aversive behavioral side-effects. The last six procedures reduce misbehavior through more positive or productive teacher-student interactions. In Section III we summarize and discuss some implications and conclusions derived from the other sections.

Through studying these issues, the reader should gain *practical expertise* in the following areas:

1. Analyzing and defining misbehavior.
2. Measuring misbehavior.
3. Implementing a misbehavior reduction program following one of the ten suggested procedures.
4. Evaluating the effects of a misbehavior reduction program.

Within each section, the book is divided into a number of Units. Each Unit presents a complete discussion of one or more *specific* skills necessary for the effective reduction of misbehavior. The Units are short enough to be mastered in a relatively brief period of time but complete enough so that the reader will have accurately and thoroughly mastered a useful skill. To help the reader gain that skill, each Unit is preceded by a list of study questions. They attempt to guide the reader to the most important aspects within the Unit. At the end of each Unit is a list of suggested projects the reader should try to complete. They promote active practice of the skill. If the reader can accurately answer the study questions and complete the projects, he or she can be sure the skill has been mastered. The skills presented through Section I should be mastered first. But, after that, the reader may choose to master the remaining Units in any order. He or she should read the brief introductory pages before the section on the ten procedures and first master those procedures which are of most interest. We hope everyone tries to master each skill, but the order in which they complete them is unimportant.

Once a skill has been mastered, the reader should be able to implement it, and if he or she can implement each skill as it is mastered, the authors have been very successful in their goals: Practitioners will be able to effectively, efficiently, and ethically reduce misbehavior problems.

Obviously, the Units covering the misbehavior reduction procedures are the most important ones of the book. It is essential that the reader be able to effectively use a procedure after mastering that Unit. Therefore, as in all other parts of the book, we have de-emphasized technical vocabulary and stressed practicality. While we cannot anticipate all misbehavior problems, we have tried to make it explicit that not all procedures work for all types of problems, so we have included sections on the advantages and disadvantages of each procedure. We have also tried to tie our suggestions to the important findings of applied researchers.

As stated earlier, it is very important that teachers have a large variety of practical solutions. This book, therefore, is not just a series of case studies. All teachers face different problems. Even the similar problems contain differences. If we presented our solutions only to our own list of specific problems, we would be doing you an injustice. What we have done is to present a method for approaching the problem and many potential solutions for solving the problem. Each reader will be able to find out how to solve his or her particular problems by mastering the contents of this book. Also, certain teachers are more comfortable using only certain types of solutions. The ten effective procedures presented in this book should meet both of those criteria. For almost any problem common to the classroom, one or more of the solutions will be effective. For almost any teacher—from the most firm to the most relaxed—some of the procedures will be ones with which he or she will be comfortable.

We have attempted to write a book which is informative, interesting, and above all else useful. Of course, the main criterion on which the success of this book can be judged is how well readers solve their misbehavior problems after having completed the text. While we have not figured out a way to measure this, we are interested in hearing from any reader who has comments along these lines. Hopefully, all practitioners reading this book will be rewarded many times over for their effort. Happily, part of that reward will be the benefits derived by students enrolled in classrooms where misbehavior is at a minimum and acquisition of academic and social skills is at a maximum. When that happens, teaching will still be tough, but no longer for the wrong reasons.

We've had a lot of wonderful people help us to get to the point where we could write this book and others who helped us get the task finished. Our families and friends deserve thanks; our graduate students with whom we discussed many issues and without whom much of our research would never have been completed also deserve thanks. One special secretary, Janet Ferguson, worked hard and long and allowed us to meet our deadlines. We would like to mention everyone, but we cannot. So, to all of you who helped, thanks, and to any of you whom this book helps, thank these others as well as the authors.

S.M.D.
J.H.H.

TABLE OF CONTENTS

xiii

DISCIPLINE IN THE SCHOOLS
A Guide to Reducing Misbehavior

Section One

**APPROACHING THE PROBLEMS
OF MISBEHAVIOR**

Section One

APPROACHING THE PROBLEMS
OF MISBEHAVIOR

Misbehavior must be approached with the same dedication to preparation and planning as any other aspect of teaching. As in teaching someone to read, there is no magic, immediate answer to many problems of misbehavior. A teacher must confront misbehavior objectively and systematically. The problems of misbehavior can be solved, but any solution requires that the necessary preparatory tasks be completed. Through this first section, the reader should gain those skills required to begin a program in the reduction of misbehavior in his or her classroom.

Unit 1 stresses the importance and extent of the problems of misbehavior in today's schools. It also covers an explanation of how to choose a misbehavior to reduce, how to "target" it, and how to operationally define it. Without those early skills, it is difficult to effectively change the misbehavior. *Unit 2* presents information on the consequences of behavior. By analyzing the consequences of misbehavior, you can often discover why children are engaged in misbehavior so frequently. The ten solutions to be covered later are all ways to rearrange or supplement those consequences in order to reduce or eliminate the misbehavior. Through *Unit 3* the reader will learn how to measure the targeted misbehavior. By accurately measuring a misbehavior, you avoid the difficulties of relying only on your opinion as to the extent of the problem and whether or not there has been a reduction. Unit 3 also provides the reader with some evaluation skills. Through the designs presented in this Unit, the teacher can answer the very

5

important question, "Was my solution, or some other factor, mainly responsible for the change?" Without the answer to that question, the teacher may be wasting a great deal of time and effort.

Having completed this section, you will have the skills to begin using any of the procedures described in the next section of the text. With practice, an essential ingredient, you will find each step easier to complete and each problem easier to solve.

Unit One

THE NATURE OF
THE PROBLEM

Study Questions

1. What are four problems that misbehavior presents to educators?
2. Why is a good definition of misbehavior difficult? What are some criteria for defining misbehavior? To what must the eventual decision be left?
3. Describe the ends and middle of the misbehavior continuum. List at least five behaviors under each.
4. Describe the extent of the problems of misbehavior occurring in today's schools.
5. List 10 procedures which can be solutions for problems of misbehavior.
6. List the seven steps for using the 10 behavior reduction procedures.
7. What is a target behavior? How is one identified? What is an operational definition and what should it include?
8. List and operationally define three misbehaviors.

Classroom misbehavior presents many important problems for educators. First, it is difficult to come to agreement as to what exactly constitutes classroom misbehavior. Like creativity, misbehavior is difficult to define, but you know it when you see it. Second, serious criminal problems are multiplying rapidly in

7

today's educational institutions. These problems are more hazardous for all involved than the common forms of less serious misbehavior. Third, solution systems exist but are often only in the hands of researchers; these solutions have not yet been made readily available to the practitioner. Fourth, it is crucial that our schools maintain pleasant, productive atmospheres. If the solutions for the problems of misbehavior were of a sort to increase the aversive nature of education, the cure would be at least as bad as the disease.

This book attempts to address each of the four problems. The stress, however, is in providing practical solution systems. If teachers have a wide variety of procedures at their disposal, one or more of them should work for almost any problem. The procedures should not be isolated, however, from the rest of a teacher's tasks. To be effective they should be incorporated into a total, and hopefully positive, educational environment.

What Is Misbehavior?

Since so many types of behavior can be labeled inappropriate, depending on the specific situation, a good definition for misbehavior is difficult, if not impossible, to obtain. Generally, misbehavior can be described as an action of the child which interferes with his or her learning of either academic material or appropriate social behavior. But that description is both too broad and not inclusive enough. Misbehavior might also interfere with others' learning. Or, while most often misbehavior is an action, it may be the *omission* of an action. Not doing something, like not turning in homework, may be labeled a misbehavior. Injuring oneself or others may not interfere with appropriate learning, but it should surely be considered a type of misbehavior. Another type of behavior which may neither interfere with the child nor other children, but is often labeled misbehavior, is an action which interferes with the teacher's teaching behavior.

It would be wonderful if we could summarize all of the above instances, categorize behaviors, and come up with a foolproof definition of misbehavior. But, we cannot. The best we can do is give the teacher general guidelines. If a behavior of a student has a *measurable* adverse effect on classroom learning, or has a *measurable* adverse effect on an individual's appropriate behavior, it can be defined as misbehavior and probably should be reduced or eliminated. This does not always hold true, however, and in the last resort we must leave the decision of labeling a certain action, "misbehavior," to the individual practitioner's professional judgment. Try to be objective and fair. Be sure the misbehavior has that adverse effect. Once you have decided that an action or the omission of an action is a misbehavior, there are several, more certain, steps to follow. We will come back to those later in this chapter, but now let's try to get more specific while moving on to our second problem.

How Serious Is the Problem?

Types of misbehavior can be viewed as being on a continuum with one end labeled "usual" and the other, "serious." Until relatively recently, most of the problems in the schools were to be found more toward the "usual" end of the continuum. These included such behaviors as talk-outs, out-of-seats, and unprepared assignments. Toward the middle of the continuum are behaviors like cheating, fighting, and minor vandalism. On the serious end are such crimes as assault, rape, and serious vandalism, such as arson. While some educators might be hesitant to include the latter group in a list of "misbehaviors," they do fall within our loose definition given above. Table 1.1 shows some examples of misbehaviors and their possible places on such a continuum.

Historically, schools have always been associated with a certain level of misbehavior, but incidents have been relatively sporadic and minor. "As recently as 1964, a survey of the nation's teachers found that only 3% of their students could be considered discipline problems. Overall, teachers were able to rate 70-80% of their classes as exhibiting good to excellent behavior" (Bayh, 1975, p. 3). Today, most adults see misbehavior as the school's

TABLE 1.1: A CONTINUUM OF MISBEHAVIOR

Usual			Serious
Talking	Teasing	Fighting	Murder
Out-of-Seat	Poor Sportsmanship	Lying	Rape
Littering	Crying	Stealing	Vandalism
Showing-off	Screaming	Chronic Failure	Arson
Time to Start	Not Doing Work	Rebelliousness	Drug Use
Ignoring Rules	Sleeping	Swearing	Assault

most important problem. A recent poll conducted by George Gallup (1975) showed that lack of discipline was named as the foremost problem presently facing our schools and has been for six of the preceding seven years (1968-75). Results were based on a random sampling of adults in more than 300 localities across the nation. All participants were asked the following question: "What do you think are the biggest problems with which the public schools in this community must deal?" The problems mentioned most often were, in order:

1. Lack of discipline.
2. Integration-segregation problems.
3. Lack of proper financial support.
4. Difficulty of getting "good" teachers.
5. Use of drugs.
6. Size of school classes.
7. Crime-vandalism-stealing.
8. Poor curriculum. Pupils' lack of interest.
9. Parents' lack of interest. Lack of proper facilities.
10. School board policies.

The focal point of a recent U.S. Senate Subcommittee's investigation (1971-1975) into juvenile delinquency also attempted to ascertain the present level or state of misbehavior within our school systems. The report, titled, "Our Nation's Schools—A Report Card: 'A' in School Violence and Vandalism," was chaired by Senator Birch Bayh (1975). The express purpose of the report was to "direct the attention of Congress and the American people to a most disturbing and costly problem—violence and vandalism in the schools of our nation" (p. 1). The report discusses the information obtained from: (1) questionnaires sent to 757 superintendents of public school districts across the nation; (2) 55 days of Senate hearings; (3) the testimony of 419 witnesses that included 50 school security directors; and (4) various additional studies focusing on school violence and vandalism that were reported to the subcommittee.

The subcommittee's findings indicate that misbehavior is no longer characterized by infrequent disruptions (such as a fist fight) among or between individuals and groups that are confined to isolated instances. "Instead, our schools are experiencing serious crimes of a felonious nature including brutal assaults on teachers and students, as well as rapes, extortions, burglaries, thefts, and an unprecedented wave of wanton destruction and vandalism. Moreover, our preliminary study of the situation has produced compelling evidence that this level of violence and vandalism is reaching crisis proportions which seriously threaten the ability of our educational system to carry out its primary functions" (p. 3).

A survey of urban secondary schools, conducted by the Syracuse University Research Corporation and described in the Senate Subcommittee report, found that 85% of the schools surveyed reported student disruptions between 1967 and 1970. The report concluded, "The disruption of education in high schools is no longer novel or rare. It is current, it is widespread, and it is serious" (p. 3).

The result of the questionnaires sent to the 757 school districts across the nation indicated that violence in the schools is both pervasive and on the increase. Between 1970 and 1973:

1. Homicides increased by 18.5%.
2. Rapes and attempted rapes increased by 40.1%.

    3. Robberies increased by 36.7%.

    4. Assaults on students increased by 85.3%.

    5. Assaults on teachers increased by 77.4%.

    6. Burglaries of school buildings increased by 11.8%.

    7. Drug and alcohol offenses on school property increased by 37.5%.

    8. Dropouts increased by 11.7%.

These statistics and individual cases do not tell or represent the entire story. The Senate report stresses, "that the Subcommittee's survey findings, as well as those of other surveys on violence within the school system, are only estimates of the nature and extent of the problem" (p. 5). Many schools do not maintain records of violence committed on school personnel or students, and the Subcommittee has recommended that a uniform, nation-wide system of reporting violence and vandalism be developed and initiated. It also may be that many schools and school systems ignore or do not report incidents in order to promote the belief that, "Discipline is not a problem here."

The cost of vandalism, according to testimony received by the Subcommittee, has also been increasing. Dr. Norman Scharer, President of the Association of School Security Directors, stated: "A conservative estimate of the cost of vandalism, thefts, and arson to schools in this country this year will reportedly be over a half a billion dollars" (p. 6). Types of vandalism span from carved initials in desk tops to fires that destroy entire buildings.

It may be stated summarily that there are problems in our schools and in our society which have not been present previously. Children are different; rules and home environments are different. "We are becoming aware that the attitudes of today's children, regardless of age, are quite different from what they were in 'the good old days.' Children no longer accept parents' judgments as absolute. Indeed, in many cases they pay little or no attention to them at all. Parents are called upon to justify their actions in ways which were not expected of them in the past. In addition, defiance and even outright rebellion are becoming more characteristic of even very small children" (Dreikurs and Grey, 1970, p. 4). Open and structured classrooms suffer the effects of misbehavior as do upper and lower class schools. Both black and white, ghetto and non-ghetto children misbehave. Punishment is frowned upon and is often illegal. Teachers and principals are frustrated. School boards and superintendents are frustrated. Parents are both frustrated and angry. Misbehavior is obviously a problem of major proportions.

The problem exists and it is serious. More teachers than ever before see at least the serious types of misbehavior as their largest difficulty. The important question is whether we have humane but useful solutions. The answer is complicated and somewhat speculative. We can solve the problems on the continuum from "usual" through "moderate." The main part of this book explains many procedures for that purpose. At present, education has no more answers for the serious problems than do the other parts of society which also face the same types of serious difficulties.

Our speculation, hopefully empirical, is that if problems of the "usual" to "moderate" nature are stopped or avoided, the more serious problems will later decline. If we teach young children appropriate patterns of social behavior within a pleasant and productive learning environment, and if we maintain those patterns over the years, the serious problems will not occur. That is one very important basis for this book and that is why our emphasis is on solving problems in the elementary and middle schools.

What Are the Solutions?

A solution to a misbehavior problem is any procedure that works to reduce or eliminate that problem. Moving a problem child might be a solution. Rearranging the room might be a solution. Simply having a talk with the child might be a solution. The problem with most of these types of solutions is that they are often temporary. Not long ago, we conducted two research studies assessing the effectiveness of having a "good talk" about "usual" misbehavior with misbehaving students. In all cases the teachers were patient, understanding, and nonthreatening. Some of the students stopped misbehaving; others did not. All of the students, however, were exceeding their previous rates of misbehavior within two weeks. Second talks with some of the students worked, but for even shorter lengths of time. In these cases, talking with the students was not effective and, in fact, increased the problems (Deitz, Hummel, Sundrup, Meeks, and Butler, 1977).

What we need are solutions which more *permanently* change the behavior patterns of misbehaving students. These solutions are presently available, but there has not been widespread dissemination of their use to practitioners. Researchers have been examining their efficacy, and those reported in this book have been found effective.

All the procedures are applicable by teachers in their classrooms, although some are a bit more cumbersome than others to implement. Each has advantages and disadvantages and some are more suited for certain types of misbehavior than are others. If a teacher masters the use of each or many of the procedures, all usual problems with misbehavior, most moderate problems, and even some of the serious problems are solvable. Also, since many of the procedures require the use of positive interactions with the students, discipline, as well as learning, can become a pleasant experience. Table 1.2 summarizes the procedures for reducing or eliminating misbehavior which are discussed in this book.

TABLE 1.2: THE TEN PROCEDURES FOR REDUCING MISBEHAVIOR

1. Punishment	6. Satiation
2. Response Cost	7. Positive Practice
3. Timeout	8. Reinforcing other behavior
4. Extinction	9. Reinforcing low rates of behavior
5. Overcorrection	10. Reinforcing incompatible behavior

Some of the procedures are aversive because they have been found to be either aversive in their own right, or to produce undesirable, behavioral side-effects. Other procedures either produce no undesirable side-effects or actually require the use of positive teacher-student interactions for their effectiveness. Units 4 through 11 explain the status of each procedure in terms of aversiveness.

The proper use of these procedures requires following several steps mentioned earlier in this Unit. If the steps are followed, the procedure should provide each teacher with excellent success. They are not difficult but require some practice to insure efficient use of a teacher's time as well as effectiveness. But, if a teacher has determined that the problem is serious enough to handle, that decision should be an important incentive for following the steps. Table 1.3 lists the steps for using the behavior reducing procedures.

TABLE 1.3: THE SEVEN STEPS IN
THE BEHAVIOR REDUCTION PROCESS

1. Decide to reduce a behavior (Unit 1).
2. Specify the behavior (Unit 1).
3. Determine the present level of the behavior (Unit 3).
4. Decide which procedure seems the most appropriate (Units 4-11).
5. Implement the procedure (Units 4-11).
6. Evaluate the effectiveness of the procedure (Unit 3).
7. Make changes if necessary (Unit 3).

The earlier discussion in this Unit about what misbehavior is should help the teacher complete step one. Unit 3 explains step three, as well as steps six and seven. Steps four and five are explained through the Units on the procedures, themselves. We will spend some time now clarifying *step two*.

Specifying Behavior

The first step in changing a previously chosen behavior is clarifying exactly what that behavior is. This step is often referred to as *targeting* or *pinpointing*. Rather than reducing a child's "disruptions," you would reduce his talk-outs or out-of-seats or hitting or cursing. A target is a short but specific label for the exact misbehavior you want to reduce. If a child does many or all of the above examples, you might still target each one individually. A target is the exact *action* the child makes which needs to be reduced.

A target is usually obtained by carefully watching the child to observe exactly what it is that he does which you consider misbehavior. The target behavior you choose should be *observable* by you, the teacher. Obviously, it would be quite difficult to reduce a behavior that you could not observe. Without its observability you would never be sure if it occurred or not; and, without being sure, you would not know what to do to it, or when to do it. For very young children, observable target misbehaviors might be whining, toileting problems, selfishness, aggression, or even nose-picking. You might need to work on all of those for some individuals. Since not behaving (omission) may be the problem, you might target isolation, sleeping, or excessive silence. With older children, emission targets could include talking, interruptions, hitting, stealing, cheating, swearing, desk-marking, or throwing objects. Omission targets might include avoiding group interaction, not completing homework assignments, or answering "I don't know" quite frequently (especially if you are fairly certain that the child *does* know). Each of these targets also meets a second requirement: the target must be *measurable*. Measuring misbehavior is step three in the process and is covered thoroughly in Unit 3.

To be even more accurate in specifying a behavior, you need to "operationally define" the behavior. An *operational definition* is a definition which refers specifically to the separate actions which make up the behavior. For example, a talk-out may be defined as any noise the child makes during reading period without the permission of the teacher. It might include talking, whistling, and humming. In the definition, it is often helpful to specifically exclude some actions. In the case of talk-outs, you might not want to count quiet comments to oneself about the material being read. Within this definition of talk-outs was the phrase, "during reading period." This was included because some of the behaviors might be appropriate during recess, music, or free periods. An operational definition should list and describe, (1) the behaviors to be counted as inappropriate; (2) the behaviors which are similar but not to be counted; and (3) the setting in which the specific behaviors are considered inappropriate.

Since hitting is a fairly common misbehavior with young children, it might be helpful to give an example of an operational definition for that target misbehavior. Table 1.4 shows a good way to present your targets and definitions for your records.

TABLE 1.4: TARGET BEHAVIOR AND DEFINITION

Target Behavior: Hitting Others

Operational Definition:	Striking others with fist, palm, feet, or objects. Does not include accidental hitting or throwing during recess when "contact" sports are played. This target holds during all parts of the day and across all activities.

Some targets are more easy to operationally define than others. Targets which are labeled with a judgmental type of name, such as insubordination, are very general and thus require very explicit definitions. The closer the target is to labeling a single action, the easier it is to operationally define. Out-of-seats are easier to define than talking back, but talking back is easier to define than disruptions. Be sure that your operational definition is complete and broken down into observable behaviors. An excellent way to rate the completeness of your definition is to have someone else read it and tell you if they think they could identify when the child is doing the target behavior. If they cannot, or if they are unsure and ask about exceptions, the definition is not yet complete.

The best way to see what should be included in your operational definition is to again watch the child very carefully for a day or two and jot down all the specific behaviors the child does which relate to your target label. Once you have accomplished the task of constructing an operational definition, you are in a good position. You know exactly what it is that the child does which you are labeling inappropriate. You have a good head start toward success because your attention is directed toward the specific behaviors you want to reduce. You will be less tempted to get "off target" and it will be easier to keep your eye on the goal. It will also be fair for the child. Other, more minor, misbehaviors will not be attended to, for you are concentrating on the larger, targeted problem.

You have accomplished the first two steps. You have decided to reduce a behavior, and you have specified the behavior. You have an operationally defined target. You know what you want to change. Your target includes all the related misbehaviors you have decided are important to change. Now you begin the change process itself. But keep in mind that you should know extremely well the procedure you are about to use. You must be careful to implement it properly and accurately. Care in the reduction of misbehavior is as important as is care in the teaching of academic skills.

And Speaking of Care . . .

The fourth problem listed early in this chapter concerned maintaining pleasant and productive learning environments in our schools. That is one of the most important goals of education today. Whenever possible, students should be happy, busy, and productive. So much pleasant learning should be occurring that misbehavior never occurs. We know some ways to do that and many texts concentrate on that information. If schools met that goal, this book might be unnecessary.

But, unhappily, this is a very necessary book. There are many problems in schools, and teachers need to learn to solve them. Since many of the solutions add to pleasant events occurring in schools, maybe this book will, in its own way, move us toward the goal of pleasant, interesting schools which we all seek. Since the solutions presented will eliminate some of our most difficult and time-consuming problems—problems which far too many teachers face, attempt to solve, and give up on—maybe this book is the first, most necessary step in reaching the goal of happy, productive, and well-educated students.

SUGGESTED PROJECTS

1. Join with some of the other teachers in your school and discuss the following:
    A. What do you consider misbehavior to be?
    B. How serious is misbehavior in your school? Where do most misbehaviors in your school fall along the "usual" to "serious" continuum?
    C. How many different ways do you know to reduce misbehavior?
2. Watch the children in your classroom. List the target misbehaviors done most frequently. Count the number of children who exhibit those target behaviors. Why did you decide to target, thus label, those specific behaviors? Rank order the targets you listed from most serious to least serious. Star those targets you intend to change. (Are there any "omissions"?)
3. Operationally define the targets you starred. Be sure to include the actions or lack of actions which you can observe. Include

similar but non-target behaviors and settings. Remember: a target like "insubordination" or "disrupting" is very general and must be more carefully and explicitly defined.

REFERENCES

Deitz, S.M., Hummel, J.H., Sundrup, D., Meeks, C.M., and Butler, S.C. The effectiveness of talking to children about the reduction of their misbehavior. A paper presented at the meeting of the American Educational Research Association, New York, April, 1977.

Dreikurs, R., and Grey, L. *Parents guide to child discipline.* New York: Hawthorne, 1970.

Our nation's schools—a report card: "A" in school violence and vandalism. Birch Bayh, chairman, U.S. Senate Subcommittee Report on Juvenile Delinquency. Washington, D.C.: U.S. Government Printing Office, 1975.

The Atlanta Journal/Constitution. Discipline No. 1 School Crisis. George Gallup, Field Enterprises, Inc., December 1, 1975.

Unit Two

ANALYZING THE CONSEQUENCES OF BEHAVIOR

Study Questions
1. In what way does psychology interest most teachers?
2. What is an environmental event? When is it a consequence of behavior? What are consequences of behavior?
3. Explain the differences between long-term and immediate consequences. How does each affect behavior?
4. When is a consequence contingent on behavior? Explain the difference between an accidental and a contingent consequence.
5. What is a functional definition? Why is it important to know the effects of a consequence?
6. Define, explain, and give an educational example of each of the following:
   a. positive reinforcement
   b. negative reinforcement
   c. escape and avoidance behaviors
7. Explain the four important rules for using reinforcement.
8. Explain the difference between primary and secondary reinforcers. List, explain, and give examples for the five types of secondary reinforcers.
9. Defend the use of a large amount of positive reinforcement in the classroom.

Misbehavior presents educators with many problems, but before we can discuss the solutions it is important to understand the psychological basis for those solutions. Most teachers look to psychology for help in learning to identify why certain types of behavior occur. Why do some children learn so much more quickly than others? Why do some children avoid social interaction with other children, thus losing the opportunity to learn appropriate social skills? While general answers to these questions are available, specific, useable answers are obtainable only after a thorough analysis of the current situation.

One branch of psychology provides a theory and a methodology for the analysis required to answer questions like those asked above. Unlike in most other branches of psychology, human behavior is viewed as a function of external, environmental events, both past and present. A particular behavior is examined primarily in terms of the environmental events which occur immediately *after* the behavior. The branch of psychology associated with this orientation is most often referred to as applied behavior analysis. The remainder of this text presents that part of the applied behavioral methodology which is relevant to the reduction of misbehavior. This Unit covers how the consequences of a behavior influence the future occurrence of that behavior. Or, to return to the point, why children do some things and avoid doing others.

Environmental Events, Consequences, and Contingencies

In order to accurately understand how behavior is learned or changed, it is essential to know how certain events occurring outside of the learner influence his or her behavior. These external events are important for two reasons. First, they can exert very powerful influences which change behavior. Second, these external events can be controlled by the teacher. Obviously, it is quite necessary that those events which can change behavior be accessible and controllable by a teacher; lacking that accessibility, the teacher is left without a direct, useful method for insuring that students learn to behave appropriately and learn to cease misbehaving.

External events should more appropriately be called environmental events, since they are occurring in the environment of the learner. An environmental event is any event which occurs in the learner's environment and effects some form of change in the learner. These events may affect the learner through any of the five senses (hearing, sight, touch, taste, and smell). The events could come from the physical environment (buildings, trees, and classrooms) or from the behavior of another person. The changes these events effect may be quite simple—just having heard the event—or quite complex—beginning to solve a complicated problem posed by the event. Environmental events may occur before, after, or during a particular behavior. They may be pleasant, unpleasant, or neutral. Our behavior is always in contact with our environment in all its complexity, and that contact is with environmental events.

Many types of environmental events are evident in the classroom but only some of them have strong effects on behavior. The bulletin board display the students notice is an environmental event. A loud noise which startles or frightens students is an environmental event. Music is an environmental event; a direction to turn to a certain page in a text is an environmental event. The line made by a pencil is an environmental event. Such things as the arrangement of the room, and instructions, rules, and praise by the teacher are all examples of educational environmental events.

Not all of these events, however, directly influence changes in behavior. Bulletin boards, music, and classroom arrangements guide certain behavior rather than alter it. They are mostly the settings in which behavior occurs. Rules, directions, and instructions influence behavior, but consist of the type of event which can be ignored. While all of those are important classroom events, they lack the ability to increase or decrease the strength of any particular target behavior.

Probably the most important type of environmental event is one which occurs *after* the behavior occurs. These events are labeled the *consequences* of behavior. Consequences of behavior are important because, when properly used, they can alter the future rate or frequency (strength) of a behavior. We say a behavior has increased in strength if the consequence causes the behavior to reoccur more often in the future. A decrease in strength is evidenced by a decrease in the future occurrence of that behavior. The teacher who has the necessary skills to alter the strength of a behavior by dealing with the consequences of behavior can be certain that his or her students will meet the classroom's academic and social behavioral objectives.

An environmental event is a consequence only if it occurs after the behavior has occurred, or if it is removed after a behavior has occurred. Saying "good" after a student gives a correct answer is a consequence of the student's behavior. It will probably increase the strength of the behavior. Taking away a privilege after a student has misbehaved is also a consequence of the student's behavior. In this case, the strength of the misbehavior will probably decrease. Both occurred after the behavior, thus were consequences of the behavior. These types of consequent events (presentation or removal) are quite commonly used in classrooms and are important for understanding and changing targeted behavior.

Explaining behavior in terms of its consequences is not an unusual phenomenon. Parents have always tried to teach their children to weigh the future consequences of each choice during a decision-making process. Looking toward the future, or making plans, involves an attempt to determine the consequences of certain ways of behaving. Normally, we hope that those decisions are followed by pleasant, rather than aversive, consequences; but, either way, the consequences are an important part of our action.

The applied behavior analyst does not limit the examination of consequences of behavior to anticipated long-term events. In fact, he has found that consequences which occur in the distant future rarely influence behavior very much. For example, almost every smoker knows that the chances of getting lung cancer increase with the behavior of smoking. Still, almost one-third of the adults

in the United States continue to smoke. The long-term consequences of over-eating, besides the unpleasant appearance of
obesity, include heart problems among others. Nevertheless, much
of our population is overweight. Long-delayed consequences just
do not affect our *current* behavior as strongly as we would hope.

Applied behavior analysts have found that the effects of
immediate consequences are much more powerful for increasing or
decreasing the strength of a behavior than are those of long-term
consequences. Much of the research completed by these analysts
in the field of education has investigated the various effects of
pleasant and unpleasant consequences on academic and social
classroom behavior. The results have demonstrated quite clearly
that a teacher can institute dramatic changes in the classroom by
learning to vary the immediate consequences of the student's
behaviors.

Immediate consequences can have a strong effect on behavior.
To accurately understand how they have that effect, however, it is
important to understand the term, "contingency." A *contingency*
is an if-then relationship between a behavior and its consequence.
If the behavior occurs, then the consequence will occur. If the
behavior does not occur, neither will the consequence. A
consequence is *contingent* on behavior when the event occurs only
if the behavior has already occurred. If you turn on a radio, then
you hear music. If you move a pencil across a piece of paper, then
you will produce a line. In those cases, the effect or consequence
of the behavior is contingent upon the occurrence of the behavior.
Hearing music is contingent on turning on the radio; forming a line
is contingent on moving the pencil.

Consequences which are evident in the classroom are most often
contingent on certain behaviors. Praise is contingent on a correct
answer if it is delivered only after a correct answer occurs. The
removal of a privilege is contingent on talk-outs if it is removed
only after a talk-out occurs. If a target behavior must occur in
order for the consequence to be provided, or delivered, or
produced, or removed, then we can say that a contingency exists

between a behavior and its consequences. If you want to insure that the consequence has a strong, steady, lasting influence on the strength of a behavior, it must be contingent on that behavior.

Not all consequences are contingent on behavior. Very often a consequence will occur immediately after, but not contingent upon, a behavior. A consequence of this type may have an influence on behavior even though, technically, it occurred independently of the behavior. It was neither planned to occur by you nor a normal result of that specific behavior. This type of event is called an *accidental* consequence. If it establishes or changes the strength of a behavior, that behavior is referred to as "superstitious" behavior. When a gambler yells, "Come seven," just before rolling a seven with the dice, he has experienced an accidental consequence and will probably yell that expression before other tosses of the dice. The roll of a seven accidentally strengthened a superstitious behavior.

In the classroom, if a teacher is not careful to consequate behavior contingently, he or she may be accidentally establishing superstitious behaviors. If, although unplanned, you only praise a student for his good reading when he raises his head to look at you, you might be accidentally teaching him to pause and look up when reading. Your praise is a strong consequence. You planned it to be contingent on good reading, but it is also accidentally occurring after looking up. Both behaviors might increase: good reading intentionally, pauses unintentionally. Care in the use of consequences is important, because without specifically contingent consequences, a teacher may accidentally establish or strengthen a behavior which is actually counterproductive to the classroom. In some cases, a teacher may even be accidentally strengthening misbehavior.

Superstitious behavior produced by accidental consequences is often only temporary. It tends to disappear after a time. If it does not entirely disappear, superstitious behavior will tend to change. Since the consequence occurs accidentally, it will rarely occur after very many instances of the behavior or will also occur after variations of the behavior (or even entirely different behaviors). Under these circumstances, it is hardly likely that the behavior would become too strongly established. For misbehaviors or other counterproductive classroom behaviors, that is good news. If those types of behaviors are established through accidental consequences, it is nice to know they will probably disappear or change. For appropriate classroom behavior, however, it presents a problem. We do not want those behaviors to change or disappear.

The problem can be avoided by insuring that there are specific, contingent consequences occurring for appropriate behaviors. Consequences which are contingent do not allow the behavior to drift or disappear. They have a more direct and lasting effect on the strength of a target behavior and you are sure which behaviors you are changing. Since the relationship between the target behavior and the consequence is real, or planned, rather than accidental, the target will be regularly affected for a more permanent change.

Since change in the strength of a behavior is often a function of more than one experience with the consequence, a contingent consequence is also much more likely to reoccur. In general, then, if a consequence is contingent on a behavior, it will have both an immediate and long-term as well as a more powerful effect on behavior. You can be much more sure you are making a productive change in your classroom if you are using consequences contingently.

To summarize, all types of environmental events are potentially important to the classroom. The teacher must be aware of the events they use and know how to control them. Those events which occur after the behavior occurs are the consequences of behavior. They are probably the most important type of environmental event because they directly cause increases or decreases in the strength of a behavior. To be effective in altering a specific behavior, the teacher must be sure the consequence is contingent on the target behavior. It should be contingent only on those behaviors he or she wants to change. In other words, the teacher must try to insure that the consequence occurs only after a specific behavior occurs, and not without its occurrence.

Types of Effects

It has been explained that consequences, whether contingent or accidental, can be pleasant, unpleasant, or neutral. Depending on how the pleasant and unpleasant consequences are made contingent on behavior, that behavior can be increased, decreased, or maintained. Also, entirely new behavior may be established through the systematic use of the consequences of behavior. In any case, the effect of a consequence is always very individual and always very important. For some children, praise, contingent on (given only after) appropriate math problem-solving, will increase that behavior; for others, it might decrease it; for still others, it will have no effect.

Therefore, when analyzing consequences, one must examine the *effect* of a certain contingency on a certain behavior. Only then can we determine exactly what we should label that particular consequence in technical terms. Also, only then would we know if we are meeting our goals. If a certain consequence can produce different types of effects, a label for that consequence is accurate only after the effects have been determined. Consequences, when analyzed in this manner, are said to be defined by their effects, or functionally defined. A *functional definition* in applied behavior analysis is a definition for a term which includes, in the definition, an indication of the direction of the change that the consequence has on the behavior. The two most important terms in applied behavior analysis which are functionally defined are positive and negative reinforcement; both terms are defined so as to include the direction in which they change behavior and both are also very important for continuing our discussion about consequences.

Reinforcement

Reinforcement is the most important way to increase the strength of a response. It is a technical term which is used only when we know both (1) that a type of contingent consequence has occurred, and (2) that the direction of the change it produced in the behavior was an increase. In the cases of both positive and negative reinforcement, the direction of behavioral change is always the same; with either type of reinforcement, behavior is always *increased* or maintained at its current level. If one always remembers that, the common confusion about positive and negative reinforcement can be avoided.

Positive reinforcement is defined as the contingent presentation of an environmental event after the behavior occurs which increases the future rate or frequency of that behavior. The contingent consequence of the behavior is the presentation of the event. Also, the behavior must then increase. If it does not increase, you have used a contingent consequence but it does not qualify as positive reinforcement. If one thinks about the term, positive, as an addition sign, a plus (+), rather than a word implying, "pleasant," it is easier to understand what happens in positive reinforcement. The behavior causes the event to be added to the situation. The event which is presented is usually pleasant, but does not have to be. The important point is that it is presented and the behavior increases. If you spanked a child every time he threw a rock at another child, and his rock throwing *increased*, you would be using positive reinforcement—that would not have been your intention, but it would have been the effect. Still, you presented a contingent consequence (spanking) after the behavior *and* the behavior increased. More common would be the case where you told a child how nice he has been immediately after he had been playing appropriately with another child. If his appropriate play increased or remained high, you would have used positive reinforcement.

It is important to remember that after a behavior occurs, a consequence is added to that behavior either by someone, like the teacher, or naturally produced by the behavior. If the behavior increases, the interaction has been one of positive reinforcement. Everyday life, as well as the classroom, provides innumerable examples of interactions which, if we know that the behavior increases, or is maintained, are examples of positive reinforcement. When pleasing compliments occur after you have behaved in such a way as to make yourself look good, you have been positively reinforced. When you place an "A" on the top of an excellent paper or test, you are using positive reinforcement. When you praise a child, or allow him extra privileges, or supply a gold star, or touch him warmly on the shoulder, or say, "terrific," you are usually doing those things after a behavior that you'd like to see increase—if it does increase, that is positive reinforcement.

Negative reinforcement is a little more difficult to understand. Negative reinforcement is defined as the contingent removal of an environmental event after the behavior occurs which increases the future rate or frequency of that behavior. In negative reinforcement an event is escaped or avoided by a behavior. It is removed after the behavior, *and* the behavior increases. The removal of the event is contingent on behavior (it would not have been removed if the behavior had not occurred), thus the contingent consequence in this case involves the removal of an event if the behavior occurs. Think of negative as subtraction, the minus (-) sign. The behavior causes an event to be removed or subtracted from the situation. In most cases the event which is removed is unpleasant or aversive, so it is easy to understand why a behavior would *increase* if that occurs. But, as with positive reinforcement, the type of event is not the criterion. What is important is that a behavior occurs, an environmental event ceases or is removed, and the behavior increases.

Negative reinforcement is easier to understand when you know that it produces what is called *escape* or *avoidance* behavior. Escape behavior removes the person from direct contact with what is usually an aversive event. So, the consequence of escape behavior is the direct removal of an event, or negative reinforcement. Your behavior of removing your hand from a fire is escape behavior; you have escaped the contact with fire. Your behavior removed an aversive event, so you experienced negative reinforcement. The behavior of turning down a radio that is too loud is escape behavior. You have terminated an aversive event. Turning off a bad TV show or leaving a bad movie are escape behaviors. You are negatively reinforced by terminating ongoing aversive events (terminating them, at least, for you). The negative reinforcement will increase the chances that you will do the behaviors again in the future when the same situation arises.

With avoidance behavior, you have learned to behave so as to avoid what you either expect will be an aversive situation or have learned through escaping *is* an aversive event. By avoiding, you postpone or remove the chances of encountering an aversive event, so avoidance, too, fits the negative reinforcement paradigm. Deciding not to go to a movie because someone whose opinion you trust warned you that the movie is bad is avoidance behavior. Skipping school on a day when a test for which you are unprepared is scheduled is also avoidance behavior. Since negative reinforcement increases behavior, it becomes easier to understand why some children are "selectively ill" so often. The behavior of claiming illness is negatively reinforced if it allows the child to escape or avoid an aversive classroom event.

Escape and avoidance behaviors are important, though often less valuable, parts of school-related actions. Understanding how negative reinforcement works to produce what are usually, but not always, counterproductive behaviors in school children is a necessary but not sufficient step in overcoming the problem. The problem is the generally aversive nature of most schools. As long as certain of the events occurring in schools are aversive, many counterproductive escape and avoidance behaviors will persist. Cutting classes, skipping school, delaying test taking, and even dropping out of school are a few of the more important examples of escape and avoidance behaviors. Less obvious, but equally as important, for they may be seen as precursors of the above, are such behaviors as not answering questions, the "I don't know" syndrome, "wallflower" behavior, and self-isolation. In each case, the student is avoiding a possible aversive interaction with the teacher; thus, negative reinforcement maintains an important set of behaviors which more definitely interfere with appropriate social and academic learning in the school. According to our general definition from Unit 1, these are examples of misbehaviors which are learned through negative reinforcement.

Negative reinforcement is also responsible for an important set of teacher behaviors, ones which neither teachers nor students enjoy. Many teachers who have not been trained in a variety of ways to reduce misbehavior resort to various forms of punishment (see Unit 5). The most common form of punishment is "yelling" and the most frequent effect of yelling at a group of noisy students is that they, at least temporarily, become quiet. Since the noisy behavior of the students is aversive to the teacher, and since the teacher's behavior of yelling has removed, or stopped, the noise, the teacher has been negatively reinforced for yelling, thus he or she will tend to yell again when the group becomes noisy again. After a number of years, many teachers become so upset because they have become "yellers" that they leave the profession. This natural interaction between teachers and students can have extremely deleterious side-effects. Negative reinforcement often provides undesirable teacher and student behavior and in many ways provides one rationale for this text. If the teacher knows more positive methods for reducing misbehavior and knows how negative reinforcement can be responsible for many objectionable student behaviors, that teacher can begin to reverse the trends.

Effective Reinforcement

When using positive or negative reinforcement in the classroom, four rules which govern their effectiveness are essential. Although these are not the only rules, they are sufficient for use in the classroom. Carefully following these four rules will make any behavior reduction program you try more effective. First, reinforcement should be as *immediate* as possible. The longer the delay between the target behavior and the reinforcement, the greater the chance of the reinforcer losing its effectiveness. This rule is especially important with both younger children and anyone who is learning new ways to behave.

The second rule which, if followed, makes your reinforcement program more effective is that reinforcement is always *individual*. A positive reinforcement program which will be effective for some children, or one child, may not work at all for other children. When setting up any reinforcement program, be prepared to experiment, and to experiment individually. Don't be afraid to ask children what they'd like to earn or avoid, but don't be surprised if what they choose turns out to be ineffective. A good rule of thumb is to try at least three different reinforcement programs before even questioning your chances of success.

Third, you must be *consistent*. Don't reinforce a behavior sometimes and ignore it at other times. If you have a well defined target behavior, this problem can be more easily handled. Write the target behavior down, memorize your definition, and remind yourself to attend to it when it occurs. Posting clear classroom rules and leaving reminders in your notes for yourself to reinforce students also helps overcome the difficulty in being consistent. Since it so often feels unnatural for a teacher when he or she begins using a large amount of positive reinforcement, practice is essential. Within a relatively short period of time it will begin to feel comfortable and you and the students will like the results. Pleasantly commenting on a student's appropriate behavior creates a much happier classroom than aversively attending to inappropriate behavior.

The last rule tells you to *comment on the behavior* you are reinforcing. Reinforce the behavior as well as the child. By doing this you can be more sure that the student knows exactly what he is doing that has earned your reinforcement. "Good, Bob," is not as effective as saying, "Bob, I really like the way you're working on your math." Practice such expressions as "Good, your writing is very neat," and "What a pretty picture you've drawn, Mary." Becoming proficient at reinforcing the behavior you want to increase is an important skill for any teacher.

Types of Reinforcers

Reinforcement is usually divided into two major types: primary and secondary reinforcement. *Primary reinforcers* are events which are necessary for the maintenance of life, such as food, air, and other necessary biological events. These reinforcers work naturally. No learning or experience is necessary for their effectiveness. However, since primary reinforcers are rarely used in the classroom, they are not too important to teachers. For educators, a far more important type of reinforcer is the *secondary reinforcer.* Any event which increases or maintains a behavior but is not a primary reinforcer is a secondary reinforcer. It might be argued that secondary reinforcers are events which are necessary for the maintenance of the "good life." Money, smiles, praises, hugs, confirmation of being correct, and other pleasantries are examples of secondary reinforcers. These reinforcers have gained their effectiveness through the experiences of the students; and, since those experiences are so different, it is natural to assume the individual nature of secondary reinforcers.

Secondary reinforcers can be classified into five categories, each of which is useful in classrooms. Table 2.1 shows several examples of each of the five categories of secondary reinforcers. The most useful and important category is made up of *social* reinforcers. Pleasant words, expressions, or physical contacts are powerful, easy, and inexpensive for increasing certain appropriate social or academic target behaviors. Any human contact which increases or maintains behavior is a social reinforcer. Telling Mary her writing is neat or praising Bill and Mary for cooperative play are examples of social reinforcers, as are hugs for making up after an argument and smiles for good in-seat working.

Another useful category of secondary reinforcers is made up of *activity* reinforcers. Any activity in which a child desires to participate can be used to reinforce an activity the child dislikes. This is often referred to as the Premack Principle (after David Premack, who first stated this) or Grandma's Rule (after Grandma, who first used it—you can go out to play as soon as the dishes are

TABLE 2.1: EXAMPLES FOR THE CATEGORIES
OF SECONDARY REINFORCEMENT

Social	Activity	Material	Consumable	Exchangeable
"Good"	Playing games	Stars	M&M's	Points
"Terrific"	Recess	Puppets	Soft drinks	Poker chips
"Yes"	Captain	Art supplies	Cookies	Star cards
"Great"	Line leader	Rope	Ice Cream	Punch cards
"Thank you"	Run errands	Cards	Candy	Checking
Closeness	Movies	Paint	Fruit	Savings
Smiles	Trips	Marbles	Juices	Credit
Hugs	Stories	Flowers	Crackers	Play money
Laughs	Pet care	Beads	Life Savers	Money

washed). Appropriate academic or social target behaviors can be increased by making an enjoyable activity contingent upon their completion. When access to recess is only available after completion of a certain assignment, or when choosing an art project is contingent on proper lining-up, or if moving to the reading table is available only after working at the math table, activity reinforcers are being used. In each case, access to a desired activity is contingent on completion of an undesired activity.

The opportunity to avoid an unpleasant activity shows that negative reinforcement can be used in an activity reinforcer situation and that negative reinforcement is not always only a problem in the classroom. One negative activity reinforcer which is usually quite successful is the "homework pass." If students complete assignments regularly (for example, five days in a row) they earn a homework pass. On a day when they are unprepared, they can turn in the homework pass instead of the assignment and still receive credit. Other rules are usually employed in that situation, such as no more than one pass per week may be used and some assignments cannot be avoided with a homework pass. Generally, however, they are quite effective and enjoyable. To use activity reinforcers, you only need to know what you want the students to do and what you have found the students enjoy doing (or avoiding).

Material, consumable, and *exchangeable* reinforcers constitute the last three categories of secondary reinforcers and are used much less frequently in most classrooms. In difficult cases or when other systems fail, they can be powerful tools for helping to influence change in students. Material reinforcers are objects which the students can earn which usually are of some value. Small toys, games, and other such things are material reinforcers. Consumable reinforcers are edible, such as candy, gum, juice, and cookies. The famous behavioral M&M is the most often used consumable reinforcer in classrooms. It is a good choice, for it has the advantages of being small, easily dispensable, usually enjoyed, and tends not to melt while being handled.

Exchangeable reinforcers offer the most variety and potential for learning while experiencing reinforcement. An exchangeable reinforcer is an object which has value only in that it can be traded for other objects which in themselves have some value. Money is the most frequently used exchangeable reinforcer in situations outside the classroom. In classrooms, tokens such as poker chips or punch cards serve the same purpose. (See Unit 5 for a complete explanation of token economies.) They are earned when students do appropriate social and academic target behaviors. Any of the other categories of secondary reinforcers may be the items for which tokens are exchangeable (back-up reinforcers). To use exchangeable reinforcers to build a learning system is a bit unwieldy but can be much fun. You can set up a store which students operate and through which basic economic principles such as inflation, supply, and demand can be learned. With this store as a basis, you can also teach banking and finance. Students can have checking accounts, savings accounts, and even credit cards. They can learn about balancing a checkbook, interest, and finance charges. While initiating the system may be cumbersome, the payoff in student effort and learning may make it quite worthwhile.

Most teachers prefer to remain with social and activity reinforcers, but the other categories provide useful alternatives depending on your needs and goals. When properly administered, all secondary reinforcers help maintain academic progress, appropriate social behavior, and a pleasant, happy attitude in the classroom. Without reinforcement, much of our lives would be less satisfying.

Conclusions

Analyzing the consequences of behavior provides teachers with an excellent method for determining why certain children behave in certain ways. If behavior occurs because of reinforcing consequences, a teacher's first step is to decide how to use or change those consequences. Reinforcing appropriate behavior and eliminating reinforcement for inappropriate behavior can go far toward solving most common classroom problems.

One of the greatest problems with education today is that teachers, untrained in the analysis of consequences, often do things exactly the opposite of what they should. The student behaving properly is often ignored, while the problem child is attended to—often with mild punishment but still receiving much attention. A teacher following the principles of behavior analysis would attend to the child who is behaving well and, when possible, ignore the inappropriate behavior of the problem child. If the inappropriate behavior is severe or dangerous, however, ignoring would be inappropriate—that's why many other alternatives are presented in this book. All of us too often attend to inappropriate behavior. We learn early to criticize and condemn. If teachers would only criticize if they are sure they have praised at least ten times, schools would be much more pleasant places for students and teachers—and much more academic behavior would be learned.

To stop problems from developing in the first place is an important goal for all teachers. The most potent solution is to make the classroom a reinforcing environment. Teachers should reinforce children frequently; a good goal is to praise someone for appropriate academic or social behavior at least several times every hour. That is a difficult goal, and it takes much practice, but it is one which pays off in numerous dividends. Misbehavior will almost disappear and appropriate social as well as academic behavior will greatly increase. Is there a teacher who has different objectives for the classroom?

SUGGESTED PROJECTS

1. List five target misbehaviors occurring in your classroom and identify the immediate consequence for each. Observe carefully, for the consequences may not be readily apparent.
2. List ten pleasant events you say to or do for your students. Do you do them contingently? How often are you consistent?
3. List five unpleasant events in your classroom. Can students behave appropriately to escape or avoid those events?
4. For at least two weeks try to praise two appropriate target behaviors of each student every day. Then try to increase slowly the number of praises. Follow the rules of effective reinforcement.
5. Arrange at least one situation where students can appropriately behave to avoid or escape an unpleasant event.
6. For the group of individuals, arrange an activity for them to earn. Be sure they must do specific appropriate behavior in order to earn it.

Unit Three

MEASURING MISBEHAVIOR AND EVALUATING CHANGE

Study Questions

1. Briefly define measurement and evaluation. List the four reasons why measurement and evaluation are important.
2. What is a behavior reduction project?
3. What is observational recording? What are the two decisions you must make before you begin counting misbehavior?
4. Explain the differences among frequency, rate, duration, and time-sampling. When is each most useful? How do you convert a frequency to a rate? Why would you do it? How does duration become more useful when presented as a percentage? How is data of time-sampling converted to a percentage?
5. Explain how you can count group misbehavior.
6. Why should teachers graph data? Explain the horizontal and vertical axes, the data points, connecting the data points, and phase change lines.
7. Why is evaluating change important?
8. What is a baseline, and why is baseline data collected?
9. Explain the four phases of the ABAB reversal design. How does this design show that your procedure, rather than other factors, is responsible for change in the misbehavior?
10. Explain the reasons for using a Multiple baseline design. What alternatives are available in selecting how you will measure more than one baseline? In this design, when do you

introduce treatment on the first baseline, on the second, etc.? How does the Multiple baseline design show the effectiveness of your procedure?

11. If your design demonstrated your effectiveness, what advantages have you gained? If your design showed your procedure to be ineffective, what advantages have you gained?
12. List the steps to follow for measuring and evaluating misbehavior.

Teachers are continually trying to change the behavior of children. They want to increase appropriate or academic behavior and decrease inappropriate behavior. When Mary turns in a correct math worksheet, she is praised by her teacher with the hope that the praise will strengthen Mary's math behavior. When Jeff throws food in the cafeteria, he is sent to the principal's office with the hope this will reduce his food-throwing behavior. The approaches these teachers are taking, however soundly based on the principles of behavior, may or may not be effective. Without *measurement* and *evaluation,* the teacher can never be sure.

Measurement and evaluation are interrelated aspects of one of the more important areas of teaching. Measurement is the process of determining the level of behavior which is occurring at any given time. It answers the question, "How many times was something done?" Evaluation allows you to determine whether or not a particular procedure you are using is responsible for a change that occurred. Evaluation answers the question, "Was it my procedure, or possibly something else, which accounted for a change in behavior?" It is important to know if your procedure is working and, if so, how well it is working. Since this book explains many different procedures for reducing misbehavior, it is essential that you learn how to measure misbehavior and evaluate those procedures. So, this Unit explains several ways to measure misbehavior and to evaluate behavior reduction procedures.

The processes of measurement and evaluation are important for several reasons. The first reason concerns measurement. It is important to measure misbehavior early in a program because you can gain a clear, accurate conception of the problem. Measuring the amount of misbehavior presently occurring removes much of your subjective, and often unreliable, judgment. For one thing, as Poteet (1973) mentioned, measurement may reveal a discrepancy "between your perception of the situation and the situation as it exists" (p. 13). Measurement focuses your attention on what the student is doing rather than what you think the student is doing. You may think that Bobby talks out more than anyone else in your class, but when you systematically count the number of talk-outs for each student, you could find that Bobby does not talk out more than anyone else. So measurement can clearly be useful for determining what the problem really is and how important it is.

The second reason is also related to measurement and is derived from the first reason. A clear conception of the extent of the problem allows you to choose a behavior reduction procedure more accurately. When you know how serious or minor the problem is, you can prescribe a solution much more accurately. As the later Units in this book explain, specific procedures are more suited for some problems than they are for others. Measurement allows you to select a solution with a higher probability of success for solving a misbehavior problem.

As Poteet (1973) has suggested, a related issue is that a graph of your data can reveal a pattern of behavior which may, in turn, suggest solutions that may not have been apparent. Suppose you wish to reduce the amount of time it takes your students to "get ready" for class (getting books and having pencils and paper ready). After collecting data for several days, your graph may show that it only takes an abnormally long time to "get ready" at various times in the day: after morning recess, after lunch, and after milk and cookies in the afternoon. With such a situation, you would probably only have to measure the target misbehavior and implement the behavior change program after those three activities, a finding which would save you time and effort. Not only can measurement help you select a behavior reduction procedure more accurately, it can also help save you time and effort in the long run.

The third reason for measurement and evaluation is that they provide one with empirical evidence that a program is working. This is important because frequently the initial reductions are slight and would not be noticed unless data were being collected. Being able to detect these small changes can strengthen *your* commitment to continuing a behavior reduction program. It keeps you from dropping a procedure which, although it is requiring some effort on your part, will eventually be quite beneficial for you as well as your students. "If a student's behavior is to be changed, those responsible for the program must also carefully maintain their own behavior. They must continually make the effort to structure the situation designed to bring about the change. When the teacher and behavior specialist see their plan beginning to take effect, as they do when keeping records, they are encouraged to maintain their efforts" (Sulzer and Mayer, 1972, p. 18).

The final reason for the necessity of measurement and evaluation is mostly related to evaluation. However, since evaluation is impossible without measurement, all the previous reasons strengthen this final component. Through evaluation you learn whether your procedure is *responsible* for the change in a misbehavior, and without that knowledge you can neither account for your efforts nor be sure you are not wasting your time. Through measurement you may come to think that your procedure is working, but only through evaluation can you be sure. Evaluation can provide you with sufficient information so that you can prove your accountability. You have demonstrated that it is what you are doing which is effective. When the evaluation shows your accountability, you are in a good position when discussing your procedures with peers, parents, students, or supervisors. When evaluation shows your procedure to be ineffective, you are fortunate that you no longer need to implement a particular procedure. Specifically, you no longer need to waste your time. A procedure which proves ineffective should be dropped and another one used instead. This is especially true when aversive procedures, such as punishment, are found to be ineffective. So, evaluation which shows effectiveness justifies your action, while evaluation which shows ineffectiveness saves you time and effort and opens other options. In either case, evaluation can only strengthen your teaching performance.

To summarize, measurement and evaluation are important components of classroom teaching. Through their use you can (a) obtain a clear conception of your problem, (b) select the best procedure for that problem, (c) strengthen your resolve to continue your efforts, and (d) demonstrate either that what you are doing is worthwhile or that modifications are necessary. These issues should justify your use of measurement and evaluation; now we will move to the specifics of how they are done.

A Behavior Reduction Project

We have mentioned previously in this book that it is important to approach problems of misbehavior in much the same ways you approach the other parts of your teaching job. You should attempt to handle misbehavior by being thorough and systematic. One way to accomplish those goals is to deal with misbehavior by completing what can be called a behavior reduction *project.*

To properly complete a project aimed at reducing misbehavior, you must carefully follow the seven steps outlined in Table 1.3 (in Unit 1). Referring to that Table, you will see that Steps 3, 6, and 7 refer you to this Unit, and upon completion of this Unit you should be able to accomplish those three steps. Before you can complete all the steps of a project, however, you must have mastered some of the procedures (Units 4-11). Still, after this Unit, you can begin completing the necessary prerequisite steps and be well on your way to becoming effective at reducing misbehavior. So, in this Unit, when we refer to your "project," we are referring to the plan you are beginning to evolve to handle your problems of misbehavior.

Measuring Misbehavior

Applied behavior analysts use a large variety of methods to measure misbehavior. Some of these methods are quite complex; others are relatively simple. We have decided to discuss only those methods which meet two conditions, however. First, for inclusion in this book, a measurement method must be useful to a teacher working alone in a self-contained classroom. Second, the measurement method must be suited for misbehavior. Following these conditions, we will only discuss a few of the more useful methods of *observational recording.*

Since misbehavior occurs most often without a permanent result which could be measured (unlike academic behavior which can be measured through worksheets or test scores, for example), the teacher must learn to measure misbehavior while observing it. Observational recording includes several different methods, all of which have this single common feature: the teacher must measure the level of a misbehavior by observing an ongoing behavior within a specific situation. Really, all the observational recording methods we will discuss are ways to *count* that misbehavior while it is occurring. Before you can count misbehavior through observation, however, two questions must be answered by the teacher. First, who is to be the observer, and second, when should the observations take place?

The most feasible observers in classrooms are obvious: students and the teacher (and possibly teacher-aides and student teachers). There are times during the school day when the teacher is either not able to observe (for example, when out of the room) or when active observation may reduce teaching effectiveness (for example, when working with a small group or an individual). In such situations, students have been used as observers with excellent results.

To illustrate, Surratt, Ulrich, and Hawkins (1969) trained a fifth-grade student to modify (using DRO—see Unit 9) the maladaptive behavior of four first-grade students. The teacher and the behavior analysts who conducted the study periodically checked the student observer's accuracy and found that they agreed with the student about 95% of the time. Additionally, being allowed to serve as an observer was a positive reinforcer for the student. He increased his academic behavior as a requirement for being given the opportunity to participate in the study.

Still, there are drawbacks encountered when using students as observers. Vargas (1977) has cautioned that students are more apt to count and record accurately when the students themselves have had input as to the goals and objectives of the behavior change program. When reducing misbehavior, however, students and teachers may disagree as to what is inappropriate, and some students may resent being monitored by their peers. If such a situation exists in your classroom, the responsibility for collecting and recording accurate data must remain yours.

When to observe and the length of the observation must be answered on the basis of preliminary observations. Once you have operationally defined a misbehavior, you should count how often it occurs and note the time of each occurrence for a few days. Such a strategy, as mentioned earlier, may indicate a pattern to the behavior. For example, if talk-outs are a problem in your class, you may find, through your observations, that the greatest number of talk-outs occurs during English and social studies. If so, you would probably only want to count talk-outs during those two periods. If a misbehavior occurs during the same time each day, that is when you should count it. If a misbehavior occurs only now-and-then, and with no apparent pattern, then you probably need to count during the entire day.

When a misbehavior occurs on a fairly constant basis (for example, it is stable in that it occurs as often in math as in reading) it is acceptable to count and record for only a specified period during the day as long as two stipulations are met. First, the time period during which you count must be the same each day (for example, between 10:30 AM and 11:00 AM each day) and second, you should count for a long enough period of time so that you observe a representative sample of the misbehavior (Vargas, 1977). If, for example, your initial counting demonstrated that about 25 talk-outs were being emitted over the *entire day*, but now you have been counting for 10 days in a row for only one-half hour per day and have not observed anyone talking-out, then your observational interval is too short.

Now that you have the information to make decisions about who should count the misbehavior and how long the observation session in which the counting occurs should be, it is time to discuss *how* to count misbehavior. The methods we discuss which meet the previously stated two conditions are (1) frequency, (2) rate, (3) duration, and (4) time-sampling. Armed with these four measurement methods, applied practitioners should be able to accurately measure the great majority of misbehaviors they will encounter.

Recording the *frequency* of a misbehavior is probably the easiest, among the most useful, and a quite accurate way to measure misbehavior. The teacher need only count the number of misbehaviors which have been observed. Frequency is useful for measuring a large majority of types of misbehaviors. However, it is only appropriate when the misbehavior is *discrete* and when the times during which the observations were made are the same length each day. To be discrete, each incident of the misbehavior must be of short duration and have an obvious beginning and end. A talk-out, for example, is usually a discrete misbehavior, while sleeping in class is not. Sleeping has an obvious beginning and end but is usually not of short duration. So, for discrete misbehaviors that you are counting across the same length of time each day, frequency is an appropriate measure. Frequency gives you the total number of occurrences of a misbehavior—Frank hit Billy six times, Mary was late to class twelve times.

If you want to know more than the total number, and

especially if you count the misbehavior for varying lengths of time each day, you should convert your frequency measure to a *rate* measure. Using rate is a way to control for time. If Frank hit Billy six times, it would be useful to know if it was done during a 30 minute recess period or over the whole day. Was Mary late for class 12 times during a two-week period or for the whole school year? Converting the frequency of a misbehavior to a rate is important, since there is an obvious difference in doing something once a day versus once a minute. As Reese (1977) has stated, "Frequency counts by themselves have little meaning unless they are turned into rates; it makes a difference if something is happening twice a minute or twice in a lifetime" (p. 45).

It is easy to convert a frequency to a rate. All you need to know in order to calculate rate is the total number of times the misbehavior was observed (the frequency) and the length of the observation period (the time). To compute the rate, you divide the frequency by the time. Rate, then, can be reported as "misbehaviors per day," "misbehaviors per hour," or even "misbehaviors per minute." As long as you are consistent, the rate each day is comparable to the rate of any other day. For example, if David hit his classmates 11 times during a 45 minute History class and 11 times during a 60 minute recess period, the frequencies are the same but rate measures would show the difference. The rate (per minute) during History would be .24 hits per minute (11 divided by 45) and during recess it would be .18 per minute. By using rate, you can detect that his hitting behavior was actually less during recess, not the same. So, rate can give you more information than frequency and allow you to be more accurate. If you are measuring discrete misbehaviors and count for different lengths of times, rate is a much more useful measure than frequency.

The third method of measuring misbehavior is called *duration*. It involves timing how long a misbehavior lasts. Recording the duration of a misbehavior is useful when a misbehavior has an obvious beginning and end, but each episode of the misbehavior lasts a relatively long time. For example, sleeping in class may only occur once per day, but the frequency of sleeping behaviors does not tell you nearly as much as the length of time the student slept. You might not be interested in the number of "sobs" of a crying child, but you could be interested in the duration of a child's crying behavior.

One would measure the duration of a misbehavior when it is the duration of that misbehavior rather than its frequency which is important. For example, merely reducing the number of times a student is out-of-seat is unimportant if the total amount of time spent out-of-seat remains the same. The student is out-of-seat less often but each out-of-seat lasts longer. In this case, it would make more sense for a teacher to time (perhaps with a stopwatch) the cumulative number of minutes the student is out-of-seat and institute a behavior reduction program to reduce that total.

It is sometimes useful to convert a duration figure to a percentage. What percent of the class time was the student sleeping? If two students each slept 30 minutes but one was only in your class four hours while the other was in your class six hours, the percentage of time slept shows the difference while the duration does not. To determine a percent with duration, all you need to do is divide the time the misbehavior lasted by the total time it could have happened. For the above case, we would divide 30 minutes by four hours for student one and 30 minutes by six hours for student two. After converting hours to minutes and dividing, we would see that the first student slept 12.5% of the available time while the second student slept only 8.3% of the time. As with the conversion of frequency to rate, the conversion of duration to a percentage can make the data more useful as well as more accurate.

The fourth method of recording observational data that teachers can easily use in their classes is called *time-sampling.* Through time-sampling you do not count or time misbehavior, you only try to get an accurate sample of the misbehavior. To time-sample, you divide the observational period into smaller intervals and observe whether or not the misbehavior is occurring at the end of each interval. So the teacher periodically observes (at preset times) to see if the misbehavior is occurring. The length of the intervals is usually fixed, for example every two minutes, but it can vary.

Data collected through time-sampling is reported as a percentage of intervals in which misbehavior was observed. The total number of intervals in which the misbehavior was observed is divided by the total number of intervals in which observations were made. For example, Mr. Jones was having trouble with inattentiveness by his students when he was working with an individual. The students were not working on their assignments, they were just wasting time waiting for their turn for individual attention. Since Mr. Jones could not count or time all the inattention and still help the student with whom he was working, he decided to begin a project using time-sampling to obtain his data.

The period during which he worked individually with students lasted 30 minutes, so he decided to use 30 one-minute intervals. By checking the sweep second hand on the wall clock, he looked up to observe once every minute. If, when he looked up at least one student was not working, he made a check mark. If all were working, he made an "X." At the end of the period, he added his checkmarks and divided that number by the total of checkmarks and "X's" (he didn't just use 30 in case he had accidentally missed an interval). In this case he had 16 checks and 13 X's; dividing 16 by 29 he found that at least one student was inattentive 55.2% of the time. This was his first day of data collection, but if following days showed the same trend he knew he would have to institute a program to change that misbehavior.

Time-sampling is useful for teachers who do not have the time to continually observe and record the ongoing behavior of a student or group of students. It is also most useful for behaviors which do not have discrete beginnings and ends. However, its advantages may be outweighed by the fact that the longer the time intervals between observations, the less accurate and reliable the data (Powell, Martindale, and Kulp, 1975). In fact, Repp, Roberts, Slack, Repp, and Berkler (1976) have concluded "that time-sampling of even moderate interobserver periods does not provide data that properly represent events in the environment, and some conclusions from studies using this data collection method are clearly in question" (p. 506). In practical terms, this means that *if* a teacher does use time-sampling as a method of observational recording, there should be a relatively *short* interval between each observation. What constitutes a "short" interval is debatable. It is our opinion that the interval between observations should be two minutes *or fewer.* Intervals greater than two minutes probably means that your data is not *accurately* reflecting the behavior of the students being observed unless the behavior occurs at a very high rate.

Two additional issues need discussion before we can conclude this section on measuring misbehavior. The first concerns the easiest ways a teacher can "keep track" of the behaviors being counted. Many teachers find that a sheet of paper or note pad and pencil is the quickest and handiest method available to them for bookkeeping. Others like to use golf or wrist counters (available in most sporting goods departments or stores), especially when dealing with frequencies. An ordinary stop watch or clock with a second hand is a *must* if one is calculating duration. Choose the method that you find comfortable, accurate, and handy (remember, misplaced data or inaccurate data do you no good).

The final issue to be discussed can ease some of the measurement problems in your project. If you are thinking that you need to count the misbehaviors of 30 different children and that you know there is no way you can accomplish that feat, rest somewhat easier. When all or most of the children exhibit similar misbehaviors, you can count the behavior of the *group* rather than of the individuals.

You count the behavior of a group in much the same way you count the behavior of an individual. For example, if a teacher was concerned about how long it takes the class (as a group) to "settle-down" during the transition between math and reading, the teacher would merely note the time when she announced, "Class, get ready for reading" and the time when the last student had the appropriate book or other materials out. The elapsed time between the announcement and when the last student was ready would represent the amount of time the group, as a whole, took to get ready. If a teacher wished to reduce the frequency of talk-outs for an entire class, the teacher would count each talk-out made by any of the students in the class and total them. The total frequency, rate, duration, or time-sampled percentage would represent information about the *group's* behavior rather than any one individual. Measuring the amount of misbehavior of a group can not only give you the important data you need, but it can save you much time and effort when it is appropriate.

Measuring misbehavior through observational recording is essential to the eventual success of a behavior reduction project and is not all that difficult. Utilizing one of the four methods of observational recording provides you with sufficient data from which you can make excellent decisions concerning the reduction of misbehavior. With some practice, you will find that measuring misbehavior consumes a relatively small amount of time and is quite worthwhile.

Graphing Data

Once you have begun measuring misbehavior, you will probably find it easiest to understand if you place the data on a graph. Graphing, in its most fundamental sense, creates a pictorial representation of your data. Teachers graph data because a "picture" of one's data is easier to understand and evaluate than a table of numbers.

One should graph the rate, frequency, duration, or time-sampling of the behavior of a group or individual for all the reasons listed earlier in this Unit for measuring and evaluating behavior. Data plotted on a graph helps you to "see" clearly the extent of the problem. With that clearer conception you can more easily select the proper procedure to reduce the misbehavior. When the data show your project to be working, your efforts are reinforced. Finally, the patterns developing on the graph clearly tell you that your procedure is or is not primarily responsible for the change.

While there are many types of graphs, the one which is most useful for displaying behavioral data is the line graph. To construct a line graph you would first draw horizontal and vertical axes on a piece of commercially available graph paper. The vertical axis represents the frequency, rate, duration, or time-sample of the behavior. The horizontal axis shows when the data was collected. The top part of Figure 3.1 shows the horizontal and vertical axes for a graph on which you might plot the frequency of out-of-seat behaviors. This graph would allow you to plot the number of out-of-seats for up to 65 consecutive class days, as long as the frequency did not exceed 30 out-of-seats of any given day. Your graph might be calibrated so that more days were available or more out-of-seats able to be graphed.

The bottom graph on Figure 3.1 shows the data collected by a teacher on the talk-outs of a group of second graders. The second vertical line, marked "Phase change line," separates the data collected before the treatment began and that collected after treatment began. A phase change line is used to separate the data when any major change in a behavior reduction project occurs. Beginning a procedure or changes in the procedure are the two most common uses for a phase change line. Each dot on the graph represents the number of talk-outs by the class on a specific day. So, for example, on Day 1, 10 talk-outs were made and on Day 5, 8 talk-outs were made. Notice the dots are joined by a line (the reason this is called a line graph) except at the Phase change line.

Constructing and reading a line graph is quite easy if you know a few rules. First, the amount of the behavior is calibrated on the vertical axis. Second, the day during which you counted behavior is found on the horizontal axis. Third, place a dot on the graph where the correct place on the horizontal axis (Day 1, for

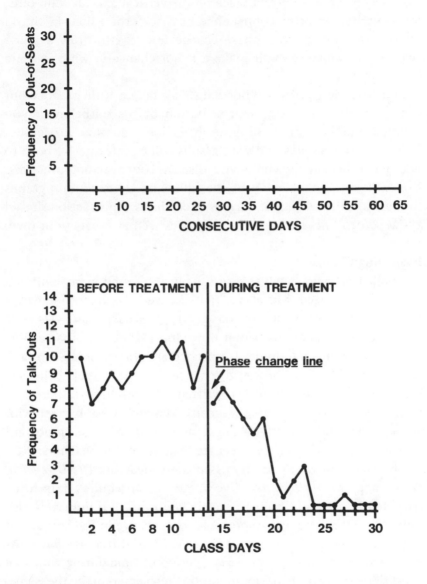

FIGURE 3.1. Two examples of graphs for behavior reduction projects. The top graph shows the labeled axes and is ready to be plotted. The bottom graph shows data plotted before and after a treatment is begun. Notice the line formed by the dots does not cross the phase change line.

example) meets the correct place on the vertical axis (10 talk-outs, for example). Fourth, connect the dots to form a line. Fifth, do not let the line cross a phase change line. Sixth, draw a phase change line whenever you make a major change in what you are doing.

Constructing graphs of your data may take a little practice but will "pay off" in a clear representation of the misbehavior you counted and the effect of your behavior reduction procedure. Follow these six rules and your graphs will be informative both to you and others with whom you discuss your teaching practices. You will notice that many of the following Units contain graphs to illustrate the effects of various procedures. This section should allow you to understand those graphs as well as create your own.

Evaluating Change

Applied behavior analysts are usually interested in not only *if* a behavior is changed, but also *why* it changed. To determine why a behavior's frequency or rate has changed, behavior analysts have developed several experimental procedures or *designs* that enable the researcher to determine if a particular intervention is, in fact, responsible for any observed change in the target behavior. However, since this book is written for teachers rather than researchers, only two of the many designs used by behavior analysts will be discussed. These are the two most important designs and the ones that we feel are really useful to teachers.

The two designs to be discussed are called the *ABAB reversal design* and the *Multiple baseline design*. Each requires data to be collected in a specific way to enable you to learn if your behavior reduction procedure was responsible for a change in the amount of the misbehavior. Each design is separated into different *phases*. As was mentioned earlier, a phase is a period of time during which all conditions of your behavior reduction project remain the same. When a condition changes, we say you have changed into a new phase of your project.

Since both designs begin with the same phase, we will begin by discussing the first phase of any behavior reduction plan—the *baseline.* Any systematic attempt to evaluate the effectiveness of a behavior reduction procedure requires the collection of data *before you implement the procedure.* In other words, you collect data on the frequency, rate, duration, or time-sampling of a misbehavior before you attempt to reduce it. The data collected before initiation of the procedure are called baseline data; the phase during which baseline data are collected is called the baseline phase. In the bottom half of Figure 3.1, the data before the phase change line constitutes the baseline of that project.

You must collect baseline data for two distinct and important reasons. First, it tells how often the misbehavior is occurring right now. This is important because it provides an objective view of the problem so that you can decide if an intervention is really necessary. Second, baseline data provide an evaluation criterion or standard. After the behavior reduction program is instituted, the frequency or rate of the target misbehavior is compared to the baseline level. If the intervention level is *less* than the baseline level, then there is some indication that the intervention is working. If the intervention level is the same or increasing, then the intervention program needs to be modified. The value and necessity of collecting baseline information cannot be overemphasized, as the following specific discussions of each design will support.

One of the more common questions we hear from teachers concerns how long baseline conditions should last in their projects. It is very hard to definitively answer such a question, since the necessary length of the baseline is dependent on the type of observation used, the length of each observation session, and the particular target behavior of interest. Because the baseline is to represent how frequently or how long a behavior occurs under normal conditions, we feel that it usually takes a minimum of 5 to 10 school days to obtain enough information about a certain behavior. Still, this is not an inviolate rule. If a behavior is dangerous for the misbehaver or others, perhaps two days or even two minutes of baseline is too much. On the other hand, we have been involved in research studies where 20 to 30 day baselines were necessary. For most nonserious misbehaviors, the deciding factor to look for in your baseline data is some sort of stability or regularity. Once you see a pattern in what the individual or group is doing, that is your signal to intervene.

Each design starts with a baseline phase, but from there on they differ. The first design, which is probably the easiest, is the *ABAB reversal design.* Each of the letters (A, B, A, B) stands for a different phase of this design, but the "A" phases are the same and the "B" phases are the same. The first "A" phase is a baseline phase—you measure the misbehavior under whatever conditions are currently occurring.

In the first "B" phase, you measure the misbehavior while you are using one of the behavior reduction procedures explained in Units 4 through 11. The "B" phase is called the treatment phase, since you are adding a specific procedure in your classroom. In the second "A" phase, the third phase of the design, you withdraw your treatment and *go back* to the original baseline conditions. In the final phase, the second "B" phase, you *reapply* the treatment.

So, basically, with the ABAB design you go baseline-treatment-baseline-treatment. Through this sequence you can find out if the behavior reduction procedure you are using as your treatment is responsible for a change in behavior. If misbehavior decreases from the baseline level when you begin your treatment (the first "B" phase), you have one piece of evidence that your treatment is responsible for your change. But that is not enough because something else may have coincidentally happened at the same time. If misbehavior increases again when you remove your treatment (the second "A" phase), you have a second, and more convincing, demonstration that your treatment is causing the change. Your final piece of evidence comes when you reintroduce the procedure (the second "B" phase). If the misbehavior again decreases, you have shown, "beyond a reasonable doubt," that your behavior reduction procedure, rather than some other factor, changed the misbehavior.

Figure 3.2 shows an example of a project of a teacher who reduced "paper-throwing" by a sixth grade boy by using the satiation procedure (Unit 8). She evaluated the effectiveness of satiation by following the ABAB design. She measured the misbehavior by counting the frequency of paper-throwing each day during a 30 minute period of individual work (since the time remained constant, she did not need to use a rate).

In the first A phase, the student threw paper an average of about 10 times per period; and, while the teacher would tell him to pick it up, no systematic procedure was being used. The data collected over the seven school days of this phase was the baseline. On the eighth day, she began to use the satiation procedure (see Unit 8 for an explanation of this procedure). As you can see on the graph, the misbehavior quickly fell to an average of less than one time per period (on most days he did none). The teacher stayed in this phase for nine days.

The reversal phase (the second "A") began on day 17. Without telling the student, she decided not to use satiation for awhile. After two days of no paper-throwing, the student threw a piece, but the satiation process did not occur. After another day of throwing only one, the student quickly began throwing paper as often as he did during the initial baseline phase. On day 23, the satiation procedure was reinstituted, so the second "B" phase had begun. Paper-throwing once again decreased to near zero levels. Since the misbehavior only changed when the treatment was either introduced or withdrawn, this teacher had satisfactorily demonstrated that her use of satiation was effective.

By systematically applying and withdrawing your treatment, you can convincingly show your effectiveness. In many cases, using the ABAB design is very helpful to teachers. They can learn that their procedures, rather than other factors, result in a change in behavior. They learn that what they are doing is effective and necessary. When implementing complicated or aversive procedures, you should withdraw the use of your procedure occasionally. If the misbehavior remains at a low level, you would learn that the

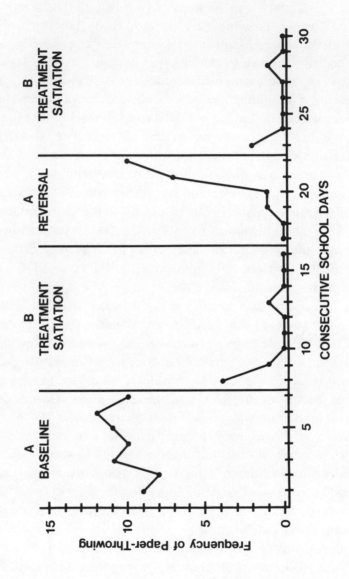

FIGURE 3.2. An illustration of the graph of a project to reduce paper-throwing where an ABAB design was used to assess the effectiveness of satiation.

procedure was no longer necessary, or that it might never have been necessary. For complicated procedures, you save yourself time and effort; for aversive procedures, stopping their use makes the classroom a more pleasant place in which students can learn.

There are times, however, that using the ABAB reversal design to evaluate change has its drawbacks. When misbehaviors are serious or dangerous, you would not want to withdraw treatment just to show that your procedure was effective. In that case, someone might be endangered if the misbehavior returned to baseline levels. Also, in cases where you have worked for a long time and have finally eliminated a misbehavior, it would be quite frustrating for the misbehavior to reappear. At these, and probably other times, a reversal would be undesirable, if not unethical. But you still need to be able to assess the effectiveness of your treatment.

When a reversal is undesirable, you can evaluate your procedure by using a *Multiple baseline design* (MB). But to use a MB design, you need to plan your project from the start so that you are collecting data for more than one baseline (the reason this design is called a *multiple* baseline design). This is commonly done in one of three different ways.

First, you can collect baseline data on *two* or more misbehaving students or groups of students if they are doing the same misbehavior. For example, you would collect baseline data on Jack's cursing and separate baseline data on Sandy's cursing. Or, you would collect separate baselines for talk-outs of your first English class and your second English class. Second, you can use a MB design when you are evaluating a procedure with *two* or more misbehaviors of the same individual or group. For example, if students in your math class got out-of-seat and did not turn in their homework, you could use a MB design. Third, the MB design can be used when you have one student (or group) doing only one misbehavior but the misbehavior occurs in *two* or more different settings. For this case, you could reduce Billy's talk-outs when they occur in both math and social studies. So a MB is appropriate when you have at least two students, or two misbehaviors, or two settings.

The key to using the MB design to evaluate a behavior reduction procedure is that you would begin the procedure on one baseline at a time. Once a reduction has occurred, you then begin the procedure on the next baseline, and the next, and so forth. Once treatment begins on a baseline, it is not withdrawn, avoiding the need for a reversal. The successive introduction of the same treatment on one baseline at a time can show that your procedure, rather than other factors, was responsible for each change.

Let's say you were working with Billy, who hit other students during free play period, recess, and individual study time. To use a MB design to evaluate the effectiveness of a DRO procedure (Unit 9), for example, you would count his hitting in each setting. Then you would begin the DRO treatment in recess, while only counting it in the other two settings. If hitting during recess was reduced but hitting at other times stayed the same, you have your first piece of evidence that DRO was responsible for the change. If hitting in all three settings fell, you wouldn't know what caused the change because DRO was only being used in one of the settings.

In this case, however, hitting fell only during recess. So, next, we would begin DRO during free play period while keeping DRO in effect during recess. If hitting fell during free play, stayed low during recess, and remained at baseline level during individual study time, our second piece of evidence that DRO results in decreased hitting is obtained. The final stage of using the MB design is adding the DRO procedure to the last setting, individual study time. If hitting fell during that time and remained low in the others, our evidence is complete. We have shown that our treatment reliably influences the misbehavior only when it is used. Since misbehaviors not yet in treatment remain at baseline levels, we know that some unknown, other factors are not responsible for the results.

Another example of using a MB design to evaluate a behavior reduction procedure is illustrated in Figure 3.3. Mr. Fredric had

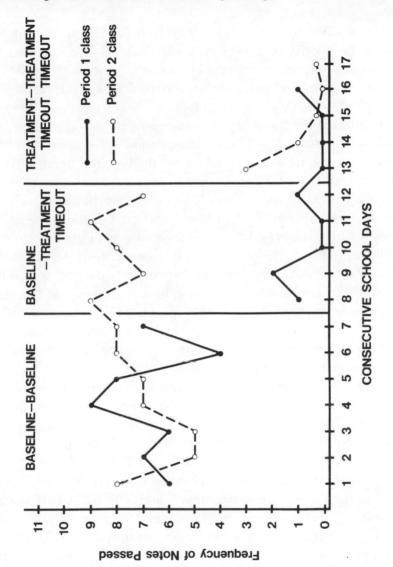

FIGURE 3.3. An illustration of the graph of a project to reduce note-passing where a Multiple baseline design was used to assess the effectiveness of timeout. Notice that the first phase change line is broken so that data for Period 2 can continue, since at that time Period 2 is still in baseline conditions. Also, the second phase change line is broken to show that Period 1 remains in treatment (timeout conditions).

problems with students passing quite a few notes in two of his classes. Each class contained different students so he decided to use the MB design to evaluate a timeout procedure (Unit 6). He had one misbehavior, two different groups, and was evaluating one procedure, so his choice was correct.

He counted the frequency of note-passing in each class. Baseline conditions remained in effect during Period 1 for seven days. At that point the timeout procedure began. Baseline began on the same day for Period 2 but, for those students, baseline conditions remained in effect for 12 days. As you can see, timeout reduced note-passing in Period 1 when it was applied, but the misbehavior remained high for Period 2. When timeout was begun in Period 2 (while continuing in Period 1), note-passing decreased there as well. Mr. Fredric effectively stopped note-passing by using timeout. More importantly, however, he was assured that timeout, alone, was responsible for the change. Since timeout is a somewhat aversive procedure and he did not want to subject his students to such a procedure needlessly, finding out that timeout was the important factor was essential to him.

Using a MB design, then, to evaluate your use of a procedure is not difficult. You must avoid the most common error—that is, do not begin treatment on any two baselines at the same time. Remember, the design tells you to have a phase where there is "Baseline-Baseline," then one of "Baseline-Treatment," and finally, "Treatment-Treatment." Since there is no reversal, you avoid the problems which are sometimes evident with the ABAB design.

Both of these designs are important. You will face many situations where only one is the "best" choice, so you need to be able to use each of them. Collecting data on the misbehavior and following one of these designs allows you to determine if the behavior reduction procedure you selected is working. Completing these tasks also provides you with some certainty that the reduction of the misbehavior stems from your use of the procedure, rather than other, coincidental factors. When reducing misbehavior, teachers need to know both types of information.

But demonstrating that a procedure is *ineffective* is also useful. It is on that type of information that teachers base their decisions to make necessary changes, the seventh and last step in the behavior reduction process (Table 1.3). If a procedure is shown not to be working, you can drop that procedure and try another one. There are ten procedures discussed in this book for that very reason. Every procedure will not work for every problem nor will it work for every teacher. Through careful measurement and evaluation, however, you will identify those procedures which are most effective for your classroom and your style.

Implementing the Evaluation Program

The proper use of the measurement and evaluation procedures previously discussed requires following several steps. Each step was mentioned either earlier in this Unit or in Units 1 and 2. If the steps are followed, the results should provide teachers with accurate, representative, and reliable information upon which they can make decisions and judge the effectiveness of various procedures. If a problem is important enough to deal with, it should be important enough to deal with in a systematic and consistent manner. The steps listed in Table 3.1 are intended to help you meet that goal if you follow them as closely as possible.

Summary

Teachers are continually changing the behaviors of their students. Teachers should observe and record the behaviors they are trying to change so they can continue effective programs or modify ineffective ones; monitor the progress of programs that work; and clarify differences between what they "think" is occurring and what actually is happening.

Once a teacher has decided to systematically observe and record misbehavior, a decision must be made about how to collect information about the misbehavior. Recording such information can be accomplished many ways, but four (frequency, rate, duration, and time-sampling) are of most use to teachers.

TABLE 3.1: STEPS TO FOLLOW TO
MEASURE AND EVALUATE BEHAVIOR

1. Specify and operationally define target misbehavior.
2. Determine method to use to measure target misbehavior (frequency, rate, duration, or time-sampling).
3. Choose observer and times when observations will be conducted.
4. Make decision about ABAB or MB design (evaluation).
5. Collect baseline data.
   (A) Graph baseline data.
   (B) Continue baseline until a representative picture of misbehavior is presented.
6. Decide which procedure is suitable to effect behavioral reduction (Units 4-11).
7. Implement procedure.
8. Compare intervention phases to baseline phase and evaluate effectiveness (if effective, continue; if ineffective, change program).

Frequency, rate, and duration recording provide the most reliable data. Since the data obtained with time-sampling methods is of questionable accuracy, its use is recommended only for those instances where the teacher absolutely could not utilize the other methods of measuring misbehavior.

The final sections of this Unit dealt with graphing and evaluation designs. Graphs are necessary because (a) they are more meaningful than tables of numbers; (b) they allow one to visually detect slow changes or trends that might otherwise go unnoticed; and (c) daily recording on a graph can serve as a positive reinforcer for your continued efforts in the behavior change program.

While behavior analysts have developed many evaluation designs, only two of these seem useful to most teachers. The ABAB and Multiple baseline designs are quite easy to use in a classroom but are also quite effective at detecting if the behavior reduction procedure was responsible for the change in the misbehavior. The

ABAB design involves a baseline phase, followed by a phase in which the procedure is introduced and used. Next, you return to baseline conditions for a reversal then reapply the treatment.

The Multiple baseline design is indicated when a reversal is undesirable and when you are studying two or more different individuals, groups, misbehaviors, or settings. After collecting baseline data on the two or more individuals (or the other alternatives), the procedure is systematically and sequentially introduced. While one individual receives the procedure the others stay in baseline conditions. When the second individual begins to receive treatment, the first remains in treatment, so no reversal is employed.

The information in this Unit, when coupled with the information in Units 1 and 2, should provide you with the necessary skills to begin a project in your classroom using one of the procedures discussed in Units 4-11. Remember, your ability to determine if a procedure is having the desired effect is influenced by two factors. First, you need to be sure that you implement a procedure properly. Ways to properly implement each procedure are discussed in each Unit, since proper implementation varies from procedure to procedure. The second factor is how well you measure the misbehavior and evaluate the change. Your measurement and evaluation systems must be systematic and accurate, or you may not be able to detect and monitor changes as they occur or to make necessary adjustments to your program. Well planned and executed measurement and evaluation systems will take the guesswork out of your program and make any behavior reduction program more efficient and effective.

SUGGESTED PROJECTS

1. Select four different misbehaviors occurring in your classroom. Two should be misbehaviors by individuals. Two can be of groups.

  A. Operationally define each one.
  B. Determine how you will measure each one. Try to use at least three of the methods of observational recording for practice.
2. Construct a graph for the data you will collect on each one.
3. Choose a design to evaluate the effects of the behavior reduction procedure you will later employ for each one.
4. For the most important misbehavior:
  A. Collect baseline data.
  B. Graph baseline data.
Does your data support or refute your original impressions of the extent of the problem?
5. For the next most important problem, complete the same two tasks (see #4 above).
6. Now you are ready to implement a behavior reduction procedure. Select one of the last eight Units, study it carefully, and begin the treatment phase of your project.

REFERENCES

Poteet, J.A. *Behavior Modification: A Practical Guide for Teachers.* Minneapolis: Burgess Publishing Co., 1973.

Powell, J., Martindale, A., and Kulp, S. An evaluation of time-sample measures of behavior. *Journal of Applied Behavior Analysis,* 1975, *8,* 463-469.

Reese, E.P., with Howard, J., and Reese, T.W. *Human Behavior: Analysis and Application,* 2nd ed. Dubuque, Iowa: Wm. C. Brown, Co., 1977.

Repp, A.C., Roberts, D.M., Slack, D.J., Repp, C.F., and Berkler, M.S. A comparison of frequency, interval, and time-sampling methods of data collection. *Journal of Applied Behavior Analysis,* 1976, *9,* 501-508.

Sulzer, B., and Mayer, G.R. *Behavior Modification Procedures for School Personnel.* Hinsdale, Illinois: The Dryden Press, Inc., 1972.

Surratt, P.R., Ulrich, R.E., and Hawkins, R.P. An elementary student as a behavioral engineer. *Journal of Applied Behavior Analysis*, 1969, *2*, 85-92.

Vargas, J. *Behavioral Psychology for Teachers.* New York: Harper and Row, 1977.

Section Two

TEN PROCEDURES FOR REDUCING MISBEHAVIOR

Section Two

TEN PROCEDURES FOR
REDUCING MISBEHAVIOR

Once you have completed the necessary planning and preparation for beginning a behavioral reduction program, you need to select a treatment strategy. Through this section of the text, you will learn ten different procedures for reducing or eliminating misbehavior. All of the procedures are effective when properly executed but not all are suited for every type of misbehavior. Each has advantages and disadvantages; for each, there is a set of rules for properly carrying out the procedures. These eight Units present thorough explanations of the procedures. Upon completion of any Unit, you should be able to begin using the procedure in your classroom with your problems.

Before presenting brief overviews of the ten procedures, one further word of explanation is necessary. Some of the procedures are more *aversive* than others. By aversive, we mean that the procedures either specify the use of aversive (unpleasant) environmental events *or* that using the procedure can produce undesirable behavioral side-effects such as emotional behavior (crying), aggression, or withdrawal. While punishment (Unit Four) is usually considered the most aversive procedure, it is difficult to rank order the other procedures by their "level of aversiveness." Response cost (Unit Five), timeout (Unit Six), and extinction (Unit Seven) have all been found at least somewhat aversive at one time or another. The extent of aversiveness of satiation, overcorrection, and positive practice (Unit Eight), or the three reinforcement

71

procedures (Unit Nine, Ten, and Eleven) is relatively unknown but probably far less than the first four procedures. The aversive nature of any procedure, however, depends on how it is applied; mild punishment may be much less aversive than severe response cost, for example. In any case, since the last three procedures employ positive reinforcement to reduce or eliminate misbehavior, we advocate their use whenever possible. Their use would more likely add to the general, pleasant nature of the classroom.

Still, since it is important that teachers have a broad range of skills with which to solve their many, different problems of misbehavior, we are explaining even the procedures which we do not advocate. *Unit Four* discusses punishment. Punishment reduces misbehavior through the contingent presentation of aversive environmental events. Mild to severe punishment is evident in most schools, in some cases to an alarming degree. The Unit defines punishment, presents the pros and cons of its use, examines when punishment is justified, explains how to use punishment effectively, and analyzes why it is probably best to avoid using punishment whenever possible. *Unit Five* presents a procedure labeled response cost. This procedure involves the removal of pleasant environmental events contingent on misbehavior. Since this process is also somewhat aversive, careful application is necessary to avoid problematic side-effects. Many of the same problems are dealt with in regard to response cost as were covered about punishment. *Unit Six* defines and explains timeout, a process through which access to reinforcement is reduced. This procedure most often is less aversive than the first two but, at times, tends to produce similar aversive behavioral side-effects. A careful examination of this procedure is made available to the reader.

A procedure called extinction is presented through *Unit Seven*. Extinction, as a procedure, involves discontinuing the reinforcement which a behavior has earned or produced in the past. The procedure, itself, is not aversive but it sometimes produces aversive side-effects. Since extinction is sometimes explained as both a procedure and a result, the Unit clarifies the distinction between extinction as a procedure and elimination as a result so that the reader gains a thorough understanding of the use of extinction. The four procedures presented up to this point are all extremely effective when properly used. Their main drawback is their aversive nature. All are thoroughly explained so that, if used, the teacher can evaluate their effectiveness and value against that drawback.

The remainder of the procedures are less aversive and possibly nonaversive. The last three procedures, in fact, employ positive reinforcement to reduce misbehavior. *Unit Eight* defines and analyzes satiation, overcorrection, and positive practice. These three procedures are similar but usually suited to different types of misbehavior. The Unit discusses how each procedure should be used and the type of misbehaviors for which each is most suitable. *Unit Nine* explains a procedure called reinforcing other behavior. This procedure uses reinforcement which is independent of (noncontingent on) the target misbehavior. The procedure is effective because the absence of the misbehavior is reinforced and thus increased. You are insuring, in fact, the omission of a misbehavior. Reinforcing other behavior is sometimes both difficult to understand and somewhat unwieldy to implement. The explanation presented through this Unit should allow readers to be able to more easily use this procedure. How to reinforce low rates of behavior is explained through *Unit Ten*. Often a teacher does not seek to entirely eliminate a misbehavior; it would be sufficient to reduce the misbehavior to an acceptable, low level. If the teacher's goals are to reduce rather than eliminate misbehavior, reinforcing low rates of behavior is an excellent procedure to use. Three different ways to implement this procedure are discussed in this Unit. The explanation and discussion should insure that a teacher has the skills to begin that implementation in his or her setting. *Unit Eleven* presents the last, and possibly most important, procedure for reducing misbehavior. Reinforcing incompatible behavior is a procedure through which a teacher increases the strength of an appropriate social or academic behavior which cannot occur simultaneously with a target misbehavior. It is important and highly useful because a teacher teaches a useful behavior to replace the misbehavior. Rather than only reducing misbehavior, the teacher is also establishing appropriate behavior.

After carefully completing any of these Units, you can begin the treatment portion of your behavioral reduction plan. Every teacher should find at least one procedure which suits his or her problem as well as his or her teaching style. Carefully conducting a behavioral reduction program specifically designed to meet your needs will hopefully give you the same attitude about misbehavior as that of the authors—after proper training and preparation, eliminating misbehavior can be among the easiest of a teacher's many tasks.

Unit Four

PUNISHMENT

Study Questions

1. Define punishment. Develop two examples (one in a home and one in a school) that illustrate the correct use of the procedure (Hint: describe the problem, why punishment was chosen, the type design you would use for evaluation of the procedure's effectiveness, and how you would record misbehaviors).

2. How is the behavioral definition of punishment different from the everyday use of the term? Describe a situation where aversive stimulation is used that does not qualify as punishment. Explain the differences between corporal punishment and corporal attention.

3. List and explain the advantages of punishment.

4. Discuss the disadvantages of the procedure.

5. What are the factors that influence the effectiveness of the procedure?

6. Explain the difference between vicarious punishment and punishment. How could vicarious punishment "backfire"?

7. Explain why one would use punishment even though its effect would probably be temporary.

8. Explain how to correctly implement punishment.

Punishment is a procedure with which we are all familiar. We

75

grow up learning to attend to the misbehavior of others, and the type of attention we pay is too often punitive. It is easy to learn to condemn, criticize, and blame when so much of our society, at least indirectly, teaches those actions.

> The most common technique of control in modern life is punishment. The pattern is familiar. If a man does not behave as you wish, knock him down; if a child misbehaves, spank him; if the people of a country misbehave, bomb them. Legal and police systems are based upon such punishments as fines, flogging, incarceration, and hard labor. Religious control is exerted through penances, threats of excommunication, and consignment to hellfire. Education has not wholly abandoned the birch rod. In everyday personal contact we control through censure, snubbing, disapproval, or banishment. In short, the degree to which we use punishment as a technique of control seems to be limited only by the degree to which we can gain the necessary power. All of this is done with the intention of reducing tendencies to behave in certain ways. Reinforcement builds up these tendencies, punishment is designed to tear them down . . . (Skinner, 1953, p. 182).

Since we live with so much punishment, it is quite easy to understand how and why we learn to punish.

Even though punishment is such a dominant control technique in our society, few people advocate its use. This has been especially true in school systems. Recently, however, there seems to be a move toward reestablishing the use of punishment in education. There are several reasons some educators are involved with this movement. First, there is the tremendous increase in misbehavior occurring in today's schools (see Unit 1). The second reason is that those educators are convinced that punishment can solve the problems. Third, too many educators are uninformed about many other solutions to those problems. So, the resurgence of punishment can be traced to the idea that punishment is *the* solution to our increasing problems.

We think that punishment is *one* solution to these problems and sometimes quite a poor one. We do not advocate the use of punishment except for special cases of very serious misbehaviors. On the other hand, we do not condemn the use of punishment either. Still, as the remainder of this book demonstrates, there are many other, equally effective, procedures for reducing misbehavior. Punishment must be put into perspective. It is neither the answer nor the problem. It has some advantages but many disadvantages. It can be used properly so that it is effective or improperly so that it is ineffective. This Unit addresses all these issues so that punishment, if selected, can be well understood and properly used.

Since punishment is such a common phenomenon, and since so many people are sure they understand it, and since it seems to be making a resurgence in education, we have decided to discuss punishment as the first behavior reduction procedure. But, it is first because we hope to show how it should be an *uncommon* procedure in schools. Also, as you will learn, punishment is a bit more difficult to properly implement than most people think. Finally, we discuss it first because we do not want that resurgence to occur. Punishment has its place, even in schools, but that place is usually last. We discuss it first so we can help make punishment the last procedure a teacher would choose for a problem of misbehavior in the classroom.

Definition and Explanation

Interestingly, although punishment is such a common technique, many people are unclear as to exactly what it is. To many people, one is punishing someone when one does things like spanking them or sending them to bed without supper. To an applied behavior analyst, however, these may or may not be examples of punishment. The behavior analyst defines punishment more narrowly than most psychologists so that, hopefully, it becomes a more useful term.

Punishment is defined as the presentation of an environmental event, contingent on a behavior, which decreases the strength of that behavior. So, like positive reinforcement (see Unit 2), punishment is defined by its *effect*. We say it is functionally defined. Not only must some environmental event be presented after a behavior, but the presentation of that event must work to reduce the strength (future occurrence) of the behavior. In other words, if you do something to a child after he misbehaves, *and* the misbehavior occurs less frequently in the future, you have used punishment. If the misbehavior does not decrease, what you have done to the child does not qualify as punishment. So, spanking or sending someone to bed without supper could be punishment, but only if they work to reduce misbehavior.

By functionally defining punishment (defining it by including its effect), we can clarify a common problem with punishment. The problem concerns the *type* of environmental event presented contingent on misbehavior. Usually we think that punishment incorporates the use of only unpleasant environmental events, but that is not the case. What we might assume to be unpleasant (for us) may not be unpleasant to a particular child. "Because of the behavioral definition of punishment, it is possible for an unpleasant event *not* to be a punisher, and it is possible for a pleasant event to be a punisher" (Miller, 1975, p. 253). So for one child, spanking might reduce "fighting," while for another child it would not. Only for the first child did spanking qualify as punishment. Also, for one child praising good in-seat work in front of her peers might increase that behavior, but for another child, that praise would decrease work. Praising the first child was reinforcement but was actually punishment for the second child. There are cases where pleasant *or* unpleasant events are punishers; if the event is presented after the behavior and the behavior decreases, punishment has been used. The type of event does not matter as long as the effect is reduction.

Usually, however, the environmental event presented after the behavior is unpleasant. Because of this, punishment is often said to be *aversive.* As was mentioned in the introductory pages to the procedures for reducing behavior, the term, aversive, is commonly used in the field of applied behavior analysis and is used in two ways. First, if a procedure calls for the use of an unpleasant environmental event, we say it is an aversive procedure. (NOTE:

Technically, the term, aversive, is *not* a synonym for unpleasant. In the experimental literature, an aversive event is an event which reduces behavior when it is made contingent on behavior. See Azrin and Holz, 1966. Our usage of aversive is intended to be more clear, more in line with common usage, and more inclusive.) So, the first use of the term, aversive, involves the type (pleasant/unpleasant) of event. The second way the term is used involves the production of undesirable side-effects by using the procedure. For example, sometimes the use of punishment not only decreases the target behavior but it also increases such problems as aggression (see Advantages and Disadvantages). Thus, punishment can be an aversive procedure for both reasons. Since punishment usually incorporates unpleasant environmental events, it can be labeled an aversive procedure. It can also be labeled aversive because punishment can produce undesirable behavioral side-effects. Because of the side-effects, however, punishment is aversive even when a pleasant event works to reduce the behavior.

This discussion of "aversive" should not confuse the issue that punishment is defined by its effect, or that if behavior does not decrease after the presentation of the event, punishment has not been used, or that the pleasant or unpleasant nature of the event is irrelevant to the definition of punishment. This discussion was only intended to show how punishment, in two different ways, can be considered an aversive procedure; and, of course, to clarify the meaning of the often used term, aversive.

To try to bring these several issues together, we must remember that punishment is the presentation of any type of event which works to reduce misbehavior. We must not get confused by thinking that punishment is presenting something we "know" the child will dislike. For example, let's say that Mr. Terry, an eleventh-grade teacher, was troubled with the amount of cursing done by his students during English class. To determine if the misbehavior (cursing) was occurring often enough to warrant an intervention, he decided to count how much cursing was actually being done. Since no individual seemed to be cursing more than any other, he simply counted the total number of curses per day for the class as a whole.

After this baseline period, Mr. Terry decided that the frequency of daily curses warranted an intervention. He had read in his local newspaper that, according to a recent Supreme Court decision, teachers could again resort to spanking students that were discipline problems. So, Mr. Terry informed his class that from that point on, anyone who cursed in his class would be sent to the principal's office to receive a spanking.

During the next fifteen days, Mr. Terry continued counting cursing and followed through with his plan. To his surprise, cursing increased rather than decreased. From an empirical and behavioral point of view (review Units 2 and 3), it is clear that instead of punishing cursing, Mr. Terry was actually positively reinforcing it. The presentation of spankings after the behavior increased instead of decreased the behavior so therefore qualified as positive reinforcement instead of punishment. He assumed spanking to be punishment but in this case it was not.

The illustration presented above has hopefully made at least two important points. First, many of the events that we commonly consider as punishment do not always qualify as punishment. What Mr. Terry considered corporal punishment would be more aptly called *corporal attention*. Second, you should always collect data that can be objectively evaluated. Too often are complaints voiced by parents and teachers that punishment (or another procedure) "just doesn't work" when either the procedure was not being used correctly or not even being used (Mr. Terry's case), or only casual observations were used to evaluate whether the procedure was or was not working.

Punishment, therefore, is not a difficult procedure to understand if you remember that (1) something occurs after the behavior and (2) the behavior then decreases. The event which occurs is most often unpleasant but it need not be. Sometimes the presentation of a pleasant event decreases behavior. Careful data collection, then, is required before you can be sure that what you are doing is in fact punishment. Before a decision to implement punishment for a particular problem is made, other issues need consideration. For now, though, hopefully you have a clear conceptualization of exactly what is meant by punishment.

Selecting Punishment

The decision to use punishment must be made very carefully. First, you must weigh the advantages and disadvantages of the procedure's use. Second, you must evaluate the misbehavior you wish to reduce. Punishment should be reserved for only very serious misbehaviors and should be used only when other alternatives have been exhausted. Third, you must be aware of the factors that influence the procedure's effectiveness. Based on the above, if punishment is still the indicated choice, you must carefully implement the procedure following guidelines as closely as possible.

Advantages and Disadvantages

Research conducted in both laboratory and applied settings shows that punishment has several distinct advantages that recommend its use for certain misbehaviors and with certain children. First, it is extremely effective across a wide variety of misbehavior. However, because of some of the procedure's inherent disadvantages, use of the procedure should be limited to misbehaviors that either were not reduced by less aversive procedures, or that pose an immediate threat to the misbehaver or another individual. For the most part, such misbehaviors will tend to be found towards the "serious" side of the behavioral continuum discussed in Unit 1.

A second advantage is that punishment can contribute to the socialization process of some children. Children who display behaviors that "turn people off" are not readily accepted in various social groups. By eliminating the inappropriate behaviors of such children, one increases the possibility that peers or other groups of children will be more accepting of the individual. That acceptance can contribute to that person's emotional and social growth. Risley (1968) has investigated instances where punishment resulted in positive behavioral contrasts or side-effects, and suggests that, "Some deviant behaviors, maintained by unknown variables, interfered with the establishment of new behaviors. This interference was not primarily due to a physical incompatibility between the behaviors. This interference, which might be termed 'functional incompatibility,' suggests that the elimination of such deviant behaviors may be a necessary prerequisite to the establishment of new behaviors" (p. 34).

Another advantage of punishment is that it may reduce misbehavior of individuals who are not punished but who watch others who are punished. Bandura (1969) calls this phenomenon "vicarious punishment." In other words, if a child watches a second child being punished for stealing, this may decrease the first child's stealing. This advantage does have a drawback, however. Punishing a child in front of classmates may "embarrass" the child and may act as a cue for intense emotional behavior (aggression) that the child would not exhibit if the punishment were not delivered in front of peers.

The final advantage of punishment is also the most important. Punishment, if implemented correctly, will not only virtually eliminate a misbehavior but it will accomplish that elimination *faster* than any other behavior reduction procedure. This is why the procedure is recommended when the misbehavior endangers the student or others. This advantage, coupled with those previously discussed, suggests that parents and teachers should be familiar with the procedure and how to use it properly but only when its use is indicated.

The *disadvantages* of punishment are *more serious* than those of any of the other reductive procedures primarily because punishment is the most aversive behavior reducing procedure. Collectively, the disadvantages of punishment are: (a) you have to determine what will work as a punisher for the individual; (b) it draws the attention of the student quite directly to the behavior you wish to reduce; (c) in many cases, punishment only suppresses rather than eliminates misbehavior; (d) in applied settings, it frequently is associated with undesirable emotional and behavioral side-effects; (e) usually, the reductive effects of punishment are specific to the situation or setting where it is administered; (f) punishment can serve as negative modeling for the individual being punished; (g) it may produce behavioral inflexibility; (h) people and places associated with punishment can also become aversive; and (i) the use of punishment causes certain problems with teachers who administer it.

First of all, since what serves as punishment for one individual might not serve as punishment for a second individual, the teacher must determine what is effective as a punisher for the particular student involved. Since there are usually legal prohibitions against severe punishers such as shock or injury which causes tissue damage (events which would probably always "work" but ones we hope no teacher would want to use), you will have to find punishers which are less "certain." Verbal reprimands, for example, are often used by teachers but are also often ineffective. In practical terms, this disadvantage simply means that you must empirically determine what is punishing for each individual by contingently presenting the event and observing if the behavior decreases or not. This disadvantage is really one of taking up a teacher's time, and having to "experiment" with aversive events in the classroom.

The next disadvantage of punishment is more serious. Since the aversive event is presented only when the misbehavior occurs, the student's attention is drawn to it, as is the attention of bystanders. This tends to make children more aware of misbehavior than they should be. Also, if the *only* attention the student receives is for misbehaving, he or she will probably continue to misbehave since the saying, "Love me or hate me, but don't ignore me," is very true, at least in a behavioral sense. Any type of attention is better than no attention at all, so in that case aversive attention would probably be a reinforcer—not a punisher.

A possible tactic that may cancel this disadvantage is to make sure that the individual is capable of emitting alternate, acceptable behaviors which do receive attention or reinforcement. In other words, try to attend to the child when something occurs which you find not to be a misbehavior (every child does do some things which are appropriate and can be reinforced). Catch the child being good and attend to that behavior.

The third disadvantage—that punishment suppresses rather than eliminates misbehavior—is based on the observation that when the punishment contingency is withdrawn, the misbehavior frequently returns to pretreatment levels. This is not surprising when the dynamics involved are analyzed. First, the misbehavior is not occurring in a vacuum. Behavior (appropriate or inappropriate) is occurring because it is reinforced. Basically, the punishment paradigm pits the reinforcing event that maintains the misbehavior against an aversive event. While the procedure is operating (if the aversive event is intense enough), the misbehavior is virtually eliminated. However, once the punishment contingency is withdrawn, the misbehavior's occurrence results in unopposed reinforcement which again increases the frequency of the misbehavior.

Punishment, however, does not always just suppress misbehavior. When punishment is properly implemented, it can eliminate behavior entirely. The problem stems from the fact that proper implementation is extremely difficult (see The Effectiveness of Punishment). Teachers in a classroom usually do not have the time, facilities, or training to properly supervise a punishment program. So, in education, punishment is often found to be only a temporary solution.

In response to the above, one may pose the question of why one would use punishment when, for the most part, especially in schools, its effects are only temporary. There are several reasons why one might. First, once the misbehavior is reduced, an opportunity is provided to teach the child socially acceptable, competing behaviors. Second, punishment *quickly* eliminates misbehavior. If children are injuring themselves or others, punishment will reduce the misbehavior and keep it down at least while it is being used. At that time, other, more positive and long lasting procedures (such as extinction [Unit 7] and DRI [Unit 11]) can be implemented.

The next disadvantage of punishment is one on which there has been much speculation but very little research. This disadvantage states that punishment produces undesirable emotional and behavioral side-effects. Among the most important side-effects attributed to punishment are aggression, such as fighting; escape, such as withdrawal (or even dropping out of school); and various types of emotional disturbances. What little evidence there is provides some support for these assumptions. There seem to be more problems caused by intense physical or verbal punishment such as paddling or sarcasm than by mild punishment such as verbal rebukes. But mild punishment is often not very effective, either.

While the evidence is scarce, we do know that the use of punishment has a greater chance of producing these side-effects than does the use of any of the other procedures in this book. And with some of the possible problems, it should be clear that it is unwise to take the chance that the side-effects will occur. Still, we cannot totally rule out punishment because the evidence also points toward less severity than once was suggested. As Walters and Grusec (1977) mentioned after a careful review of all the punishment research, "It is apparent that, although punishment does have undesirable side-effects, they are not as detrimental as some people have suggested" (p. 176).

The fifth disadvantage is not as serious as some of the others, but it can be frustrating for the teacher. The effects of punishment in one situation may not generalize or carry over to different settings. For example, if Betty is punished at home for swearing, she may learn to not swear at home or in the presence of her parents who administer the punishment, but she may continue to curse when her parents are not present or when she is in a different setting. If the misbehavior decreases in one setting but not in the other setting, then the procedure has not generalized (e.g., to reduce the misbehavior in the other settings will require the use of the procedure in those settings). Commonly, in schools, this problem shows up when a substitute teacher arrives for a day. Since the teacher who was the punisher is gone, the children misbehave at very high levels. Sometimes the children misbehave at levels even *higher* than originally. When this occurs, a related phenomenon called behavioral contrast is occurring (see The Effectiveness of Punishment); when the cat's away, the mouse not only plays, he has the time of his life.

The sixth disadvantage of punishment has not received the attention or study of the other disadvantages. Bandura (1969) has identified this disadvantage of punishment which he called "negative modeling." "If, for example, a parent punishes his child physically for having struck a playmate, the intended outcome of the punishment is that the child should refrain from hitting others. Concomitantly, with the intentional training, however, the parent is unwittingly providing vivid examples of the very behavior that he is attempting to reduce in the child" (p. 313). In other words, parents or teachers can be serving as a model for the behavior they are calling inappropriate and working to eliminate. If parents and teachers are aware of the possibility of negative modeling, the awareness should serve as a cue for them to *NOT* model behaviors they wish to reduce.

Bandura (1969) has also discussed the seventh disadvantage of punishment, behavioral inflexibility. Behavioral inflexibility can occur when a behavior that is inappropriate during one setting or time period is punished and the person, as a result of the punishment, is not able to do the behavior during a time period or setting when the behavior is acceptable or even demanded. Bandura (1969) commented about such inflexibility:

> In many instances change agents are faced with the task of discouraging patterns of behavior that are not permitted but expected at some later period of life. Such problems are most likely to occur when marked discontinuities exist in cultural demands, as in the case of sexual behavior. Thus, a child who has

been severely punished for all expressions of sexual curiosity may be rendered anxious about sex and remain sexually inhibited later in life when such behavior is socially approved and expected of him. When marked temporal or situational discontinuities exist, the use of social training procedures that result in rigid and inflexible behavior are contraindicated (p. 311).

Therefore, a teacher must be quite careful to avoid punishing a behavior which might be useful to the individual at some future time.

The eighth disadvantage of punishment is associated with all aversive procedures and is quite serious. People and places (teachers and schools; parents and homes) that are associated with aversive events can also become aversive, and children (and adults for that matter) do not like to interact with or be around aversive events (as explained in Unit 2, one tries to avoid or escape those aversive events). Schools and homes should be places that children like. If a parent or teacher becomes too dependent on aversive techniques in the management of behavior, then those children might begin to dislike the school or home, a happening we would rather not observe or be part of. To minimize this potentiality, parents and teachers should periodically evaluate what they are doing to their children or students. If they are using aversive procedures more than positive ones, then they need to try to shift to the positive methods (Units 10, 11, and 12). Aversive procedures should be used only in the short-run. Long-term behavior management should be accomplished via positive methods.

A final disadvantage of punishment is that it can create problematic teacher behavior. The problem is as much one for the teacher as for the student. Ironically, the problem starts because punishment can be so effective. Because a teacher's punishing behavior *stops* the misbehavior of the student, the teacher has been negatively reinforced (see Unit 2) and will tend to use punishment more often in the future. The effectiveness of punishment can therefore perpetuate the use of punishment. The possibility exists of a teacher using only various forms of punishment to handle misbehavior. Students are not happy in a class in which a great amount of punishment is used, and teachers are often unhappy that they punish so much. Carlsmith, Lepper, and Landauer (1974) found that children are more likely to comply with rewarding experimenters than ones who used punishment; another reason teachers, as well as students, could be happier without the use of punishment.

One way to break that detrimental cycle of too much punishment is to teach the teacher other, more pleasant ways to handle misbehavior. If the other ways are successful, reinforcement is earned for alternatives to punishment and they will be strengthened. So, a good way to get out of the punishing cycle is to stop reading and go directly to another Unit of this book, preferably either Unit 9, 10, or 11.

We have covered nine disadvantages of punishment and only four advantages. Punishment is problematic because it is so effective (when properly used) but potentially so detrimental to the student and the teacher. Even if the chances are slim for deleterious problems and side-effects, some of the problems and side-effects are so bad that it's not worth the gamble. While we will not say to totally avoid using punishment, we trust you will use it sparingly, as a last resort, and only for serious or dangerous misbehaviors.

The Effectiveness of Punishment

Once you have carefully decided to use punishment for a specific problem, we must warn you that the proper use of punishment is quite difficult. There are many factors one must consider in order to implement punishment properly. Without adequate control over these factors, it is difficult to insure the effectiveness of punishment. In one sense, an excellent reason not to select punishment is that it is so difficult (while seeming deceptively simple) to use, especially in a school setting.

Azrin and Holz (1966) have identified fourteen factors which contribute to the effectiveness of punishment. While not all of them are relevant to educational settings, most of them are. So, to properly implement punishment, a teacher must be constantly aware of these many factors. With thirty children and plenty of other tasks to do, most teachers do not have the time to properly punish.

To make the task somewhat more comprehensible, we have combined these fourteen factors, and the following explanations should help you use punishment properly when it is absolutely essential. (NOTE: Many of the following factors are similar to the rules of reinforcement from Unit 2. Punishment, like reinforcement, should be individual, immediate, and consistent. But for punishment, there is much more.)

The first factor a teacher must consider when planning a punishment program which has a high chance of success is the punishing event, itself. The event used must work to reduce the misbehavior of the particular student involved. In other words, individualized punishers must be selected. Since the majority of punishers are aversive, this factor usually involves the selection of an aversive environmental event (finding a pleasant event to be reducing behavior is usually an accidental occurrence). You should select an event you think will succeed, but remember that some events are quite unethical. Teasing, sarcasm, and criticism are poor choices for children, although they may be quite effective. While you might have planned carefully, the only way to be sure that your choice is effective is to *try* it.

The second factor influencing the effectiveness of punishment relates to the intensity of the event. In order to insure the greatest reductive effect, the punishing event should be introduced at maximum intensity. Not only must you use an intense punisher, it should be used at maximum intensity from the beginning. It is not effective to start with a mild punisher and gradually work up to an intense punisher. It is when the event is first presented at low intensity levels that the effect of punishment is usually suppression instead of elimination. Also, the disadvantageous behavioral contrast usually occurs when only mildly aversive events are used (Ferster and Perrott, 1968).

For example, suppose that Tilly hits her brother quite often and her mother decides to use punishment to reduce the misbehavior. So, each time Tilly hits her brother, she is told, "NO!," a relatively mild punisher. Tilly's hitting behavior decreases slightly (the effect of the mild punishment) when her mother is present. When her mother is absent, however, Tilly hits her brother *more* often—that is the behavioral contrast (the second effect of mild punishment).

Also, the adage, "let the punishment fit the crime," does not have an empirical base, since punishment, if used, should not be used at mild levels. "Mild punishment generally produces little change in positively reinforced performance; at intermediate levels aversive consequences have partially suppressive effects; while intense punishment typically results in large and stable reductions in behavior" (Bandura, 1969, p. 307).

The final argument against the use of punishment at low intensities is made by Fantino (1973): "It should be pointed out, however, not only that punishment is very effective in eliminating behavior while it is being applied, but also that, with sufficiently severe punishment (under which behavior is virtually eliminated), recovery is incomplete" (p. 250). For example, John and Salina, both fourth-graders, frequently "spit" on their classmates. Their classmates had endured enough and would no longer associate with them. The teacher also thought it had gone far enough and that they would not "grow out of it" so she began a program to eliminate it. She used mild punishment on John by voicing a loud reprimand each time he spit. Salina, on the other hand, had a drop of Tabasco sauce put on her lip each time she spit (the Tabasco resulted in a short burning sensation, but did not cause tissue damage). So for Salina, a more intense punisher was used.

Two types of results occurred. First, Salina's spitting was eliminated much more rapidly than John's. In fact, John never entirely stopped spitting. Second, and maybe more importantly, there were different results when the punishment procedures were stopped. When John was no longer reprimanded, his spitting behavior quickly returned to its original level. When Tabasco sauce was no longer applied to Salina, her level of spitting remained near zero.

So, this second factor is quite important if punishment is to be effective. It emphasizes the attainment of three results. When punishment is introduced at high intensity, misbehavior is more quickly reduced and behavioral contrast less likely to occur. Also, misbehavior will more likely recover after mild punishment than after severe punishment. The problem with this factor is an ethical one. To be effective, intense punishment should be used. But intense punishment also has a greater likelihood of producing undesirable side-effects. A teacher must decide at this point if effective punishment is really worth it.

The third factor influencing the effectiveness of punishment concerns how quickly the punishment occurs, or its immediacy. Immediacy refers to the amount of elapsed time between emission of the misbehavior and the delivery of the aversive event. Johnston (1972) has hypothesized that since the behavior-consequence interval is so crucial to the effectiveness of positive reinforcement, it is also probably as critical to punishment (since both procedures present an event contingent upon behavior, with reinforcement increasing and punishment decreasing the future probability of the behavior's reoccurrence). From his review of the literature, Johnston suggests: " . . . the only general conclusion which can be summarized is that delayed delivery of the punishing stimulus increases the likelihood of consequating a response other than the one being worked with" (p. 1041). In other words, if you do not present the aversive event immediately, you may end up punishing the wrong behavior.

The necessity of immediately consequating a behavior is probably the principle that parents and educators most frequently violate. How often has the harassed mother informed the oppositional child, "Just wait until your father gets home!" When the spanking (aversive event) is finally delivered it very probably is punishing a behavior other than the one with which mother was concerned. In our schools, teachers typically send the recalcitrant troublemaker to the principal's office where, after a wait, the child is finally "punished." Any delay between the misbehavior and the consequating aversive event *reduces* the effectiveness of the punishment, and, the longer the delay, the less effective the punishment. Of course, explaining to a child why he is being punished can offset this to a degree, but being informed of the contingencies of behavior are not the same as *experiencing* them.

Fourth, if punishment is to be effective, it must be consistent. Punishment works best when *every* misbehavior is consequated with the punishing event. Especially important to this rule for using punishment is to never punish a misbehavior sometimes and reward it at other times. That form of inconsistency is quite detrimental. It makes it hard for a student to understand the "rules" and damages the effectiveness of the punishment procedure. If you are not going to be able to punish the vast majority of target misbehaviors, we recommend that you select another procedure. The rationale for this recommendation is that if you do not consequate the vast majority of the misbehaviors, you are not implementing the procedure correctly. As was mentioned earlier, improper implementation increases the chances of producing undesirable side-effects.

An issue included under consistency is the rule that there should be no extended presentations of the punishment. Although punishment should occur each time the misbehavior occurs, the length of the punishing experience should be short. Extended verbal reprimands can turn into "nagging" and lose their effectiveness; more than one or two hits with a paddle does not add to a spanking's effectiveness although the person administering the spanking might think so. While punishment should be individual, intense, immediate, and consistent to be maximally effective, extended punishments are to be avoided.

Fifth, since misbehavior is occurring because it is receiving some form of reinforcement, effective punishment should be planned including some way to deal with that reinforcement. If possible, you should try to reduce the reinforcement that is supporting the punished misbehavior. If you know, for example, that the other children laugh when Jack throws stones at smaller children, and that the laughter works to increase Jack's throwing, try to stop that laughter as well as punish the throwing. Really, this involves combining Extinction (Unit 7) with punishment, and you might want to review that Unit before continuing.

The sixth factor influencing the effectiveness of punishment involves what was referred to in Unit 2 as escape and avoidance behavior. An avoidance behavior prevents the occurrence of the aversive event while an escape behavior terminates the aversive event. All aversive procedures generate escape and avoidance behaviors that are usually counterproductive, and punishment generates more of them than any of the other behavior reducing procedures. If a child being punished runs away from school and escapes most of her punishment or does not come to school and avoids the aversive event completely, then the effect of the procedure has been obviated. This is so for two reasons. First, if they are successful (wholly or in part), the effect of the punishment is diminished. Second, if they are initially *not* successful, they will quickly extinguish (Rachlin, 1976) and the misbehavior upon which punishment is contingent should be easier to reduce.

An issue related to escape and avoidance from punishment is that children sometimes misbehave because they do not know alternate behaviors which are appropriate. In other words, the child does not know what to do instead of the misbehavior. In situations where a child behaves inappropriately because he does not know an alternate, desirable behavior, the child should be taught one. Once that new behavior is well established, punishment of the misbehavior will more effectively eliminate it. This phenomenon of alternate behaviors relates to escape and avoidance because the alternate behaviors are really appropriate ways the child can behave to avoid being punished.

Perhaps an example will serve to clarify the concept of alternate behaviors. Greg, a normal 10-year-old, was usually a likeable student. However, on tests, he frequently would engage in various forms of "cheating" behaviors such as looking at another's paper and using crib sheets. Cheating on tests enabled Greg to avoid unpleasant consequences (failures) and was a strongly entrenched behavior. Greg's teacher could have adopted punishment to reduce Greg's behavior, but felt that merely punishing his cheating on tests would not be truly effective if, at the same time, he continued to fail his tests. The teacher finally decided to initiate a program designed to train Greg how to study and to reinforce him when he did study.

Once Greg learned how to study and was rewarded for studying, he no longer had to cheat to avoid failure (since he now had alternative behaviors he could employ instead of cheating). His teacher then informed the class (thus, not singling Greg out) that cheating on tests would result in an automatic, immediate "F." After being caught a few times, Greg's cheating rapidly stopped and his test performance did not appreciably suffer.

In summary, it is obvious that if a child does not have alternate behaviors that can result in reinforcement, then the effects of punishment will be limited. Conversely, if the child does have alternate behaviors, the reductive effect of the procedure will be enhanced. So, to increase the effectiveness of punishment, try teaching appropriate behaviors which can be done instead of the misbehavior. Like the reduction of reinforcement for the misbehavior, this process is one of combining punishment with another procedure; in this case, punishment is combined with DRI (see Unit 11).

The last factor to consider when planning punishment to be maximally effective is the use of instructions. Communicate what you are going to do to the students. Inform them of the misbehavior, the punishment, and how the punishment will be administered. Be sure they know all the "rules." Once you have done that, begin your program. Avoid using warnings, especially repeated warnings. All students involved should know what is going to happen, but once the program begins, let the punisher, rather than your warnings, decrease the behavior.

These seven factors, if properly controlled during the planning and administration of a punishment program, can greatly increase the effectiveness of punishment. Proper implementation also reduces the chances of disadvantageous side-effects. Still, to be individual, intense, immediate, and consistent, and to reduce reinforcement for the punished behavior, prevent escape, teach appropriate alternate behaviors, and properly use instructions is very, very difficult and time consuming. Because of the care required by proper implementation, as well as punishment's inherent disadvantages, use punishment only when it is absolutely essential.

Using Punishment

The decision to use punishment should not be made easily or approached lightly. You must carefully weigh the advantages against the disadvantages. You must determine if another, less aversive procedure could accomplish the reduction and if punishment is suitable to the child, setting, and yourself (do *you* feel comfortable using the procedure? If you feel uncomfortable, seek alternatives to punishment; if you feel *very* comfortable, examine your motives for deciding to use punishment!). Finally, you must evaluate how the factors that influence the procedure's effectiveness will bear on your particular situation.

After carefully considering the above and concluding that punishment is still the indicated procedure, you must correctly implement the procedure. To implement the procedure correctly you must follow certain steps. If the steps are followed, the reductive effect of the procedure will be enhanced. If the steps are not implemented correctly, the procedure may not work and the emotional side-effects discussed earlier have a greater chance to be generated.

Some of the beginning steps, common to all the procedures studied, were discussed in Units 1, 2, and 3. The remaining steps have been derived from the discussion in this Unit to make punishment as effective as it can be. Since each of the steps was discussed in detail earlier, the sequential steps to follow are listed in Table 4.1.

TABLE 4.1: STEPS TO FOLLOW TO IMPLEMENT PUNISHMENT

1. Specify and define target misbehavior.
2. Choose measure for target misbehavior.
3. Collect baseline data.
4. Choose design to evaluate effectiveness.
5. Determine/identify punisher (must account for individualization).
6. Inform students and begin treatment.
7. Introduce at maximum intensity, present immediately
   and consistently for each misbehavior, and limit escape.
8. Combine with other procedures—reinforce appropriate
   behaviors.
9. Follow design—evaluate your data. Make necessary
   changes based on what is happening to the misbehavior.

Conclusions

The decision to use punishment should be made carefully. Special consideration should be given to whether or not the procedure can be implemented properly. If implemented correctly, punishment will reduce a misbehavior faster and more efficiently than any other reductive technique. However, in many cases, once the procedure is stopped, there is a high probability that the misbehavior will return to its original level unless the child has been taught alternate, desirable behavior that can be done instead of the misbehavior.

Punishment, since it is so aversive, should be used only when other procedures have been attempted without success or when there is a potential for bodily injury to either the misbehaver or others. Among the reasons for limiting the use of punishment are the fact that punishment can produce side-effects and that people who use punishment and places where it is administered can become aversive. Still, there are situations where it is warranted. The successful use of punishment is dependent upon two strategies. First, implement the procedure correctly. "To be avoided is a gradual escalation in which pleading is followed by scolding, which is in turn followed by threats and finally punishment " (Anderson and Faust, 1973, p. 261). Second, do not depend on the procedure for long periods of time.

SUGGESTED PROJECTS

1. Think of two instances where your behavior has been punished. What was the aversive event? How did you feel towards the punisher?
2. List several misbehaviors that occur in your home or classroom:
    (a)   Operationally define the misbehavior.
    (b)   List other procedures tried and their effect. Is punishment indicated? Why?
    (c)   Empirically determine what is aversive to the individual.
3. List the steps you would go through to implement punishment to maximize its effect on one of the behaviors listed above. Check with your principal (if you are in a school setting) for clarification of the school's policy and local/state laws concerning the use of the procedure (you may also wish to check with your local teacher's association).
4. Implement your plan from #3 *if* it is allowed. What happened to the behaviors? Did emotional side-effects occur? If so, how did you deal with them? Evaluate your findings.
5. Describe several situations where you have used "mild" aversive events ("NO!"; "Don't do that!") and/or warnings ("If you do that one more time, you are going to get it!"). What was the effect on the misbehavior and the misbehaver?

REFERENCES

Anderson, R.C., and Faust, G.W. *Educational Psychology.* New York: Dodd, Mead and Co., Inc., 1973.

Azrin, N.H., and Holz, W.C. Punishment. In W.K. Honig (Ed.), *Operant Behavior: Areas of Research and Application.* New York: Appleton-Century-Crofts, 1966.

Bandura, A. *Principles of Behavior Modification.* New York: Holt, Rinehart, and Winston, Inc., 1969.

Carlsmith, J.M., Lepper, M.R., and Landauer, T.K. Children's obedience to adult requests: Interactive effects of anxiety arousal and apparent punitiveness of the adult. *Journal of Personality and Social Psychology,* 1974, 30, 822-828.

Fantino, E. Aversive control. In *The Study of Behavior,* edited by John A. Nevin. Glenview, Illinois: Scott, Foresman and Co., 1973.

Ferster, C.B., and Perrott, M.C. *Behavior Principles.* New York: Meredith Corp., 1968.

Johnston, J.M. Punishment of human behavior. *American Psychologist,* November, 1972, 1033-1054.

Miller, L.K. *Principles of Everyday Behavior Analysis.* Monterey, California: Brooks/Cole Publishing Co., 1975.

Rachlin, H. *Introduction to Modern Behaviorism,* 2nd edition. San Francisco: W.H. Freeman and Co., 1976.

Risley, T. The effects and side effects of punishing the autistic behaviors of a deviant child. *Journal of Applied Behavior Analysis,* 1968, *1,* 21-34.

Skinner, B.F. *Science and Human Behavior.* New York: The Free Press, 1953.

Walters, G.C., and Grusec, J.E. *Punishment.* San Francisco: W.H. Freeman and Co., 1977.

Unit Five

RESPONSE COST

Study Questions

1. Define response cost. Develop two examples that illustrate the procedure in school settings.
2. Explain how to set up a token economy in a classroom. What are two ways students can obtain tokens? Why are tangible tokens usually used? What is a back-up reinforcer? Explain how you would use response cost within a token economy.
3. List and explain the advantages and disadvantages of response cost. How can the effectiveness of response cost, at times, be a disadvantage?
4. Discuss the ethical issues of group response cost contingencies. Discuss the legal issues involving the removal of certain privileges.
5. List and explain the factors that influence the effectiveness of response cost. When and how should a cost be determined? What are the differences between a logical and an arbitrary consequence? Why would one be more appropriate than another?
6. Why should response cost be used in conjunction with other procedures?
7. What steps should be followed when using response cost?

There are several possible environmental outcomes of any

behavior. These types of consequences of behavior define the possibilities a teacher can work with when trying to change that behavior. Sometimes something pleasant occurs after a behavior, for example, teacher praise after a correct answer to a math problem. That would be an example of positive reinforcement (see Unit 2). At other times, something unpleasant happens after behavior, as when a child is spanked after he hits his brother (for an explanation of punishment, see Unit 4). Those are the two most common and best understood types of consequences.

In other cases, however, an environmental event is removed after a behavior. These cases are often more difficult for many people to understand. When a child avoids a test by feigning illness, for example, he is removing a possibly aversive event by that behavior and so is being negatively reinforced (see Unit 2). Sometimes, however, a behavior results in the removal of a pleasant environmental event. When a pleasant environmental event is removed contingent on a behavior, we have the case of response cost, which is the subject of this Unit. Response cost is fairly common in schools, can be an excellent and effective procedure, but needs careful examination before it is selected as the procedure for a particular problem of misbehavior. Still, a complete knowledge of this procedure adds one more dimension to the skills of an effective teacher.

Definition and Explanation

Response* cost is defined as the removal of specified amounts of positive reinforcement after (contingent on) a behavior. When a child does a misbehavior, some specific amount of a pleasant

---

*The term "response" cost is used because it is a common term in the literature of applied behavior analysis. We have avoided using the term, response, in favor of the term, behavior, in this book because we thought the latter to be more readily understood as well as more comprehensive. For the purpose of this book, the two terms are the same. So we could call this procedure, behavior cost, but that would be inconsistent with the literature in the field.

environmental event is removed. In other words, a teacher arranges the rules of the classroom so that there is a particular cost or fine levied for doing certain misbehaviors. The child would lose some positive environmental event for engaging in misbehavior.

There are many instances, both planned by someone and naturally occurring in the environment, in which behavior results in the loss of a positive environmental event. Because we are caught speeding, we must pay a fine to the traffic court. Clumsiness in the kitchen results in a broken glass. Misbehavior in the classroom results in the loss of a privilege. In these cases, the consequences of our behavior consist of the removal or loss of some type of pleasant event. In each case, we could say that our behavior has cost us something.

In general, when a behavior results in a cost, that consequence tends to decrease the strength of the behavior. After receiving a speeding ticket, we tend to speed less often (at least for awhile). After breaking a glass, we will tend to be less clumsy. After losing a privilege, a child will tend to misbehave less. In each case, the behavior was reduced because of its response cost.

When teachers remove pleasant events from students after they misbehave, they are using response cost in their classroom. When Fred loses five minutes off recess for hitting, his teacher is using response cost. If Mary is not allowed to play with Betty during free period because she was out of her seat during math, her teacher is using response cost. If Buster is not allowed access to the library because he did not return his last book, the librarian is using response cost.

The use of response cost demands that there be reinforcing events or items available in the classroom that can be removed after misbehavior. But these items must be ones whose loss is not proscribed by either school policy or law (it is often illegal to reduce a child's recess time). One answer to this problem presented by response cost is the use of what are called token economies in the classroom. One of applied behavior analysis' more widely recognized innovations is the token economy. Token economies have been successfully used with many different populations including the retarded, institutionalized individuals, and normal children in both public and private schools.

A token economy is a reinforcement system very similar to any monetary system. Its use incorporates a large amount of positive reinforcement in a classroom. In a token economy, children receive tokens in one of two ways. First, they can earn varying amounts of tokens by exhibiting certain appropriate academic and social behaviors. The teacher specifies the target behaviors and the specific amount of tokens each one earns. The second way through which children receive tokens is by being provided with a specific number at the start of each school day. The former is probably better educational practice since appropriate behaviors are strengthened, but it also requires more work to effectively implement (specifying the appropriate behaviors, deciding how much each is worth, reinforcing immediately, etc.). In both cases, however, this part of the token economy is referred to as the token production component.

The tokens the children receive are usually tangible items such as poker chips, checkmarks, punch cards, or stars. Technically they are tangible, exchangeable, secondary reinforcers (see Unit 2 for a more complete explanation) which derive their value from being exchangeable for particular positive reinforcers (like money is exchangeable in our society). A variety of positive reinforcers is available to the children and they can spend (exchange) their tokens for these items at particular times of the day or week. The items or events on which the children spend their tokens are called back-up reinforcers and serve to support the worth of the tokens. Each back-up reinforcer has a certain price and the available back-up reinforcers along with these prices are generally displayed in the classroom on a chart called a "reinforcement menu." Table 5.1 illustrates a possible reinforcement menu a teacher could use in a classroom. This whole exchange system is referred to as the token exchange component of the token economy.

Tangible tokens are generally used since: "(1) the number of

TABLE 5.1: AN EXAMPLE OF A REINFORCEMENT MENU

Back-up Reinforcers	Cost of Back-up Reinforcers
Choosing own seat in classroom or cafeteria for one week	10 tokens
Going to library	10 tokens
Free time for academic (reading, homework, etc.)	5 minutes for 2 tokens
Free time for games	10 minutes for 5 tokens
Raisins (1 box - 42.5 gr.)	10 tokens
Carnation breakfast bar	10 tokens
Marbles	1 token each
Balloons	1 token each
Magazine (must be returned)	10 tokens
Field trip	negotiable
Movie	75 tokens (in groups of three or more)
Sitting next to teacher	10 tokens per week

tokens can bear a simple quantitative relation to the amount of reinforcement; (2) the tokens are portable and can be in the subject's possession even when he is in a situation far removed from that in which the tokens were earned; (3) no maximum exists in the number of tokens a subject may possess . . .; (4) tokens can be used directly to operate devices for the automatic delivery of reinforcers; (5) tokens are durable and can be continuously present . . .; (6) the physical characteristics of the tokens can be easily standardized; (7) the tokens can be made fairly indestructible so they will not deteriorate during the delay; (8) the tokens can be made unique and nonduplicable so that the experimenter can be assured that they are received only in the authorized manner'' (Ayllon and Azrin, 1968, p. 77).

Kazdin and Bootzin (1972) have identified several advantages in using tokens. First, use of tokens allows one to reinforce appropriate behaviors (and fine misbehaviors) immediately. Second, they can be used when many desirable back-up reinforcers cannot conveniently be used or when the back-up reinforcer cannot be presented in small segments. Third, tokens are not dependent on an individual's being at a certain level of deprivation, thus, they are not as subject to satiation (see Unit 8 for a complete explanation of satiation) as are many back-up reinforcers. Finally, tokens can be used with individuals who have different back-up reinforcer preferences, since each individual exchanges the tokens for the back-up reinforcer of his or her choice.

Tokens, therefore, can be an excellent addition to a classroom. They solve the problem of immediate reinforcement (see Unit 2) and they add to the overall appetitive nature of the classroom. Since tokens are so convenient and valued, they can also be used to support the response cost procedure. No matter which way the child obtains his tokens at the start of each day, the teacher can withdraw a specified amount of reinforcers contingent upon a misbehavior occurring (response cost). To facilitate the procedure's effectiveness with the use of response cost, a few preliminary steps should first be done before the system is implemented. First, target misbehaviors must be defined and baseline information collected. Second, a "cost menu" should be developed which specifies how many tokens specific misbehaviors would cost. Third, after completing the above steps, the system should be explained to the child or children (a verbal explanation should suffice for school aged children of normal functioning) and implemented following the reinforcement rules presented in Unit 2.

For a complete description of a classroom token economy in action, stressing positive reinforcement aspects rather than response cost, see Lauridsen (1978).

Response Cost in a Token Economy Class: An Illustration

Ms. Clark, a third-grade teacher whose school was located in an economically advantaged community, thought she had some behavior problems with her students. She wasn't sure about the problem(s) since she had not, as yet, collected any data which she could evaluate. To determine if she did need to implement a behavior reduction program, Ms. Clark made a note of each misbehavior for a week. When a behavior occurred that was inappropriate, she would describe the behavior (hitting, talking out-of-turn, failure to turn in assignments when due, etc.) and note the time of day that it occurred.

At the end of the week, Ms. Clark found that (a) over 75% of all misbehavior was occurring after lunch and (b) talking without permission during study time was the most frequent misbehavior followed by, in order, throwing objects (paper planes, etc.), and either not turning in homework when due or turning in homework that was incomplete. Ms. Clark felt that none of these behaviors were serious, but that they were interfering with the children's learning and that they bothered Ms. Clark (possibly reducing her teaching effectiveness). She felt that if she was able to gain control of her classroom now (e.g., effectively manage it), she would probably not have to deal with more serious types of problem behavior in the future. Therefore, those three misbehaviors became the target behaviors for which she would choose a solution strategy.

Ms. Clark had studied response cost and token economies in a behavior modification class, and decided that both were suitable to her needs. Initially, she decided to give students ten points to start the day; but when students emitted a target misbehavior, Ms. Clark would fine the student one point. In later weeks, after she had established that system and regained control of her class, Ms. Clark planned to begin rewarding appropriate behavior with points as well as fining inappropriate ones. But for the first few weeks she would only use and evaluate the token response cost procedure.

In order to collect useful data, Ms. Clark kept track of each student's points on a small chalkboard that she placed on a wall of the classroom (higher than the children could reach). Each student was able to monitor the number of points he or she had at any

given time. Table 5.2 is an example of the type of bookkeeping
(data collection) system used by Ms. Clark. Each child started the
afternoon off with 10 points in column A. Each time a target
misbehavior occurred, Ms. Clark placed a tally mark next to the
offender's name under column B. At the end of the day, she
subtracted column B from A and added the result to column C
(column C indicated each child's accumulated points over one
week's plan). If column B was greater than column A, the
additional points were subtracted from column C.

TABLE 5.2: MS. CLARK'S RECORDS OF STUDENT POINTS

NAME	A	B	C
Billy	10	1111 1	47
Ted	10	111	60
Jean	10		83
Sue	10	1111	22
Terry	10	1111 1111 1	14
Bud	10	11	53
Lea	10		37

Since none of the three misbehaviors Ms. Clark wanted to
reduce were serious, she decided to eliminate each misbehavior
one-by-one using a multiple baseline design (MB). Also, the MB
design was attractive, since it did not require her to stop treatment
for a return-to-baseline phase. Figure 5.1 shows the graph of the
data which Ms. Clark used to evaluate the effectiveness of her
program.

In phase 1, Ms. Clark only counted each type of misbehavior
across the entire class and charted their daily frequencies. This was
the baseline phase. In phase 2, she continued to count all three
types of the misbehavior, but if a student talked without
permission, she fined that student one point. This started
treatment on only the first misbehavior. The other two misbehav-

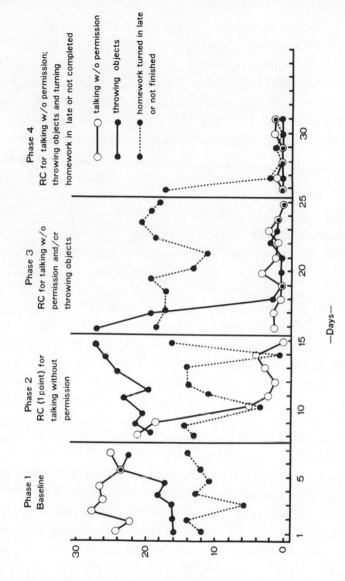

FIGURE 5.1. Ms. Clark's use of a multiple baseline design to evaluate the effectiveness of using a response cost procedure for reducing three different misbehaviors of the students in her classroom.

iors remained in baseline conditions. In phase 3, students were fined one point either when they talked without permission or when they threw objects. Turning-in-homework remained in the baseline condition. In the final phase, children were fined whenever they emitted any of the target behaviors. By that time, however, only a few of each of the target misbehaviors were occurring each day. The treatment was shown to be effective by using the design, and Ms. Clark no longer had those behavior problems. Now she can continue her plans for a classroom program that will include the reinforcement of appropriate behavior as well as the response cost of misbehavior.

Ms. Clark's use of response cost with a token economy was quite effective. Her future plan for having students earn as well as lose tokens depending on their behavior should increase appropriate behaviors and maintain the reduction of the misbehaviors. Still, a teacher need not institute a token economy to effectively use response cost. There are many items and privileges readily available in any classroom which could be removed contingent on specified target misbehaviors. Whenever a teacher removes a specific amount of positive reinforcement after a misbehavior, the response cost procedure is being used. If a teacher cannot think of any reinforcing items or events to be used with response cost, the possibility exists that the classroom is not as pleasant an environment as it should be.

Response cost, especially but not exclusively with the help of a token economy, is a useful procedure for teachers to learn. While its somewhat aversive nature provides several disadvantages, which will be discussed later, it can quickly effect behavioral reductions which are long-lasting. The use of this procedure has been widely studied in a variety of applied settings including homes, schools, prisons, mental hospitals, and industries. Such studies generally indicate that the technique is easy to use, rapidly effects a behavioral change, and seems to produce little or no side-effects—even though response cost is generally thought to be a somewhat aversive procedure.

Selecting Response Cost

Teachers intending to use the response cost procedure to manage behavior should first examine several issues. They should evaluate the advantages and disadvantages of the technique. Next, attention must be given to the various factors that partially determine whether the procedure will be effective or not. After carefully evaluating these issues, you should be able to: (1) judge if response cost is appropriate to the situation, and (2) decide how to best implement the procedure in order to achieve optimum results.

Advantages and Disadvantages

When properly implemented, response cost has several advantages which recommend its use. First, response cost reduces misbehavior effectively and quickly. The procedure has been shown to be effective in many studies, across a wide range of individuals. That response cost quickly reduces misbehavior was shown by Burchard and Barrera (1972), who found that response cost was as effective as timeout while avoiding the isolation feature required of timeout (see Unit 6).

Second, response cost is effective in widely different settings, across a wide range of misbehaviors, and with quite divergent populations. The procedure has been used with individuals and groups of most school ages. Misbehavior of normal, retarded, and emotionally disturbed individuals has been reduced by using response cost. The types of misbehaviors that have been controlled by the response cost procedure have ranged from the relatively mild (thumbsucking, talking back) to the relatively severe (fighting, destruction of property).

While response cost is effective across a wide range of types of misbehaviors, its use for any misbehavior is questionable. Long and Frye (1977) feel that response cost should be used only with the more disruptive behaviors, since they believe students must be free to make some types of mistakes. Their intent is that mild, occasional behaviors (being silly, for example) should not be treated in the same manner as fighting, cheating, or cursing. The procedure will reduce either type of behavior, but response cost for very mild misbehaviors is probably too harsh.

The procedure can also be applied on an individual or group basis. For example, each time a student runs in the halls, he could lose a specified privilege or number of points. Applied as a group contingency, however, whenever an individual misbehaves, the entire group is fined. For instance, if homework is turned in on time, the group is allowed to watch a movie on Friday. If Sally does not do her homework, instead of withdrawing the privilege from just Sally, no one is allowed to view the film. Such group contingencies are effective, since peer pressure is usually brought to bear on offenders. Still, we feel that such tactics can be quite unfair and should only be used in extreme cases and for short periods of time.

A third advantage is that response cost can be an easy procedure to use, especially when compared to some other procedures, such as timeout (Johnston, 1972). The procedure is easiest in situations where special privileges or token economies are a regular part of the classroom. Those privileges or tokens can be easily withdrawn contingent on the occurrence of a misbehavior. Record-keeping is easy, since teachers only need to keep track of the frequency of target misbehaviors, a task which can be done with paper and pencil. Even without a token economy, there should be so many reinforcing items or events available in a classroom that response cost becomes simple to implement.

A final advantage is that response cost works well in conjunction with many other procedures. When the reinforcement procedures are being used (Units 9-11), that reinforcement could be what the teacher removes when adding a response cost procedure. The combination of procedures usually reduces misbehavior more rapidly and keeps its level low for longer periods of time. Since response cost can be used with so many of the other procedures, that advantage becomes more important.

Some of the advantages, as we have noted, need careful

consideration for in some cases they can be disadvantages. Because response cost is so effective, it could be used in situations where it would be unwarranted. Using response cost for mild misbehaviors or using it through a group contingency can often be an unethical application of the procedure. Since losing a privilege can seem severe, especially to young children, any teacher must carefully judge the ethics of a choice to use response cost. There are even cases where response cost could be illegal. Withholding activities that have been established by school policy or state law is a misuse of the procedure that could turn out to be also illegal (Long and Frye, 1977).

A related use of the procedure that we believe is unethical is removing academic points or grades for social misbehavior. If a child has worked hard to earn a good grade in math, he should not lose math points for misbehaving. It is unfair for the child and unjust of the teacher. When a child is good, no one adds to his math grade; when he is not so good, he should lose nothing from that math grade. A social misbehavior should only cost a *social* event or privilege. It is difficult for us to overstress the point that academic and social costs should not be mixed.

The disadvantages of response cost are somewhat less serious than those of punishment (Unit 4) or timeout (Unit 6). Still, the teacher who plans to use the technique should be aware of them for they are more serious than many of the procedures presented later in this book. First, although this procedure is easier than some others, the teacher must still maintain adequate records, a responsibility that may, at least initially, require some effort. This is especially true when response cost is used in conjunction with a token economy. Accurate records must be kept in order to promote consistency (people often forget events not written down) and fairness (amount of the fine associated with a particular behavior should be standardized and displayed).

Second, since response cost is aversive (removal of positive reinforcers), some students may become emotional when a reinforcer is lost. In other words, response cost can produce emotional side-effects. These effects are similar to what we sometimes feel when we are caught speeding and first hear the siren behind us. Long and Frye (1977) recommend that you remain calm and ignore such outbursts. To alleviate possible emotional reactions they suggest, "Be fair in imposing penalties with all misbehaving students" (p. 98). Also, if rewards can be earned, one can explain how the student can re-earn the privilege or reinforcer. If these approaches, by themselves, do not work, you may then wish to fine the emotional outburst itself or use another procedure to reduce the outburst (for example, you might remove the child from the environment for several minutes).

It is interesting to note, however, that response cost has been found, at times, to even reduce the possibility of these emotional side-effects. Kaufman and O'Leary (1972) investigated whether response cost, in conjunction with a token system, resulted in emotional side-effects (aggression, escape behaviors) that are typically associated with more aversive procedures. They did not detect increases in aggressions or inattention (behaviors that were being monitored) nor were other behavioral side-effects noted. The behavior of students under the response cost condition was similar to the behavior of students under baseline and treatment conditions other than response cost.

The final disadvantage of response cost depends on how it has been implemented. In a token economy, where certain reinforcers or special privileges are added to a classroom, use of the procedure could be expensive. If the special events or back-up reinforcers are movies, field trips, or the opportunity to receive candy or toys, the teacher might have to spend a relatively large amount of his or her own money for these items. To avoid this potential problem, many teachers use events already available in the classroom (for example, free time, time in the library, line leader, availability of certain toys or books, and so forth).

Added to the problem of illegal or unethical implementation of response cost, these disadvantages should cause a teacher to think twice before using it. The advantages, however, show response cost to be quite helpful. For relatively serious problems, and with care in the choice of costs, response cost can be a beneficial procedure to add to a classroom.

The Effectiveness of Response Cost

In addition to the advantages and disadvantages of response cost, a teacher must be familiar with several factors which determine the effectiveness of a response cost contingency. These factors play a role in determining how fast and how effectively a target misbehavior can be reduced or eliminated by response cost. These factors which contribute to the effectiveness of response cost include the initial decision concerning the size of the cost, the type of cost to be used, communication of the rules to the students (which helps insure teacher consistency), allowing students to build up what is called a reinforcement reserve, and combining response cost with other behavioral procedures.

Deciding about the size of the cost, especially before implementing the procedure, is a difficult issue. Burchard and Barrera (1972) found that as the magnitude or size of the response cost increased, its suppressing effect also increased. This suggests that response cost, like the use of punishment, should be at maximal intensity at the onset. However, other researchers have found minimal costs to be as effective as large costs. In fact, a study by Hall, Axelrod, Foundopoulos, Shellman, Campbell, and Cranston (1972) found that merely removing colored sheets of paper with the student's name on it was sufficient to reduce certain misbehaviors (the slips were not even exchangeable). Which way should you go? Long and Frye (1977) suggest that one should penalize sparingly. "A student who has worked diligently all period to earn ten tokens should not lose his entire earnings because of a single inappropriate act" (p. 97). To an extent, this approach is endorsable.

Still, there are certain misbehaviors whose severity warrants a costly fine. Perhaps the most feasible solution to the problem is the empirical one. First, set fines for the misbehaviors that you wish to eliminate, allowing the size of the fine to reflect the severity of the behavior. If, after a period of time, the frequency of the target misbehavior has not decreased, this can be interpreted that the fine for the misbehaviors is too small and it should be raised. How large an increase should also be determined empirically. You could, though, try doubling it, and if that worked immediately, you might wish to reduce the fine. If doubling is not successful, future increases should also be reflective of what the behavior is doing according to your graph. A democratic method can also be used to first determine fines. Tell your students what the target misbehaviors are and ask them how much of a cost they think it will take to reduce them.

The "type" of cost associated with a particular misbehavior must be considered. This can be a confusing issue. Dreikurs (1971) has discussed two types of costs that can be used with the response cost procedure: arbitrary costs and logical consequences. An arbitrary cost is not a natural environmental outcome (consequence) of the behavior. For example, if a teacher fines a student two minutes of free time each time the student throws a piece of paper, the consequence is said to be arbitrary, since it is not a naturally occurring consequence of the behavior (restated, the teacher has *imposed* the consequence).

A logical consequence, too, may not be a naturally occurring consequence, but it differs from the arbitrary consequence since it logically or rationally relates to the misbehavior. For example, if a child does not finish supper, she is not allowed to snack later in the evening. There is a logical as well as a contingent relationship between the misbehavior and its consequence. An academic example that illustrates a logical consequence would be dropping a student's homework one letter (say, from a "B" to a "C") for turning it in late (this is an academic cost for an academic misbehavior, and therefore does not violate the suggestion made in the previous section).

We are not aware of any applied research demonstrating that logical costs are superior to arbitrary ones in reducing misbehavior.

Still, if one is in a position where both options are available, the logical cost *may* be preferred, since the child may be able to relate it to the misbehavior more easily than an arbitrary one. Remember, though, that each of us is continually exposed to imposed contingencies which result in little or no confusion.

It is also important to include a plan for how the response cost program will be communicated to the students. As previously stated, it can be a good idea to have the students involved in initially setting the fines. Whatever the case, though, every child should know, in advance, what a particular misbehavior's consequence (cost, in this case) will be. The reasoning behind this is fairness and consistency. Specific communication helps the teacher to be more consistent and helps the students see the fairness of the program. If, without this communication, one child is fined an exorbitant cost and another child, for the same offense, is fined a minimal cost, both children may rebel against the arbitrariness of the process. Additionally, Long and Frye (1977) state that "If students are to learn to control their own behavior, they must learn to appreciate in advance the consequences of performing specified behavior. Erratic application of behavior control techniques does not always afford them this opportunity" (p. 174).

The next factor influencing the effectiveness of response cost is the requirement of a reinforcement reserve. Reinforcement reserve means, simply, that you should plan your program in a manner that will insure each student can be successful (e.g., each student should earn or receive enough reinforcers so they do not finish with zero reinforcers or, even worse, "in-the-hole"). The rationale for the reserve build-up concept is that if students lose all their reinforcers on the first day, there will be little incentive for them to attempt to control their own behavior. Sulzer and Mayer (1972) have summarized the importance of this variable in the following manner:

> Fine the waiter too heavily for breakage, and he quits his job.
> Take too many tokens away, and the student gives up complete-

ly. Reduce his letter grade by three, and the high school junior sees no reason to work at all. The approach that seems to work best is to allow the individual to accumulate and retain enough conditioned reinforcers so that he can have access to stronger back-up reinforcers on some regular basis. The waiter should be able to end up with enough money to care for himself and his family. The student needs to retain enough tokens to buy access to the back-up reinforcers a sufficient number of times. The high school junior, motivated by aspiration to college admission, needs to maintain an average sufficient to allow him to be accepted into college if he is to remain motivated (pp. 163-164).

The final factor that can influence the success of your response cost program is how you use it in combination with other management procedures. Response cost, like all of the techniques we have or will discuss, works better in combination with another procedure than it does alone. An example of this was presented earlier when we illustrated the use of response cost within a token economy system. In the illustration, each child was non-contingently given X number of points at the start of each day and these were withdrawn as misbehaviors occurred. By itself, this is a negative arrangement, since the children are not learning which behaviors are acceptable—only which are unacceptable (the child's attention is directed to the misbehavior and not to acceptable behaviors). Since the system previously detailed is negative, we suggest a system that contingently rewards behaviors that are incompatible with the target misbehaviors (DRI—Unit 11). Non-contingently providing reinforcers is acceptable to initially familiarize the children with the system, but, in the long run, a system that teaches what is appropriate and what is inappropriate behavior (e.g., reinforces "good" behavior and reduces the "bad") is more beneficial to the child and to the "tone" of the setting.

To use response cost effectively and fairly, these factors must be mastered. The teacher must decide issues concerning the size and type of cost, communicate these issues to the students, be consistent in implementing the procedure, allow students to build up a reinforcement reserve, and when possible, combine response cost with other, more positive procedures. Having incorporated these factors into a plan, a teacher should have excellent success when using response cost in the classroom.

Using Response Cost

The final decision to use or not to use response cost is a difficult one. You must weigh the advantages against the disadvantages and evaluate the variables which will influence the technique's viability in terms of your time and ability. Once you have decided to use the procedure, however, there are certain steps you should follow to insure proper implementation. A few of the beginning steps are common to all procedures (they were discussed in Units 1-3). The remaining steps have been analyzed in this Unit. Assuming you choose to use response cost, you should sequentially follow the steps listed in Table 5.3.

TABLE 5.3: STEPS TO FOLLOW TO IMPLEMENT RESPONSE COST

1. Specify and define target misbehavior(s).
2. Choose measure for target misbehavior(s).
3. Collect baseline data.
4. Choose design to evaluate effectiveness.
5. Communicate system to students.
6. Determine special privileges/back-up reinforcers to be awarded (student involvement is recommended).
7. Associate the "price" of privileges and back-up reinforcers (student involvement is recommended).
8. Set initial "cost" for target misbehavior (student involvement is recommended).
9. Be consistent.
10. Combine response cost with other techniques if possible.
11. Follow design—evaluate your data.
12. Continue program or try another procedure.

Conclusions

Response cost quickly and effectively reduces misbehavior, and its suppressive quality is usually enduring. Since response cost is aversive, the decision to use or not to use the procedure must be made continuously. Aversive procedures can be very effective if properly and carefully implemented. Due process and the rights of students, however, must be considered before a response cost program is begun. Generally, ". . . due process has been interpreted to require that prior notice of prohibited behavior be provided" (Long and Frye, 1977, p. 175). A student's rights are, essentially, to know what he or she has been accused of (the misbehavior) and to be allowed to respond to them. The requirements of due process and student rights should not be a problem if you follow the steps which were presented in Table 5.3 and explained in this Unit.

The final consideration to remember is that response cost, by itself, does not teach children how to behave in a socially and/or academically appropriate manner. For this reason, it is suggested that you use response cost in combination with other techniques and systems that do reinforce appropriate behavior. Once again, this will add to the pleasantness of your classroom and help you reach your goals for appropriate behavior.

SUGGESTED PROJECTS

1. List three response cost contingencies that can effect behaviors in your daily life.
2. With some other teachers, list the types of costs you already use in your classrooms.
3. Evaluate those costs in terms of ethics and legality.
4. List and operationally define the misbehaviors in your classroom that would be suitable for reduction by response cost.
5. Begin collecting baseline data on one of them.
6. With your students, make a list of potential reinforcers and arrange the list into a reinforcement menu.

7. With the students involved, assign a cost to the misbehavior you are counting.
8. Arrange for the plan to begin and implement it. Note if side-effects occur. Evaluate your findings (compare treatment data to baseline data). Are your costs high enough? Too high? Rearrange your plans if they are not working.

REFERENCES

Ayllon, T., and Azrin, N. *The Token Economy: A Motivational System for Therapy and Rehabilitation.* New York: Appleton-Century-Crofts, 1968.

Burchard, J.D., and Barrera, F. An analysis of timeout and response cost in a programmed environment. *Journal of Applied Behavior Analysis,* 1972, 5(3), 271-282.

Hall, R.V., Axelrod, S., Foundopoulos, M., Shellman, J., Campbell, R., and Cranston, S.S. The effective use of punishment to modify behavior in the classroom. In K.D. and S.G. O'Leary (Eds.), *Classroom Management: The Successful Use of Behavior Modification.* New York: Pergamon Press, Inc., 1972.

Johnston, J. Punishment of human behavior. *American Psychologist,* November, 1972, 1033-1054.

Kaufman, K., and O'Leary, K.D. Rewards, cost, and self-evaluation procedures for disruptive adolescents in a psychiatric hospital school. *Journal of Applied Behavior Analysis,* 1972, 5, 293-309.

Kazdin, A., and Bootzin, R. The token economy: An evaluative review. *Journal of Applied Behavior Analysis,* 1972, 5, 343-372.

Lauridsen, D. *The Token Economy System.* Volume 19 in The Instructional Design Library. Englewood Cliffs, New Jersey: Educational Technology Publications, 1978.

Long, J.D., and Frye, V.H. *Making It Till Friday.* Princeton, New Jersey: Princeton Book Co., 1977.

Sulzer, B., and Mayer, G.R. *Behavior Modification Procedures for School Personnel.* Hinsdale, Illinois: The Dryden Press, Inc., 1972.

Unit Six

TIMEOUT

Study Questions

1. Define timeout. Illustrate the procedure in (a) a school setting and (b) a home setting.
2. What are the forms timeout generally takes in applied settings?
3. Explain when one would use timeout instead of extinction.
4. List and discuss the six advantages of timeout.
5. List and discuss the six disadvantages/drawbacks of timeout.
6. What are the factors that influence the effectiveness of timeout?
7. Describe how length of the timeout interval influences the procedure's behavior-suppressing properties.
8. Cite an example that illustrates when isolation or removal from a situation does not qualify as timeout.
9. Explain how contingent observation and systematic exclusion are different from timeout.
10. If, in removing a student from the classroom, you invariably had to first physically subdue the child, would you recommend continued use of the procedure? Explain your answer.

This Unit examines a behavior reduction procedure called *timeout*. Teachers and parents often use timeout, or variations of timeout, without knowing they are employing a specific behavior reduction procedure. When a parent sends a child to his room for a period of time after he broke a home rule, the parent is trying to use a form of timeout. The same is often true when a teacher puts a child in the corner or out in the hall after a class rule has been violated. Some teachers use the procedure for the group by having all the children place their heads on the desk for several minutes. Sometimes the misbehavior which prompted the teacher or parent to try one of these treatments is effectively reduced; often, however, it is not.

While timeout can be an effective and efficient procedure, it can be misused or used at the wrong times. The effectiveness of timeout depends on a careful analysis of the situation, the child, and type of misbehavior. Equally, the teacher must know how to implement timeout so as to maximize its effectiveness. The explanation of timeout presented through this Unit should help teachers clarify what they have been doing and help them use timeout, when appropriate, in a more effective, efficient manner.

Definition and Explanation

Timeout is a shorthand name for a procedure that is technically known as "timeout from positive reinforcement." Timeout is defined as the contingent removal of access to all positive reinforcers for a specified period of time. In practice, timeout usually means that the child is removed or isolated from the setting where the reinforcers are present. The child is placed in a setting called the timeout space, where the opportunity for reinforcement is small or nonexistent. The child is removed from the setting because it is often undesirable or difficult to remove all possible sources of reinforcement from the setting, especially a classroom.

Removing the child from access to reinforcement makes timeout one of the two procedures which attempt to directly confront one of the major causes of misbehavior. As was explained in Unit 2, misbehavior, like other forms of behavior, often is occurring because some source of reinforcement is strengthening or maintaining it. Sarah gets out of her seat because she can go over and interact with Margaret. Johnny acts up in class because the other children laugh when he does. Ralph does not pay attention because it is more reinforcing to stare at other students or out the window. In each case, the misbehavior is being maintained by a reinforcing environmental event.

Through the immediate removal of the child to a timeout area, the reinforcing environmental event does not have a chance to occur, at least not quickly enough to work to maintain the misbehavior. It is primarily for that reason that timeout is effective. When misbehavior is not reinforced, it will tend to decrease. But timeout is effective for a second reason as well. During the time the child spends in the timeout area, he is not able to earn any reinforcement (participate in an ongoing activity, complete a required assignment, or be praised for an appropriate behavior). So timeout is effective because it stops the critical reinforcement from maintaining the misbehavior and because the child must spend a period of time during which no source of reinforcement is available.

Since timeout is effective primarily because the critical reinforcement is not received, a reader could justifiably ask, "Wouldn't it be better to just ensure that the critical reinforcement does not occur after the misbehavior?" That is an astute question, for in the cases where that is possible, it is exactly what you would and should do. Discontinuing the critical reinforcement maintaining a misbehavior is a procedure called extinction. It is the second of the two procedures mentioned earlier which attempt to ameliorate a basic cause of misbehavior, and it is thoroughly discussed in the next Unit. For many instances of misbehavior, however, it is difficult or impossible to either identify the critical reinforcement or to discontinue it (for example, it is very difficult to stop the other students from laughing at Johnny). In those cases, timeout could be used where extinction could not be used. Also, timeout is often a more powerful procedure than extinction because the child must also spend a period of time in which no source of reinforcement is available.

Selecting Timeout

While timeout can be a powerful behavior reduction procedure, care must be taken in its use. The process of removing a child from the classroom setting, even for a brief period of time, presents problems. While timeout has several advantages, it has several disadvantages as well. Also, to effectively use timeout requires specific skills for its proper implementation. The remainder of this Unit examines those issues.

Advantages and Disadvantages

Timeout has several important advantages and disadvantages when used in a classroom. The advantages of timeout include its ability to quickly effect enduring reductions in misbehavior; the fact that it does not use painful environmental events; its relative ease of implementation; its effectiveness in many situations with a wide variety of types of misbehaviors; that it causes fewer and less intense emotional side-effects than found with some other procedures; and that it is easily combined with other behavior reduction procedures. Among the disadvantages of timeout are the possibility of a phenomenon called behavioral contrast, its emphasis on what the child is doing wrong instead of what he is doing right; the fact that removal from the class where appropriate behavior could be learned is required; and some possible emotional and behavioral side-effects.

Among the most important advantages of timeout is that it quickly reduces misbehavior. Both applied and experimental research have demonstrated that timeout is effective for reducing behavior in short periods of time. Figure 6.1 shows how timeout can rapidly reduce misbehavior. In this hypothetical illustration, Terry's social interactions at an inappropriate time were monitored. In Phase I (baseline), there was no intervention; the teacher merely counted and graphed the frequency of the target behavior

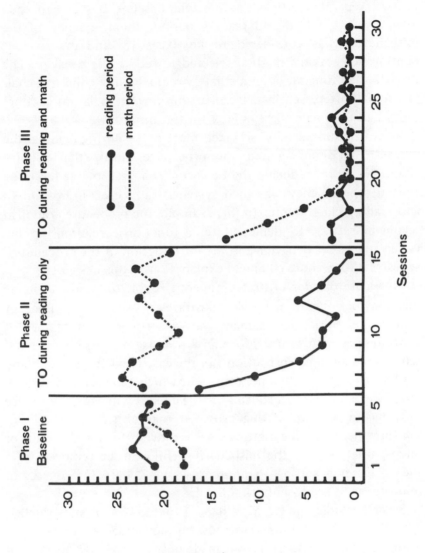

FIGURE 6.1. An example illustrating how quickly timeout reduces an inappropriate behavior in two different settings.

in two separate settings (a multiple baseline design). In each setting, math period and reading period, the frequency of the misbehavior was considered to be excessive, and the timeout contingency was the method selected to reduce the behavior. The teacher used timeout by immediately removing the child to a chair in the hall after each instance of inappropriate social interaction. Terry had to remain there quietly for five minutes.

Since the misbehavior occurred most often during reading, the teacher first implemented the procedure during that activity (Phase II). After reducing the behavior to an acceptable level, the timeout contingency was then systematically used in both math and reading class. (Note: In this example, the procedure is applied setting-by-setting to demonstrate a functional relationship between the target behavior and the introduction of the procedure— see Unit 3 for a more complete explanation of this design.)

As Figure 6.1 demonstrates, timeout is able to rapidly decrease misbehavior. Figure 6.1 also illustrates a second advantage of timeout; it works across many varied settings. This feature of timeout has made the procedure popular for use in homes, schools, and various institutions. In the case cited above, math and reading were the different settings in which timeout was systematically established as a contingency. Timeout will typically reduce misbehavior in any setting provided that either all sources of reinforcement in the setting are removed (often difficult or undesirable) or that the misbehaving child can be removed from the reinforcing setting to another setting where the sources of reinforcement are absent or minimal.

Several studies (e.g., McMillan, 1967; Tolman and Mueller, 1964) have discussed a third possible advantage of timeout. In both studies, a comparison was made between the effectiveness of contingent timeout versus contingent punishment. Results of each showed that both procedures were similarly effective (though timeout did not produce as rapid a decrement in behavior as did punishment). Since timeout is usually less aversive than is punishment, this alone can recommend it in situations where either timeout or punishment are possible choices. The import of the studies, however, is that there appears to be a more gradual and less complete behavioral recovery when timeout, as opposed to punishment, is used to reduce behavior.

Figure 6.2 illustrates the fact that a behavior reduced through a timeout procedure can recover (return to its baseline level) more slowly than the same behavior under a punishment procedure. In this hypothetical example, two identical twins with very similar reinforcement histories were studied. Both boys were in the same setting, and were doing the same misbehavior ("talk-outs") with approximately the same frequency per session. In Phase II, Tom's talk-outs were punished, resulting in an almost immediate reduction. Bill's talk-outs during Phase II resulted in a timeout period. Notice that while Tom's misbehavior decreased faster than did Bill's, both eventually reached the same low level. The contingencies established for each subject in Phase II were withdrawn during the third phase (return-to-baseline). In this phase, the punished behavior (Tom's) rapidly returned to its original level, while the behavior of Bill increased at an apparently slower rate and did not attain its original base rate.

Another advantage to timeout is also one of the factors which influences the procedure's effectiveness. Specifically, timeout works well in conjunction with other behavior reducing procedures. To the applied practitioner, this means that the effectiveness of timeout can be enhanced when appropriate alternative behaviors that will be reinforced are available to the misbehaver. This factor has been supported by research in both the laboratory (Holz and Azrin, 1962; Holz, Azrin, and Ayllon, 1963) and the applied setting (Burchard and Barrera, 1972). Probably the most productive combination of timeout with another procedure would be timeout and differential reinforcement of incompatible behavior (DRI).

DRI (the subject of Unit 11) specifies that the emission of a desirable behavior that cannot be made at the same time as the target behavior should be reinforced. For example, suppose Betty

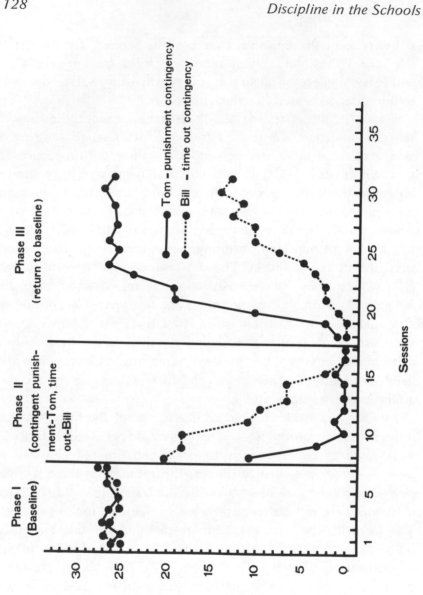

FIGURE 6.2. An example illustrating the differences between timeout and punishment in both the rate of behavioral elimination and the rate of behavioral recovery.

frequently leaves her desk during a time that she is to remain at her desk. DRI, by itself, would provide for reinforcement whenever Betty was seated at her desk *and* working or engaged in some other desirable activity. This would have the effect of increasing Betty's appropriate behaviors while decreasing her out-of-seat behavior. With a DRI/timeout combination, behaviors that are incompatible with out-of-seat behavior would still be reinforced, but additionally, emission of the target misbehavior would result in timeout.

The combination of the procedures is beneficial for two reasons. First, the behavioral reduction effected will probably be accomplished faster than if either procedure were used alone. Additionally, the behavioral outcome is constructive, since Betty's out-of-seat behavior will have been replaced by desirable alternative behaviors that have been selectively reinforced.

The last advantage of timeout may also be the most important. Clark, Rowbury, Baer, and Baer (1973) found that once a misbehavior had been reduced to a manageable level, it could be maintained at that level by making the timeout procedure contingent on the misbehavior on an intermittent schedule (versus a continuous schedule). In other words, once the misbehavior is occurring at a low rate, the timeout procedure does not have to be implemented every time the misbehavior occurs. For the teacher and parent this means that once they have reduced the misbehavior (which involves collecting data, consistently and immediately consequating, etc.) they will only have to use the procedure every now and then (allowing them to attend to other matters) to effectively keep it at a low level.

While the advantages of timeout make it sound like an excellent procedure to choose, the disadvantages of timeout must also be considered before the decision is made. The first disadvantage to be considered is an effect called behavioral contrast. Behavioral contrast can occur when a behavior or class of behaviors is exposed to certain contingencies in one setting and different contingencies for the same behavior(s) in another setting, or under different conditions in the same setting. For example, if you send Jeff to the timeout room each time he takes a neighbor's belongings (pencils), this may result in an increase in Jeff's taking-behavior when you are not around. While you are present, Jeff does not take things; however, when you are not present (the altered setting) he takes more (or more often) than he originally did (the behavioral contrast).

A second disadvantage shows that the use of timeout (although not to the extent of some other aversive procedures) may depict the teacher or parent, in the child's view, as a signal or cue for unpleasant events which follow. People, places, and things that are paired with unpleasant or aversive events often become aversive themselves, and people will actively work to avoid or escape things that are aversive (see the section on negative reinforcement in Unit 2). In the example above, Jeff may begin to treat his teacher as an aversive event to be avoided because the teacher has signaled (been paired with) the loss of access to positive reinforcement by his or her use of the timeout procedure.

We do not want children to view school or their teachers as objects to be avoided or to feel relieved when they have "escaped" at the end of the day or for the summer. Timeout is a very popular and effective behavior-reducing procedure in our schools, and because of this popularity, we feel that we must emphasize the above disadvantage and repeatedly stress the contention that schools and learning should be interesting places with reinforcing experiences rather than places which are punitive and dreary. Be consistently aware of the possibility that if you use aversive procedures to an extreme (which is difficult to define), you and the setting are likely to become aversive to the child or children.

If the teacher and the school and even possibly the subject matter become aversive to the child through the use of timeout (or other procedures), another, related issue becomes important. Once that has happened, using timeout only serves to remove the child from an aversive environment rather than a reinforcing one. Under those circumstances, timeout cannot be an effective procedure.

Timeout

For example, imagine tha
assigned extra math hom
(teachers take note: assi
suppressing inappropriat
educational practice). O\
and activities associate(
aversive environmental e\
escape. If Susie now disr
isolated from math cla:
wished to reduce (and
increase through negati

example, the child
teachers may be
ness would b
try to reinf
the beh
but tl
sp

aversive event rather than losing access to reinforcers for a period of time. Disrupting math, under those conditions, could conceivably increase or remain strong, rather than decrease.

A third disadvantage is that timeout has as its goal only the reduction of misbehavior; it does not teach the child appropriate social or academic behaviors. Timeout, by itself, neither tells the student which behaviors are appropriate to a situation nor provides for alternative behaviors that can be reinforced. Because it does not promote positive behavior, it draws the child's attention to the very behavior we wish to eliminate. That in itself may, in some instances, work to maintain the undesirable behavior.

Fourth, long or frequent timeout periods remove the child from the learning situation. Time spent outside the classroom (in timeout) is lost for purposes of instruction (since all sources of reinforcement must be absent, and, additionally, one would not want instruction/learning to be paired with an aversive event, thus, possibly, becoming aversive itself). Academic time lost during timeout should, theoretically, be made up, but usually it is not because of the burden it places upon the teacher. Also, while the individual is in the timeout area, opportunities for reinforcing acceptable academic/social behaviors in the situation are lost.

Additionally, frequent timeout, like other aversive consequences, may tend to inhibit socially appropriate behaviors. For

that is placed in timeout for arguing with
ome less assertive in situations where assertive-
 appropriate. To help prevent this from occurring,
rce appropriate behaviors that are somewhat similar to
vior being reduced. Yelling in class may produce timeout
at same child should be reinforced for cheering (yelling) at
rts events. Taking pencils in class should result in timeout, but
"stealing" a base at a ballgame should be encouraged. Watching
television may result in timeout if homework is not done, but
should be allowed if the homework has been completed.

Finally, timeout may lead to unwanted side-effects, including
aggression and withdrawal. Withdrawal is especially a potential
problem when one is dealing with a child who already interacts
with others at a minimal level. Using timeout with a withdrawn
child may further reduce the type, quantity, and quality of the
social interactions in which the child presently engages, since he is
usually isolated from social situations anyway. For some individuals, timeout may even serve as a positive reinforcer for withdrawal
forms of behavior. These infrequent instances where timeout does
serve as a positive reinforcer should be considered as a result of the
person's unique history of reinforcement. However, this possibility
must be considered before one adopts timeout as a procedure to
reduce a particular child's misbehavior.

The Effectiveness of Timeout

If, based on your knowledge of its advantages and disadvantages, timeout appears suitable for a particular child, behavior, or
setting, you must now consider various factors relevant to the
proper use of the technique. At least five factors have been
identified which, if attended to, can contribute to a program's
success or, if ignored, may account for its failure.

Communicating the Procedure

Explaining the rules or contingencies under which the children
will be operating generally will enhance the timeout procedure's

effectiveness for several reasons. First, telling the students which behaviors are unacceptable *may* influence how quickly the procedure decreases the occurrence of the behaviors, since the students will not have to "figure-out" which behaviors result in timeout. Second, informing children of the rules or parameters within which they may operate is always good pedagogy, since it reduces the possibility of error and uncertainty as to what is acceptable and unacceptable. Finally, the consequence itself (removal from sources of reinforcement) should be explained. This explanation should include a visit to the timeout room or area, specification of the length of the timeout period, and a description of how the child must act prior to leaving the timeout area and regaining entry to the classroom.

Duration of the Timeout

Length of the timeout period in applied studies has ranged from several seconds to several hours. In general, most behavior analysts recommend short (five to ten minutes) intervals for timeout. Johnston (1972) has identified two excellent reasons for brief timeout periods. ". . . all responses occurring during the timeout are unavoidably paired with the aversive stimuli in the situation. Thus, the longer the timeout period, the greater the probability of pairing desirable responses with aversive stimuli. Longer timeout periods also serve to remove the subject from treatment sessions for greater periods of time, thus lessening the opportunity for reinforcement of appropriate behavior" (pp. 1039-1040).

Removing the Misbehaver

The offending child must be removed to the timeout area immediately upon emission of the misbehavior. The removal should be done in a natural, non-hostile manner, but firmly. It is recommended that you say the child's name and verbally relate the behavior to the consequence. For example, "John, since you hit Marie, you must go to the timeout room." Try *not* to say anything more to the child. Social attention directed towards the child while being removed may reinforce the original targeted misbehavior and possibly act as a cue or reinforcer for further misbehavior. If you find that the removal of an individual results in physical resistance that you are not able to handle comfortably, then timeout should not be used (try a different procedure).

Leaving Timeout

The child should not be allowed to leave the timeout area while the timeout period is in effect. The child should also not be allowed to leave the timeout area soon after engaging in any disruptive behavior. If the timeout period has elapsed and it is time to allow the child back into the classroom but the child is, for example, screaming, do not allow the child out. If you allow him to leave the timeout area, you will have negatively reinforced screaming (you have increased the probability of a behavior—screaming—that terminated an aversive event—the timeout; you may want to review negative reinforcement, which is explained in Unit 2). Because the process of negative reinforcement is operating when you terminate timeout, you should stop timeout immediately after the child does a behavior that you want to increase in frequency. A rule-of-thumb to follow is that the child cannot display any disruptive (operationally define this term to the child) behavior during the final thirty seconds of timeout (if you use this rule, you should, of course, explain it to the child).

Consistency

There are two aspects of consistency that relate to the implementation of the timeout procedure. First, at least initially, every occurrence of the misbehavior should result in timeout. If you do not consequate each occurrence of the behavior, it is being reinforced on an intermittent schedule (those times you don't use timeout) and behavior maintained on such schedules is more difficult to decrease. Second, parameters of the procedure (which behaviors result in timeout, length of timeout, etc.) should be the same for all children in the class. Differential treatment in the application of the procedures may produce problems for the teacher; the point to remember is that the same rules of conduct should apply to all students.

Variations of Timeout

At least two procedures have been used in applied settings that are variations of the timeout paradigm: systematic exclusion and contingent observation.

Bandura (1969) and Clarizio (1976) have both discussed the concept of systematic exclusion. The procedure is generally used by schools as a final effort for children that have not responded favorably to other procedures (used by themselves or in combination with other procedures). Before implementation, Bandura (1969) suggests that the child, teacher(s), parents, and school administrator confer to determine which behaviors will result in exclusion. Once these parameters are decided, whenever the child exhibits a target misbehavior, he is sent home for the rest of the day. At the home, the child should remain in the house (the parents' responsibility). The parents should "refrain from punishing, scolding, or applying other disciplinary measures" (p. 345), since the misbehavior is currently being consequated.

The rationale behind this variation is based on the observation that school, especially for young children (grades 6 and below), is a "fun place" to be (which, hopefully, is true). Unfortunately, there are at least three difficulties associated with this variation of timeout. First, the timeout period would, in most cases, be longer than what is currently considered optimal by behavior analysts. Second, the child is away from the learning situation which entails certain ethical (and possibly legal) considerations. Finally, and possibly most importantly, systematic exclusion is most often used with older children (grades 7 and above) who frequently do not view school as favorably as do younger children. Worse, many schools even further extend this variation to what is commonly known as "expulsion." When expelled, a student is denied access to the classroom for a specified amount of time (usually three days to an entire academic year!). Clearly, expelling a student that already discriminates schooling as aversive is not a viable method of reducing that student's misbehavior—in fact, it may strongly reinforce it.

The second variation of timeout, contingent observation, was first investigated by Porterfield, Herbert-Jackson, and Risley (1976). Contingent observation specified that ". . . when interesting activities or strong extrinsic reinforcers are not provided, a more prolonged timeout to a barren room would be necessary; but for undesired behaviors occurring in a context of highly reinforcing activity or strong extrinsic reinforcers, a brief timeout from active participation should be sufficient" (p. 56). The key to this variation on timeout is that, while the misbehaver is not allowed to participate in the ongoing activity, he is allowed to observe the activity.

Porterfield *et al.* (1976) reported a behavioral improvement with 15 of the 19 children who were exposed to this variation. Still, comment on the efficacy of the variation is limited since all the children were also praised when they were readmitted to the activity and displayed appropriate behavior (a combination of the timeout variation and DRI—Unit 11—was thus being used which limits the generalizability of contingent observation by itself).

However, contingent observation, by itself, is used in our society. In hockey, one of our more popular contact sports, when a player fouls another, he is sent to a penalty box for X amount of time. During this period, the player is able to watch the activities of the other players, and, hopefully, when allowed back into the game, will not commit the foul again.

Contingent observation is also the way most lifeguards enforce rules at swimming pools. For example, running in the pool area is not allowed (it is easy to slip on the wet concrete and be hurt). Leslie runs and is warned by the lifeguard to not run again. The second time Leslie runs, she is told that she is not allowed back into the pool for half an hour. During the half hour timeout period, Leslie is able to watch other swimmers, but she is not allowed back into the pool until her timeout period is over.

Using Timeout

Based on the information previously presented, it is obvious that the decision to use timeout should not be made lightly. For each individual (and setting) you must consider the factors that influence the procedure's effectiveness and decide if the procedure's advantages offset its disadvantages. In addition to the above, you should also review whether the use of timeout is legal in your school. The reason you must attend to this aspect is that, ". . . the use of timeout has been eliminated or severely curtailed in many institutional settings due to recent court action (Wyatt v. Stickney, court case, 1974)" (Doleys, Wells, Hobbs, Roberts, and Cartelli, 1976, p. 471). If timeout is illegal in your system, or if there is much verbal administrative and parental complaint, use another procedure.

Parents and administrators who are not familiar with the technique are especially apt to recoil and become emotional over rooms or settings that are labeled as the "isolation" or "timeout" room. One can easily avoid this potential problem by calling the procedure and room (or setting) a name other than timeout. For example, instead of labeling the cloak room the timeout area, call it the "cooling-off room" or some other such name that does not carry the emotional connotations of timeout or isolation.

If you have decided to use timeout to eliminate a misbehavior, there are certain steps you must follow to assure proper implementation. Since they have already been discussed, Table 6.1 lists the steps you are to follow in sequential order.

Conclusions

Timeout is both efficient and effective in reducing misbehavior. Timeout is generally used in situations where one is unable to identify or control reinforcers that are maintaining a target misbehavior. The decision to use timeout must be made carefully, since it is usually an aversive procedure. The timeout contingency (removal from sources of reinforcement) may be aversive to some individuals in some settings. The procedure can, at times, also produce unwanted behavioral side-effects in certain individuals.

TABLE 6.1: STEPS TO FOLLOW TO IMPLEMENT TIMEOUT

---

1. Specify and define target misbehavior(s).
2. Choose measure for misbehavior(s).
3. Collect baseline data.
4. Choose design to evaluate effectiveness.
5. Determine if there is a suitable environment for the timeout area.
6. Decide how you are to remove the child from the setting.
7. Decide the length of timeout for each misbehavior.
8. Explain procedure to concerned child(ren)/parent(s)/administrators—begin procedure.
9. Initially, be consistent; after the misbehavior is reduced, shift to an intermittent schedule.
10. Combine procedure with others if possible.
11. Evaluate your data.
12. Continue or adopt another procedure.

One of the variations of timeout, contingent observation, seems to be particularly appropriate for very young children (ages 5-8) or settings that do not have a suitable area for the timeout period. A second variation, systematic exclusion, would not seem to benefit children academically, and should be used only when other procedures have failed.

Remember, since timeout is an aversive procedure, people (parents and teachers) who use it and the setting in which it is used may also become aversive. Finally, because timeout only reduces behavior, it is recommended that it be used in combination (if possible) with more positive procedures such as DRI (Unit 11). Timeout can be an excellent part of a teacher's behavioral reduction skills. Still, it must be used with caution and we recommend its use only in circumstances where other, more pleasant, procedures are either not feasible or have been found to be ineffective.

SUGGESTED PROJECTS

1. Suppose a child frequently throws food at other children during lunch at the school cafeteria. How would you use timeout to reduce this behavior? List several of the characteristics of the child you would first examine before attempting to utilize the procedure.
2. Pick two misbehaviors that occur in your home or school:
   A. Operationally define them.
   B. Explain why you would use timeout to reduce them.
   C. Describe (in detail) how you would implement the procedure (the timeout environment; the discussion with the child; communicating with parents and/or administrators (if indicated); data evaluation; design; etc.).
3. Implement your plan for one of the misbehaviors in #2 above. Explain what happens (Were there negative consequences? What? etc.).
4. You have implemented timeout, and, according to your data, it has not been effective. What do you do?

REFERENCES

Bandura, A. *Principles of Behavior Modification.* New York: Holt, Rinehart, and Winston, Inc., 1969.

Burchard, J.D., and Barrera, F. An analysis of timeout and response cost in a programmed environment. *Journal of Applied Behavior Analysis,* 1972, *5*(3), 271-282.

Clarizio, H.F. *Toward Positive Classroom Discipline,* 2nd ed. New York: John Wiley and Sons, Inc., 1976.

Clark, H.B., Rowbury, T., Baer, A.M., and Baer, D.M. Timeout as a punishing stimulus in continuous and intermittent schedules. *Journal of Applied Behavior Analysis,* 1973, *6,* 443-455.

Doleys, D.M., Wells, K.C., Hobbs, S.A., Roberts, M.W., and Cartelli,

L.M. The effects of social punishment on noncompliance: A comparison with timeout and positive practice. *Journal of Applied Behavior Analysis,* 1976, *9,* 471-484.

Holz, W.C., and Azrin, N.H. Interactions between the discriminative and aversive properties of punishment. *Journal of the Experimental Analysis of Behavior,* 1962, *5,* 229-234.

Holz, W.C., Azrin, N.H., and Ayllon, T. Elimination of behavior of mental patients by response-produced extinction. *Journal of the Experimental Analysis of Behavior,* 1963, *6,* 407-412.

Johnston, J.M. Punishment of human behavior. *American Psychologist,* November, 1972, 1033-1054.

McMillan, D.E. A comparison of the punishing effects of response-produced shock and response-produced timeout. *Journal of the Experimental Analysis of Behavior,* 1967, *10,* 439-449.

Porterfield, J.K., Herbert-Jackson, E., and Risley, T.R. Contingent observation: An effective and acceptable procedure for reducing disruptive behavior of young children in a group setting. *Journal of Applied Behavior Analysis,* 1976, *9,* 55-64.

Tolman, C.W., and Mueller, M.R. Laboratory control of toe-sucking in a young rhesus monkey by two kinds of punishment. *Journal of the Experimental Analysis of Behavior,* 1964, *1,* 323-325.

Wyatt *versus* Stickney. In B.J. Ennis and P.P. Friedman (Eds.), *Legal Rights of the Mentally Retarded,* Vol. 1. New York: Practicing Law Institute, 1974.

Unit Seven

EXTINCTION

Study Questions
1. Define and explain extinction. Develop two examples in which you might use extinction from your teaching experience.
2. On what assumption is the effectiveness of extinction based?
3. Explain the problem of identifying reinforcers, and discuss contingency analysis as a solution.
4. Briefly describe the Williams (1959) experiment. What was the reinforcer for the tantrum behavior?
5. List and describe the advantages and disadvantages of extinction.
6. List four misbehaviors for which it might be appropriate to use extinction and four for which it would not. Defend your choices.
7. List and explain each of the six factors which influence the effectiveness of extinction.
8. List the twelve steps for implementing extinction.
9. How does extinction answer the question of the "cause" of misbehavior?

Extinction is probably one of the most useful procedures for teachers to master when trying to reduce misbehavior. Although there are some drawbacks inherent in extinction, which will be discussed later, it is very effective, and the resulting elimination of misbehavior can last indefinitely. Extinction is one of the behavioral reduction procedures which has been extensively investigated in both laboratory and applied settings, and behavior analysts have learned how to use extinction in effective and efficient ways. The conclusions usually derived from the research state that extinction is one of the better behavioral elimination procedures for classroom use, and probably the best of the more aversive procedures.

Some teachers are initially confused about extinction because the term is commonly used to describe a result or product, rather than a process. Geologists say that a volcano has become extinct if it is no longer active. To a biologist, a species of animal is extinct if no members of the species are currently living. Adding to this confusion, some psychologists say that a behavior which no longer occurs is extinct, or, more commonly, has been extinguished. These types of geological, biological, or behavioral extinction are products. Each of those products can be traced to certain causes, but extinction, when used in this way, is the result, not the cause.

A behavior analyst uses the term, extinction, much more precisely. Extinction is one of many procedures by which a behavior can be eliminated. The resulting elimination is not called extinction; instead, it is referred to as behavioral elimination. Extinction, then, is a *process* which can result in the product of behavioral elimination.

Definition and Explanation

In Unit 2 it was explained that behaviors which are reinforced increase strength. If the reinforcement no longer occurs after the behavior, the behavior will decrease in strength. Extinction is the procedure of insuring that reinforcement does *not* occur following a behavior. When extinction occurs, the frequency or strength of that response will decrease. Since we are interested in misbehavior, insuring that reinforcement does not follow a misbehavior is an excellent way to reduce that behavior.

Extinction, then, can be defined as withholding reinforcement after a behavior. It is an operation by the teacher of insuring nonreinforcement. During extinction, a behavior which was previously reinforced is no longer reinforced. When no conse-quence follows a certain behavior, eventually the behavior will not occur; Ferster and Perrott (1968) have stated that, "Simply withholding reinforcement (extinction) is the most important way of reducing the frequency of a previously . . ." (p. 22) learned behavior. That would indicate that a working knowledge of the procedure—its advantages, disadvantages, properties, and the con-ditions influencing its effectiveness—is very important to teachers, and to other practitioners as well.

The effectiveness of extinction is based on the assumption that almost all behavior which a person does with some frequency is at least sometimes reinforced. If reinforcement were discontinued, the person would cease doing those behaviors. If a certain door was always locked, knob-turning behavior on that door would eventually cease. If whenever you passed a friend in the hall your salutation received no reaction, you would eventually cease your greeting behavior. If you never called on a child in your class, he would eventually cease raising his hand. In each case nonreinforce-ment occurred and the behavior decreased. All learned behaviors either currently receive reinforcement or were reinforced in the past. When reinforcement is completely discontinued, the behavior disappears.

A problem many teachers face when first using extinction is *identifying the reinforcer*. Extinction will work only when the reinforcer for that behavior is no longer available. Sometimes many consequences follow a behavior but only one is a reinforcer. If a teacher rearranges the situation so that one of the conse-quences, but not the actual reinforcer, no longer occurs, the behavior will continue at full strength. Eliminating the effective reinforcer is the crucial aspect of extinction.

The problem of identification of reinforcers is best exemplified through the example of "ignoring." Quite often a teacher's attention is the reinforcer which maintains a misbehavior. Even when the attention is thought to be punishment (see Unit 4), if it increases or maintains the misbehavior, it is, in fact, reinforcement. For some reason, the child sometimes misbehaves to earn this aversive attention. Probably aversive attention is better than no attention. In this case, if the teacher ignores the misbehavior, pays no attention to it, in other words provides no consequence for it, it will eventually disappear. Scolding, for example, might be intended to decrease the misbehavior but instead reinforced (strengthened) it; ignoring the misbehavior, however, eliminated it. Under those circumstances, the teacher has properly used extinction.

Ignoring misbehavior becomes a problem when the teacher's attention is *not* the reinforcer for the misbehavior. Jimmy may be talking and the teacher scolding him for each occurrence of his talking. Other consequences are also occurring, however, for Jimmy's talking. The other students are giggling occasionally, and after class his friends commend him on his "bravery." If one of these other consequences is the reinforcer, the teacher ignoring Jimmy would be ineffective. In fact, it would not even be extinction. Extinction requires the elimination of the reinforcer, and in the case of Jimmy's talking, the reinforcer has not been eliminated.

With young children it is surprising how often a teacher is inadvertently reinforcing misbehavior by attending to it. But one must remember that the attention is not always the reinforcer. Ignoring misbehavior is often one good way to use extinction but only if teacher attention has been identified as the actual reinforcer. If one confuses ignoring with extinction, however, one can run into the problem of "I tried extinction but it doesn't work." Since teacher attention was not the reinforcer, extinction wasn't really tried. Obviously, insuring you are stopping the reinforcer of the misbehavior is the most important aspect of extinction.

Identifying the reinforcer maintaining a misbehavior is often a very difficult task. Unit 2 discussed contingencies. By analyzing those contingencies we have an excellent way to determine which particular environmental events maintain a certain behavior. This process for identifying reinforcers is referred to as *contingency analysis.* For review of this area, a contingency specifies an "if-then" relationship between a behavior and the consequences of the behavior:

    (a) *If* one places one's hands in a fire (behavior); *then* one's hand is burnt (consequence).

    (b) *If* one goes out into a rain storm without an umbrella, rain coat, etc. (behavior); *then,* one gets wet (consequence).

Perhaps the most feasible method teachers can use to determine the environmental consequences for a particular behavior is to *observe* and *record* where, when, and what happens when the child emits the target behavior. If Jean burps during math time, do you attend to it? Do others (Jean's peers) attend to it? How? By observing and recording how you and others behave in response to a specific misbehavior, you should be able to define what the consequences for that behavior are.

After collecting this information for several days, one can analyze and evaluate what were the consequences for a target behavior of a specific child. For example, Mrs. Jones wants to reduce a student's behavior of "wandering away" from her while on field trips. She would like to use the extinction procedure to reduce this behavior and has reached the stage where she must determine what the environmental consequence is that reinforces this behavior in the student.

On their next two trips, Mrs. Jones takes a pen and pad of paper with her. Each time her student "wanders away," Mrs. Jones records what happens to the child. When she analyzes the consequences of wandering-away behavior, Mrs. Jones finds that on every occasion, she has either (a) called the child back, (b) physically brought the child back to her side, or (c) done both.

In this instance, it appears that it is Mrs. Jones' attention to the wandering-away behavior that is the controlling reinforcer for the behavior. However, Mrs. Jones failed to record *where* they were when her child would wander away. If they were always at or near something particularly interesting when the child left, and the child sometimes was able to examine or touch it before being called back, then this information must also be considered before deciding that Mrs. Jones' attention is the controlling reinforcer. This careful analysis of the contingencies or environmental conditions present at the onset of the misbehavior is sometimes tedious but is an excellent and thorough way for a teacher to correctly identify the reinforcers controlling the misbehavior.

A second important and related problem in using extinction is the *ability to control the reinforcer* once you've identified it. It is not advisable to try to use extinction unless you are sure you can control the reinforcers maintaining the misbehavior. In an earlier example of Jimmy's talking, if the giggling of the class is the reinforcer and you cannot stop the giggling, you cannot use extinction. Not only must you be able to identify the reinforcer, you must also be able to control it. If you cannot accomplish both tasks, extinction will not eliminate the behavior, since extinction, by definition (withholding reinforcement), is not being used.

Extinction has been shown to be effective by a large number of research studies and is commonly used. An excellent example was reported by Williams (1959), who used extinction to reduce the tantrums of a 21-month-old child. When the child was put to bed, he would scream until the parents or an aunt returned to the room. In order to prevent a tantrum, whoever put the child to bed remained in the room until the child went to sleep, which was often one-half hour to two hours after the initial bedtime. To remove social reinforcement (attention) for the tantrum, the parents were told to put the child to bed and leave the room. When the tantrum began, it was ignored. The child cried for 45 minutes the first night of extinction. However, the next day there was no tantrum. In the remaining days, tantrums were of less than ten minutes' duration. After a week, the child had a severe tantrum. The aunt erred and reinforced this by going in the child's room and staying with him until he fell asleep. Extinction was carried out again on subsequent nights. By the ninth session there were no tantrums. Moreover, no further tantrums were reported over the next two years.

In everyday life, extinction may contribute to behavior problems as well as ameliorate them. Often, desirable behavior is accidentally extinguished. For example, parents sometimes ignore their children when they are playing quietly and provide abundant attention when the children are noisy. Essentially, quiet play may be extinguished while noisy play is positively reinforced. Merely altering parental attention so it follows appropriate play is often sufficient to develop appropriate play and to eliminate inappropriate behavior.

Scott and Bushell (1974) demonstrated how teachers should reinforce appropriate academic behavior instead of attending to "off-task" behavior. Their investigation showed that teachers often attend to students displaying off-task behavior and ignore (extinction) those students who are appropriately attending to their academic studies. These findings suggest that teachers and parents should monitor the types of behaviors that they reinforce (e.g., "pay attention to") and develop a schedule to follow that would require them to praise or otherwise contingently reinforce each child a specified number of times each day for their appropriate behavior.

In other research studies, such different problem behaviors as self-destruction (Lovaas and Simmons, 1969), aggression (Pinkston, Reese, LeBlanc, and Baer, 1973), and feminine behavior of a boy (Rekers and Lovaas, 1974) were all reduced by using extinction. Extinction has been shown to be a very effective procedure which is useful across a wide range of misbehaviors. There are, however, more issues than effectiveness which need to be discussed before anyone can decide to use this procedure. The following sections present this information.

Selecting Extinction

If a teacher is trying to decide whether or not to use extinction to reduce a misbehavior, several considerations must be closely examined. First, the advantages and disadvantages of the procedure should be weighed. Second, the type of misbehavior for which extinction is being considered is important. Third, you need to know if you can identify and control the reinforcer of the particular target behavior. Fourth, you need to know the factors which will influence the effectiveness of extinction. After considering those four issues, you can begin to implement extinction if you have decided it is the appropriate procedure for your problems.

Advantages and Disadvantages

The research literature shows extinction to have several excellent advantages. It is an extremely effective procedure which is useful across a wide range of misbehaviors. If a teacher can identify and control the reinforcer of the misbehavior, it is usually a fairly easy procedure to use. It requires no special equipment and costs nothing. Once behavior has been eliminated by extinction, it tends to remain eliminated; the effects of extinction on misbehavior are usually quite long-lasting. These advantages strongly suggest that extinction should be an important part of any teacher's behavior-reducing skills.

The disadvantages of extinction are often less serious than those of punishment (Unit 4), response cost (Unit 5), or timeout (Unit 6), but still present the teacher with some possible difficulties. Misbehavior first exposed to extinction tends to initially *increase* in frequency. If you have identified teacher attention as the reinforcer for a misbehavior, for example, the misbehavior will probably increase when you first begin ignoring it. The increase does not occur every time and seldom lasts for very long but occasionally is fairly significant. If Margaret has been out-of-seat about five times per class period, that behavior might increase to eight or ten times per period for several days after you start using extinction. If a temporary increased level of the behavior cannot be tolerated because of the severity of the behavior (i.e., hitting) or its disruptive influence on the class (i.e., yelling), extinction is probably not a good procedure to choose.

A second disadvantage of extinction is that behavioral elimination effected by extinction is gradual rather than immediate. At first, the behavior will usually increase in frequency, then begin a slow but relatively steady decline until it is eliminated. The decline is typically a continuous change over time as opposed to a sharply differentiated change that can be produced by some of the other procedures. If you are counting the behavior each day (Unit 3), you should be able to observe a steady, if not a drastic, change.

These first two disadvantages often cause the most problems for teachers, especially when they are unexpected. The initial increase in the behavior or the gradual change often cause a teacher to terminate use of the procedure before its effectiveness has been demonstrated. Don't be too easily discouraged; be patient; if you are going to try extinction, allow it sufficient time to work before deciding to change to another procedure.

A phenomenon called "spontaneous recovery" is the third disadvantage of extinction. Sometimes, after a behavior has been eliminated, the behavior will reappear even though it has not been reinforced. The reappearance of the behavior should not be cause for alarm, however, because the behavior will quickly disappear again *if it is not reinforced.*

Spontaneous recovery is not uncommon in applied settings such as the classroom and home. For example, suppose a teacher eliminated the "out-of-seat" behavior of a student by ignoring (the teacher's attention was identified as the controlling reinforcer for the behavior) the student whenever he was out-of-seat without permission. Several weeks have passed, during which the child has not emitted the target behavior when, during reading class, the child suddenly gets out of his seat and walks to the side of the teacher's desk. If the teacher is not completely "taken by surprise" and continues to ignore the behavior, the longevity of the spontaneously recovered behavior will be short. However, if the teacher reinforces the recovered behavior by attending to the child (via a scolding or asking why the child is out of his seat), the behavior may be reestablished at its initial, or even greater, level.

A final disadvantage of extinction should be considered before deciding to use the procedure. The extinction process may initially produce emotional behavioral side-effects. These effects are similar to but less serious than those discussed earlier when punishment was examined (Unit 4). Various investigations (Kelly, 1969; Viney, Clarke, and Lord, 1973; Blist and Ley, 1969) have reported forms of "aggression" as a probable temporary side-effect of the extinction process. Harrell (1971) found that both the frequency and magnitude of an aggressive behavior (punching a padded cushion with a minimum of 20 pounds force) increased when extinction was introduced. Therefore, the possibility of aggression, or other side-effects such as withdrawal or frustration, as a result of the procedure being used is present. These behavioral side-effects are usually not very serious, but careful observations should be planned to see the extent to which they occur. The decision of whether or not to use extinction should, however, consider the possibility of these side-effects.

Primarily because of the first two disadvantages discussed above, one must consider the type of misbehavior for which extinction is being planned. In general, extinction is best suited for behaviors toward the "usual" end of the continuum discussed in Unit 2. An initial increase and a slow decline would create serious difficulties when attempting to change such misbehaviors as fighting, vandalism, and self-harm. Misbehaviors such as stealing present problems, not in identifying the reinforcer but in controlling it. If someone steals, they have already obtained their reinforcer so you cannot stop it from occurring. Also, since extinction may cause some aggressive behaviors, it seems unsuited to aggressive misbehaviors; the problem might only worsen. Children who tend to be withdrawn might not benefit from extinction either, for the procedure could produce further withdrawal. With most children and most common misbehaviors, however, its advantages can make extinction a very good choice.

The Effectiveness of Extinction

Maybe the most important issue concerning the choice of extinction as a behavioral reduction procedure is the decision of whether or not it is possible to use it. This decision involves the two questions raised earlier in this Unit. First, can you identify the reinforcer or reinforcers which is keeping the misbehavior active? Second, can you control the occurrence of the reinforcer or reinforcers which you have identified? Identifying the reinforcer is often very difficult, for it may be too occasional or quite obscure. Controlling the reinforcer is a different, but possibly an equally difficult, task. The reinforcers provided by other children are often the hardest to control. Obviously, your attention is hopefully the reinforcer, because you can learn to ignore the misbehavior and thus use extinction quite easily and effectively. If you can accomplish both tasks, you *can* use extinction. The other issues in this section help you decide *if* you will use extinction.

Once you have decided that extinction is possible, you must now consider the factors which influence the effectiveness of extinction. These factors influence how quickly and effectively a target behavior can be reduced or eliminated when extinction is being used. The factors are: the length of time that the misbehavior has been reinforced, the schedule under which the misbehavior has been previously reinforced, the individual's level of deprivation, the effort needed to do the misbehavior, the use of other behavior-reducing procedures in combination with extinction, and how easily the child is able to discriminate a change in the conditions of reinforcement.

The first factor concerns the length of time over which the misbehavior has been previously reinforced. Behaviors that have been reinforced for a long time in the past take longer to eliminate by extinction than behaviors that have been reinforced for only a brief time. Common sense should indicate to one that the longer a behavior has been reinforced the stronger it is and thus the more "resistant to extinction" it will be (e.g., the longer it will be done under extinction conditions). Perhaps an example that illustrates how the length of time a behavior has been previously reinforced influences the rate of elimination will further clarify this factor.

Imagine that there are two first-grade teachers that attempt to reduce the same target behavior ("off-task" verbalizations during story time) by ignoring the students' inappropriate comments (teacher attention has been identified as the reinforcer maintaining the off-task comments). The first teacher institutes the extinction procedure near the beginning of the school year, while the second teacher waits until the middle of the year before initiating the technique. It took the first teacher five days to eliminate the target behavior of the students by extinction, while it took almost three school weeks before extinction effectively reduced the same behavior for the second teacher (see Figure 7.1).

The differing lengths of time it took for the procedure to reduce the behavior are due to the differing lengths of times over which the target behavior had previously been reinforced. The second teacher did not start using extinction with the behavior of her students until six months after the first teacher had started the procedure. The second teacher was using extinction on a more firmly established behavior which had been reinforced more often.

The second factor which influences the effectiveness of extinction is *the schedule of reinforcement* by which the misbehavior has been reinforced in the past. Simply stated, a schedule of reinforcement indicates how probable it is that a particular instance of a behavior is reinforced. There are two broad categories of schedules. The first specifies that every occurrence of the behavior is reinforced. This type of schedule is called a continuous reinforcement schedule (CRF). A CRF schedule indicates that each behavior is reinforced immediately after it occurs. The second category of schedules are collectively called *intermittent* schedules of reinforcement. This category specifies that some of the target behaviors are reinforced and some of them are not.

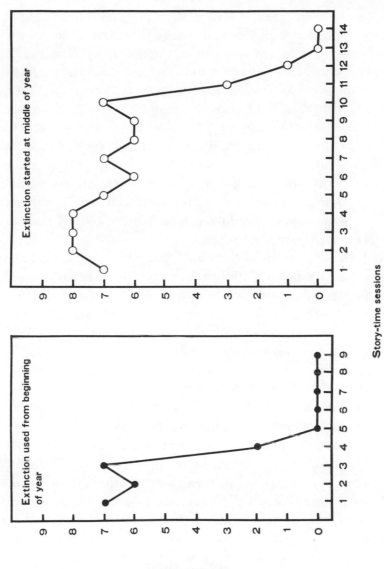

FIGURE 7.1. An example illustrating how the number of times the misbehavior was previously reinforced can influence the rate at which the misbehavior will decrease during extinction.

Research conducted both in the laboratory and in applied settings indicates that those behaviors that have been on a CRF schedule are eliminated faster by extinction than those that have been reinforced only now and then (on an intermittent schedule). For example, when you deposit a coin in a vending machine you typically receive a reinforcer for that behavior (i.e., you get a candy bar for your quarter). If, however, you deposit your coin and do not get the reinforcer (the reinforcer for the behavior is withheld—extinction), you may deposit another coin, but the probability of your depositing a third or fourth coin without getting your candy bar are slight. Your behavior is eliminated rapidly because your vending machine behavior has been reinforced on a CRF schedule.

Still, there are types of "vending" machines that reinforce one's coin-depositing behavior intermittently. These machines, called slot machines, dramatically illustrate how a behavior reinforced on an intermittent schedule is more resistant to extinction than a behavior reinforced on a CRF schedule. If at some point in time the slot machine broke down and no longer paid anything, your coin-depositing behavior would last much longer than when the vending machine broke down.

Often, a teacher will begin extinction on an inappropriate behavior but will not be consistent. Occasionally he or she will attend to or otherwise reinforce the target behavior. This lack of consistency, or lapses in applying the procedure, is a way of reinforcing the unwanted behavior on an intermittent schedule, and can maintain or even increase the frequency with which the behavior is being done. The end result will be to make the behavior very resistant to extinction and very difficult to eliminate.

Since a CRF schedule is less effective in maintaining a behavior under extinction conditions than is an intermittent one, it seems reasonable to speculate that if one wished to reduce a behavior that was being reinforced on an intermittent schedule, one should reinforce the behavior on a CRF schedule for a period before beginning the extinction process. The changing of reinforcement schedule from intermittent to CRF could possibly reduce the amount of time the procedure eventually takes to eliminate the behavior.

Level of deprivation is the third factor influencing the effectiveness of extinction. It is the amount of time that has passed since the individual last received a certain type of reinforcement. Generally, the greater the level of deprivation, the more resistant to extinction is the behavior. This applies especially to those behaviors maintained by primary reinforcers and to many tangible secondary reinforcers (such as money).

However, Johnston (1972) has speculated that behaviors maintained by social reinforcement (smiles, praise, etc.) do not become more resistant to extinction as a function of the level of social deprivation. This is important when misbehavior is being reinforced by teacher attention. Misbehavior maintained by that social reinforcer should not be very resistant to extinction, so it could be eliminated with that procedure. Therefore, the level of deprivation is in respect to reinforcers other than social reinforcers. When choosing extinction, then, the amount of control you have over the level of deprivation is an important part of your decision.

A fourth factor involves the ease with which a target misbehavior can be done. Behaviors that are easy for the child to do are more resistant to extinction than are behaviors that require a great deal of effort. Perhaps an example will best serve to illustrate this variable. Assume that every time you meet a particular friend or relative that you chat with them for several minutes bringing them up-to-date as to what you have been doing. One can cover many topics in a few minutes time when speaking (a behavior that is relatively easy to do). Now assume that your friend or relative has moved to a different state and the only economical method of exchanging information with him or her is through the mail. The behavior of writing a letter requires more effort than does speaking, and if you are not reinforced for writing your letter (probably by receiving a return letter), your writing to this individual would most likely be eliminated more quickly than would your speaking.

The fifth factor states that when the extinction procedure is combined with other behavior-reducing procedures, the target behavior will usually disappear more rapidly than if you had used the extinction procedure alone. This holds true for many of the behavior-reducing procedures that are discussed in this book. Restated, the reduction rate for any specific procedure will increase if that procedure is used in combination with one or more other, different procedures.

For example, a teacher wishes to eliminate the "out-of-seat" behavior of a second grade student. If the teacher "ignores" each out-of-seat occurrence (and teacher attention has been identified as the reinforcer for that behavior), the number of out-of-seat behaviors will eventually decrease. However, if the teacher not only ignored each occurrence of the target behavior, but also praised the student whenever he remained at his desk working on his assignment and informed him as to *why* he was being praised (because he was working at his desk), the frequency of his out-of-seat behavior would decrease even more quickly (see Figure 7.2).

In the above example, the combination of procedures more effectively decreased the target for two reasons. First, the student's inappropriate behavior (out-of-seat) was not reinforced. Second, an appropriate behavior (at-desk-working) that could not occur at the same time as the target behavior was reinforced. The target behavior decreases more rapidly because there is an alternative behavior the student can emit that requires approximately the same effort and will be reinforced. Simultaneous reinforcement of a desired behavior while extinguishing an inappropriate one will often achieve a more rapid decrement in the target behavior than would extinction alone.

Bandura (1969) has explained the sixth and last factor influencing extinction. He suggested that the length of the period of resistance to extinction may be related to how easily or how

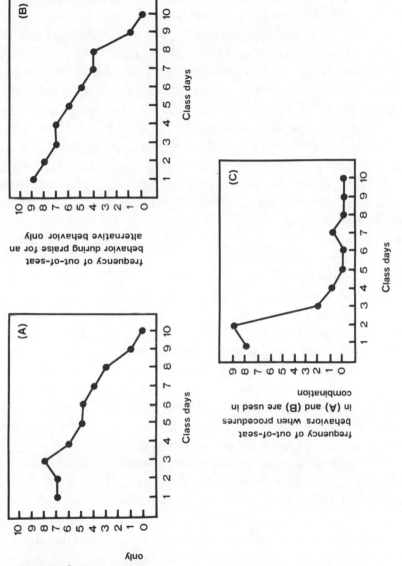

FIGURE 7.2. An illustration of how a combination of procedures can reduce a behavior faster than either procedure is able to do by itself.

long it takes the individual to figure out that the environmental change from reinforcement conditions to nonreinforcement (extinction) conditions has occurred. This final factor states that resistance to extinction is reduced when the child learns reinforcement will no longer occur after a given behavior. In some instances, given that the individual whose behavior we wish to reduce is verbal, if we explain or tell the individual that a particular behavior will no longer be reinforced, these instructions *may* reduce the period of time the extinction process would normally have taken (without the instructions). In effect, we are making it easier for the individual to learn changes in the conditions of reinforcement. Telling the student what you are about to do often increases the speed of the reduction of the misbehavior.

Using Extinction

When presented together, all of the above areas influencing your choice of extinction seem to make the decision extremely difficult. You must weigh the advantages against the disadvantages, figure out if it is possible to use the extinction in a given situation, decide if your target misbehavior is appropriate for extinction, and examine your target behavior in light of the factors which influence the effectiveness of extinction. With practice, however, and with some of your own experience using extinction, the decision becomes easier and easier to make.

Once you have made the decision to use extinction to eliminate a target misbehavior, you must follow certain steps in order to implement this procedure properly. Some of the beginning steps are common across all the procedures; those are the preliminary steps discussed in the first three Units. The remaining steps are necessary for the implementation of extinction. Assuming that you have decided to try extinction, you would follow those steps. Since aspects of all the steps have been discussed previously while explaining extinction, the steps are listed in order in Table 7.1.

TABLE 7.1: STEPS TO FOLLOW TO IMPLEMENT EXTINCTION

1. Specify and define target misbehavior.
2. Choose measure for target misbehavior.
3. Collect baseline data.
4. Choose design to evaluate effectiveness.
5. Identify reinforcer(s) of misbehavior.
6. Decide how to control reinforcer(s).
7. Stop the reinforcer(s) — begin extinction.
8. Be consistent.
9. Be patient—allow for initial increase, slow decline, and spontaneous recovery.
10. Combine extinction with other procedures if possible.
11. Follow design—evaluate your data.
12. Continue extinction or try another procedure.

Conclusions

Extinction is an efficient and effective behavior-reducing procedure. If the decision to use the procedure is made with care and if implementation is done properly, the misbehavior will be eliminated, and, except for sporadic spontaneous recovery, the elimination should be permanent. If a teacher does not have reason to worry about an initial increase in the frequency of the misbehavior or a slow decline, extinction is a useful tool for the classroom.

An interesting question posed in Unit 1 is also answered by examining extinction. The question concerned why children misbehave. According to the analysis presented through this Unit, one very significant answer is that misbehavior occurs because it is reinforced. The reinforcement is rarely planned in any way, may even be accidental, but is nonetheless effective. This reinforcement can establish, increase, or maintain misbehavior at levels quite counterproductive for the classroom. The use of extinction, then, eliminates the causes of the misbehavior. By getting to the sources of the problem, extinction may be one of the procedures most helpful to a teacher.

This Unit, like all the Units in this section on the solution strategies, presents its case cautiously. While extinction does not utilize aversive environmental events, it can sometimes produce some aversive behavioral side-effects. All the procedures, when properly used, can be quite effective. But that is not the only issue. As we have said, schools should be pleasant and productive environments where happy children learn appropriate social and academic behaviors. If the use of the more aversive procedures does not help reach that goal, they should be avoided when possible. In favor of the aversive procedures, though perhaps somewhat sadly, it must be said that avoidance is not always possible.

SUGGESTED PROJECTS

1. Think of two examples of your own behavior. How would someone else plan to use extinction on you? Might it be a good procedure to choose?
2. List four target misbehaviors in your classroom.
    A. Operationally define them.
    B. Analyze each as to choosing extinction to eliminate them. Would extinction be a good choice of procedures?
    C. Complete a contingency analysis to identify the reinforcers of the behavior.
    D. Can you control the reinforcers you identified?
3. For one of the misbehaviors identified and analyzed above, list all of the steps you would go through to effectively use extinction.
4. Implement your plan from #3. Is there an initial increase? A slow decline? Spontaneous recovery? Aggression? Withdrawal? Evaluate your findings.

REFERENCES

Bandura, A. *Principles of Behavior Modification.* New York: Holt, Rinehart, and Winston, Inc., 1969.

Blist, S., and Ley, R. Force-contingent reinforcement in instrumental conditioning and extinction in children: A test of the frustration-drive hypothesis. *Journal of Comparative and Physiological Psychology,* 1969, *69*(2), 267-272.

Ferster, C.B., and Perrott, M.C. *Behavior Principles.* New York: Meredith Corp., 1968.

Harrell, W.A. Effects of extinction on magnitude of aggression in humans. *Psychonomic Science,* 1971, *29*(4-A), 213-215.

Johnston, J.M. Punishment of human behavior. *American Psychologist,* November, 1972, 1033-1054.

Kelly, J.F. Extinction induced aggression in humans. Unpublished master's thesis, Southern Illinois University, 1969.

Lovaas, O.I., and Simmons, J.Q. Manipulation of self-destruction in three retarded children. *Journal of Applied Behavior Analysis,* 1969, 2, 143-157.

Pinkston, E.M., Reese, N.M., LeBlanc, J.M., and Baer, D.M. Independent control of a preschool child's aggression and peer interaction by contingent teacher attention. *Journal of Applied Behavior Analysis,* 1973, 6, 115-124.

Rekers, G.A., and Lovaas, O.I. Behavioral treatment of deviant sex-role behaviors in a male child. *Journal of Applied Behavior Analysis,* 1974, *7*(1), 173-190.

Scott, J.W., and Bushell, D. The length of teacher contracts and students' off-task behavior. *Journal of Applied Behavior Analysis,* 1974, *7*(1), 39-44.

Viney, L.L., Clarke, A.M., and Lord, J. Resistance to extinction and frustration in retarded and non-retarded children. *American Journal of Mental Deficiency,* 1973, *78*(3), 308-315.

Williams, C.D. The elimination of tantrum behavior by extinction procedures. *Journal of Abnormal and Social Psychology,* 1959, 59, 269.

Unit Eight

SATIATION, OVERCORRECTION AND POSITIVE PRACTICE

Study Questions

1. Define satiation. Develop an educational example that illustrates the procedure's proper use.
2. List and explain the advantages and disadvantages of satiation.
3. List and explain the four factors which influence satiation's effectiveness.
4. List the steps one should follow to properly implement satiation.
5. Define overcorrection and positive practice. Develop an educational example that demonstrates each.
6. How do overcorrection and positive practice differ from punishment as it was discussed in Unit 4?
7. Explain when one might use positive practice but not overcorrection.
8. Define the reverse Premack principle. How does it differ from positive practice?
9. List the advantages and disadvantages for overcorrection and positive practice.
10. List and explain the factors which can influence the effectiveness of the two procedures.
11. List the steps one would follow to correctly implement either overcorrection or positive practice.

If Samantha stops hitting her sister when her mother yells at her, Samantha's hitting behavior has been punished (Punishment, Unit 4). Jeffrey forfeited half of his allowance because he stayed out past his curfew, which decreased his occurrences of staying out so late (Response Cost, Unit 5). Leslie is required to stand in the corner for five minutes because she interrupted the teacher (Timeout, Unit 6). Johnny likes to burp in class because, in his words, "it gets Ms. Denny mad." Today, though, Ms. Denny is "ignoring" Johnny's burps (Extinction, Unit 7).

All of the behavior reduction procedures illustrated above share certain characteristics. They all reduce a wide variety of misbehaviors, are quick and effective with different children in different situations, but, unfortunately, do not teach the child appropriate ways of behaving. Additionally, they can all be rather unpleasant to use in academic environments since most of them (Units 4-6) utilize aversive consequences to effect the behavioral reductions. Even extinction (Unit 7), which does not, per se, use aversive consequences, is sometimes associated with unfavorable behavioral side-effects.

There are several behavior reduction procedures, however, that can reduce or eliminate many misbehaviors without using aversive consequences, or by using potentially aversive consequences but at least also teaching the child appropriate alternative behaviors. One of the procedures which accomplishes the former is called *satiation* while two accomplishing the latter are called *overcorrection* and *positive practice*. This Unit discusses satiation, then positive practice and overcorrection. While there are some similarities in how all three are implemented, the reasons they are effective differ. Because of the similarities, we include them in the same Unit; because of the differences, we discuss them separately.

SATIATION

Definition and Explanation
Satiation is a procedure which is derived from the principle that

all behavior occurs because it has been strengthened by some type of reinforcement. This is as true for misbehavior as it is for other types of behavior. So, if misbehavior is being done because it receives some form of reinforcement, it will not occur if the student already has a sufficient amount of that reinforcement. Through satiation, we insure that a sufficient amount of reinforcement is provided the student. With no lack of that reinforcement, misbehavior no longer needs to be done in order for the student to receive that reinforcement.

Specifically, satiation is defined as a procedure through which an oversupply of a particular reinforcer is presented so that the effectiveness of the reinforcer for strengthening a misbehavior is diminished. The key to satiation is knowing what reinforcer to oversupply. Since behavior occurs to produce reinforcement (review Unit 2), you need to know the specific reinforcer which is strengthening a specific target misbehavior. Once you identify that critical reinforcer, you oversupply it. The misbehavior will decrease because the student will no longer misbehave for something of which he now has enough (or too much).

Identifying the critical reinforcer is not always an easy task. Sometimes it is an external environmental event, like the teacher's attention. Other times, however, the act of doing the misbehavior, itself, is the critical reinforcer. In the former situation you would insure that the misbehaver received an oversupply of your attention. In the latter case, you would have the student repeat the action over and over until that action was no longer a reinforcer. If, for example, a child is reinforced by the loud noise produced when a door is slammed, to reduce door-slamming, you would have the student slam the door many, many times until that activity ceased to be reinforcing for the child (in fact, eventually, it would most likely become a boring activity for the child).

It is quite important that you identify the reinforcer responsible for the misbehavior. You cannot oversupply just any reinforcer, it must be the critical reinforcer. We behave for food (eat) when we're hungry but not when we're full (satiated). We drink when thirsty, not after having consumed a glass of water (satiated). To decrease an episode of eating behavior, the person needs to be satiated on food, not some other reinforcer. To decrease drinking, satiation on water is required. So, satiation oversupplies the reinforcer which is maintaining the misbehavior. If a student is satiated on the correct reinforcer, he will no longer misbehave in order to earn that reinforcer.

The ability of satiation to reduce misbehaviors has been known for a very long time. For example, centuries ago, in various Western European monarchies, it was considered very gauche for one to continue eating after the King had finished. Individuals who ate after the King had stopped were sometimes required to eat far beyond the point where they would have liked to have stopped, beyond the point where they were satiated with respect to food. This practice, unfortunately, frequently resulted in the death of the King's subject.

Satiation is also commonly used in our day-to-day lives, though, hopefully, not to the extreme mentioned above. To illustrate, the procedure is regularly used by some therapists to help people quit smoking. Typically, the therapist's client is placed in a small room with four or five packs of cigarettes. The client is instructed to smoke *all* the cigarettes, one-after-another, as fast as possible with no breaks. The client generally loses the desire to continue smoking after one or two packs (e.g., the client becomes satiated after one or two packs) but keeps smoking until all the cigarettes are gone. As you can imagine, it seldom takes more than a few such "treatments" to effect a substantial reduction in smoking. A mild, but often effective, variation of this technique is used by some parents when they make a child who was caught smoking, smoke cigarettes until nauseous.

Perhaps the most frequently cited research study that employed satiation was conducted by Ayllon (1963) to reduce towel hoarding in a hospitalized female psychiatric patient. Before the intervention began, the patient would take towels from around the hospital and would store them in her room. The staff repeatedly asked her to not take the towels because of the problems encountered when other patients took baths and there were not enough towels.

In the first intervention phase, the staff were told not to ask the patient for the return of the towels she had collected. They were also instructed not to remove towels she had hoarded in her room. Additionally, the patient was presented with an average of seven towels per day. Later in the experiment, the number of towels presented to the patient was increased to 60 per day!

Initially, the patient was happy to get the extra towels. However, after there was in excess of 700 towels stacked in her room, she became less enthusiastic about additions to her collection. Eventually, the patient began to take towels from her room, but the towels she removed were replaced by the hospital's staff.

After a month of treatment, the patient threw several towels into the hallway. When they were not returned, she removed all but a few of the towels from her room. Several months after the behavior change program, a follow-up indicated that she was now averaging 6 or 7 towels in her room, which was far below her baseline average. She had become satiated on towels so no longer hoarded them to the extent she had previously.

There are not many studies available that report on teachers using satiation to reduce misbehaviors in their classrooms. One study that used satiation to reduce misbehavior in a school setting was reported by Deitz (1973). The project was done because the teacher had a problem with students wadding up scratch paper and throwing the paper wads from their desks to the trash can in the back of the room. The teacher took baseline measures in two classes on the number of times paper was thrown at the can. (It was of no matter to this teacher whether or not a "shot" was successful.)

The teacher decided to first try "yelling" to determine what effect it would have on paper-throwing. She started using verbal reprimands after 8 baseline sessions for class A and after 15 baseline sessions for class B. Her reprimands were of the nature: "Stanley, the class does not appreciate your distracting our attention while we are trying to learn. This is math class, not basketball practice!"

After a total of nine "yelling" sessions with class A, it was suggested that the teacher try something new. Paper-throwing itself was, obviously, a reinforcing activity, so satiation was explained to the teacher and its use was recommended. In this case, each day, one of the most prolific paper-throwers was told to stay after school. During detention he was forced to shoot every piece of paper from the trash can in front of the room into the trash can in the back of the room. He did this continuously for 30 minutes, throwing paper back and forth from one garbage can to the other. After four sessions of "yelling," class B was also moved to satiation. On the day the classes were changed to satiation, the satiation procedure was explained to the students.

The graph in Figure 8.1 illustrates the differences and similarities between class A and class B. During baseline, class A averaged 20.0 paper-throws per 50 minute class. During "yelling" the average *increased* to 22.8 throws (obviously, yelling was a positive reinforcer for paper-throwing in this situation). The satiation technique decreased the average number of throws to 5.6 and, in the last four experimental sessions, no throws occurred.

Class B averaged 14.4 throws per day during baseline but they were affected by the "yelling." Contingent "yelling" (punishment for class B) reduced the average throws to 4.0 per session. Satiation further reduced the average number of throws to 0.1 with the last 8 sessions containing no throws.

The data from class B demonstrates that "yelling" can sometimes work, but it is a type of behavior that most teachers would rather avoid having to rely on to reduce misbehaviors. Both classes were affected by the satiation technique. Since occasional detentions were used during baseline (and did not seem to affect the data) for both classes, it is probable that satiation rather than the detention caused the resulting decline in the misbehavior.

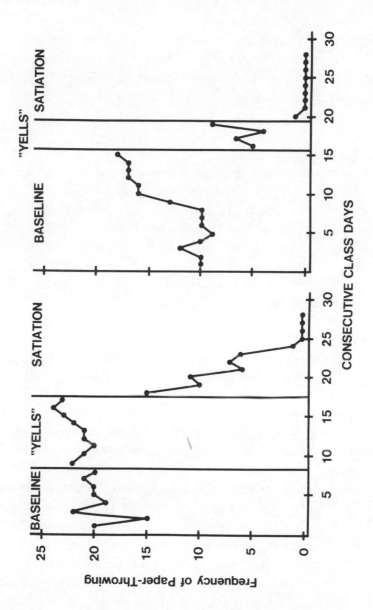

FIGURE 8.1. The frequency of paper-throwing for two elementary school classes. After baseline and teacher reprimands (yells), satiation was used to reduce the misbehavior in both classes.

So, when you can identify the critical reinforcer which is strengthening a particular misbehavior, you can oversupply it to use satiation to reduce that misbehavior. The effectiveness of a reinforcer is greatly diminished when it is in abundance. Therefore, students will not misbehave to earn or produce a reinforcer that is no longer effective.

Selecting Satiation

The decision to use satiation to reduce a particular misbehavior should involve several considerations. First, you need to compare the procedure's advantages against its disadvantages. Next, you must consider the type of misbehavior which you wish to reduce. Finally, you must evaluate the factors which will influence the procedure's effectiveness. After carefully weighing these issues, you can begin to implement satiation if you have decided it is an appropriate technique for your problem.

Advantages and Disadvantages

The advantages of satiation frequently outweigh the disadvantages. The primary advantage of the procedure is that it is a relatively easy, positive approach to behavior problems. It does not depend on aversive events to effect the behavioral change. This "positiveness" is a definite benefit in a school, since neither the teacher nor the academic setting becomes associated with unpleasant events.

The remaining advantages of satiation are all partially related to its primary advantage. Because it is nonaversive, there are generally no prohibitions (legal or administrative) against its use. This is an important advantage when considered in light of lawsuits filed against teachers and schools that have established or maintained discipline through aversive procedures such as punishment.

The third advantage is that students generally do not object to the procedure's use and frequently even enjoy it (what you should do in the few cases in which children refuse to repetitively emit the misbehavior will be discussed later). The final advantage of satiation is that few, if any, undesirable side-effects are associated with the procedure (again, because it is not aversive).

The disadvantages of satiation are not as serious as those associated with the more aversive procedures (Units 4-6), but they must still be considered before deciding to use the procedure. First, the reductive effects of satiation are often temporary. This is especially true when one becomes satiated with respect to primary reinforcers such as food. "Even the individual who gets up from the banquet table and swears that he will never eat again, usually skips no more than a meal or two" (Sulzer and Mayer, 1972, p. 204). Satiation's temporary effect may be a reason why many teachers have not used satiation as extensively as the other procedures we have discussed (Reese, 1978). Still, this disadvantage may not be so important when the activity itself is the reinforcer. In such cases, satiation can effect a long lasting reduction as in the previously cited studies (Ayllon, 1963; Deitz, 1973).

The second disadvantage of satiation is that it is not useful for many types of misbehaviors. Certainly, no teacher would want to satiate the hitting misbehavior of the class bully. You would have to make the bully hit the other child until he tired of it, a most unethical decision. You could have the child continually hit a punching bag but that action might not be effective if the actions (crying, running away, etc.) of the other child, rather than the behavior of hitting, were the critical reinforcers.

So satiation would be a poor choice for such misbehaviors as aggressiveness, self-injurious behaviors (headbanging or playing with matches), those classes of misbehavior which may entirely disrupt or prevent the learning process (screaming), or those behaviors that cause permanent physical damage to property (carving one's initials in a desk). For the most part, then, misbehaviors that can be reduced via satiation would tend towards the "usual" end of the misbehavior continuum mentioned in Unit 1. In any event, no matter how "usual" the misbehavior, each teacher, on a case-by-case basis, must decide if satiation is really the most appropriate choice of behavior reduction procedures.

The Effectiveness of Satiation

The final issue to examine when deciding about using satiation concerns the factors that influence the effectiveness of satiation—how quickly and efficiently a target misbehavior can be reduced or eliminated when satiation is being used. These factors include: deprivation conditions of the student, willingness of the student to cooperate, presenting sufficiently large quantities of the reinforcer, and characteristics of the misbehavior.

Deprivation conditions of the individual have been partially analyzed earlier. Essentially, people satiate faster on primary reinforcers such as food than they do on secondary ones like social attention or money.

The next variable, the willingness of the student to cooperate, is crucial, especially when you are having a student repeat an activity until it becomes boring. It should be obvious that the procedure will not work if the student refuses to repeatedly emit the target misbehavior or accept the reinforcer. Still, as noted earlier, an advantage of satiation is that, usually, students are more than willing to do the misbehavior. If a student refuses to do the misbehavior, you have two options. You can forget satiation and attempt another procedure, or you can combine satiation with a more aversive procedure like response cost or timeout. For example, if you wished to decrease "finger-snapping" by having the child snap her fingers for 10 minutes, and the child refused to comply, you could revoke a privilege or send the individual to timeout until she would comply. Such an approach, however, can obviate the procedure's primary advantage of positiveness.

The third factor that influences satiation's effectiveness is whether sufficient quantities of the reinforcer are presented (or if the reinforcing activity is required of the misbehaver a sufficient number of times). If a child "swipes" a cookie, it is very difficult to definitively state how many cookies the child should eat to reduce future cookie-swiping episodes (we would not want a child to eat so many that physical damage was suffered). On the other hand, to only require the child to eat one or two more cookies would be reinforcing the child's stealing.

Determining how long an individual should emit a particular activity is somewhat easier to answer because guidelines can be established. As a rule-of-thumb, it is imperative that the student emit the misbehavior beyond the point where he or she "tires" of it (if the child does not tire of the behavior, you have probably only reinforced it). Long and Frye (1977) recommend that the child continue the activity several times beyond the point when the child indicates he or she would like to stop. For example, Terry likes to cup his right hand under his left armpit while vigorously flapping his left arm. Such a maneuver resulted in a sound which evoked giggles from his classmates. After one such episode, however, his teacher remarked, "Swell! You did that well. Please do it again." Terry complied and the class again laughed. This continued for several more times until Terry said he did not want to do it anymore. At that point, his teacher told him to do it for two more minutes as fast as he was able, then he could stop (the class had stopped laughing much before Terry indicated he was tired). The next day, Terry again emitted the noise and the process was repeated. The only difference was that, this time, Terry tired earlier (as did the class). Still, he was required to continue for the same amount of time as he had on the first day. From the third day on, Terry did not make the sound.

The final factor that influences the procedure's effectiveness, characteristics of the misbehavior, is related to the third factor. If a misbehavior is very easy to do, it will take the individual longer to satiate on it. If the misbehavior is one that requires much effort on the part of the misbehaver, he or she will satiate in a relatively short period of time. Sulzer and Mayer (1972) suggest using a behavior reducing procedure other than satiation for those activities that are very easy (whispering, for example) for the misbehaver to do.

Using Satiation

When collectively considered, all of the above information may seem to make the decision of whether you should try satiation difficult. You must weigh the disadvantages against the advantages, determine if satiation is appropriate to the particular target misbehavior, and examine the misbehavior, misbehaver, and setting in view of those factors which will influence how effective the procedure will be. All of this is not easy, but it is a task that must be accomplished if the procedure is to be used properly.

If the decision to implement satiation is made, you must follow certain steps in order to use the procedure properly. Some of the steps are common to all Units and were discussed in the first three Units. The remaining steps are unique to satiation and must be followed to implement satiation. The steps are listed in Table 8.1.

TABLE 8.1: STEPS TO FOLLOW TO IMPLEMENT SATIATION

1. Specify and define target misbehavior. If misbehavior is appropriate to satiation, continue.
2. Choose measure for target misbehavior.
3. Collect baseline data.
4. Choose design to evaluate effectiveness.
5. Explain procedure to students.
6. Be consistent.
7. Be patient—go beyond point where student(s) are saturated with reinforcer(s) or "tired" of activity.
8. Consider combining satiation with timeout or response cost if students refuse to comply (or, adopt alternate procedure).
9. Evaluate data.
10. Continue program or modify based on evaluation.

OVERCORRECTION AND POSITIVE PRACTICE

The remainder of this Unit explains two procedures labeled *restitutional overcorrection* and *positive practice* by the behavior analysts who first investigated them (Azrin and Foxx, 1971). Technically, overcorrection and positive practice are both variations of punishment (Unit 4). We have elected to discuss them with this Unit rather than the punishment Unit, however, because they are not the contingent presentation of some *event* after the misbehavior but, rather, *activities* required of the misbehaver contingent on the emission of a misbehavior. Additionally, the procedures usually teach the child appropriate behavior, while punishment only draws the student's attention to the misbehavior.

Overcorrection and positive practice have been used successfully to decrease a wide variety of inappropriate behaviors and to increase correct forms of behavior with quite a few different types of individuals. For example, Foxx and Azrin (1973) decreased self-stimulation of retardated and autistic children by using overcorrection procedures. Epstein, Doke, Sajwaj, Sorrell, and Rimmer (1974) used positive practice with two children diagnosed as schizophrenic. Azrin and Wesolowski (1974) used the procedures to eliminate stealing, and Barton and Osborn (1977) increased the physical sharing of toys with kindergarten children using positive practice. Based on the findings of these and other studies, it is apparent that teachers should be familiar with the various facets of these procedures which are necessary for their proper and effective use.

Definitions and Explanations

Foxx and Azrin (1973) have designated the two procedures as "restitutional overcorrection" and "positive practice." Restitutional overcorrection requires that the misbehaver "overcorrect the environmental effects of an inappropriate act" (Foxx and Azrin, 1973, p. 2). For example, if a child throws a piece of food on the floor, the child would not only have to clean the food up, but would also have to clean the entire floor. You would require the extra cleaning (the *over*correction) because the procedure stipulates that the physical environment be restored to a condition that is *better* than it was *before* the misbehavior occurred.

According to Foxx and Azrin (1973), positive practice would "require the disrupter intensively to practice overly correct forms of relevant behavior" (p. 2). For the child that threw food, perhaps that child would have to practice putting leftovers away properly or scraping plates into the garbage can after a meal. Foxx and Azrin view positive practice as a lesson designed to teach the misbehaver the correct manner in which to treat the object of the misbehavior.

Sometimes overcorrection and positive practice are used together; sometimes only one is used. That decision depends on the type of misbehavior involved. If the environment has been physically altered (food thrown, initials carved in a desk top), overcorrection is typically used before positive practice. If, however, no damage is done to the environment (the environment is not altered when a child will not share toys with others), overcorrection is omitted and only positive practice is employed.

Some educators confuse positive practice with a procedure which could more appropriately be labeled the *reverse Premack principle.* Normally, the Premack principle states that you can increase a low probability behavior, such as doing homework, by reinforcing it with access to a high probability behavior, such as watching TV (this concept was discussed under activity reinforcers in Unit 2). To reverse this, a teacher could make a child engage in a low probability behavior (such as running laps) because the child had done a high probability misbehavior (such as showing poor sportsmanship at recess).

An often used example of the reverse Premack principle would be requiring a child to write "I will not throw erasers during reading" one thousand times *after* the child had thrown an eraser (writing the 1000 sentences is the low probability behavior and throwing the eraser is the high probability behavior). Such a tactic *may* decrease the probability of the student throwing erasers, and would surely serve to teach the child how to spell "eraser," but it is not an example of positive practice. You might find variations of the reverse Premack principle useful to you but you should not confuse it with positive practice.

The reverse Premack principle is not positive practice for several reasons. First, it is not positive. Requiring a child to write a thousand sentences may be aversive and, consequently, you may be training the child to view writing (and possibly schooling in general) as an aversive event.* Additionally, positive practice is supposed to be *relevant* to the misbehavior and should teach the individual *what to do* instead of the misbehavior. It should be obvious to you that having a child write sentences for throwing an eraser is only somewhat relevant or related to the misbehavior and will not teach the child what is an acceptable alternative action for using erasers.

So, overcorrection requires the student to restore the normal environmental condition, and positive practice requires the student to practice proper, alternative actions. Perhaps an example will serve to further clarify the differences between overcorrection and positive practice. Ms. Skinner taught a fourth grade special education class. All of the students in the class were classified as educable mentally retarded (EMR). The difficulty of teaching her students was compounded by the fact that one of the children (Lucy) frequently disrupted the class by knocking her desk over, which invariably elicited a startle-reaction from the other EMR students (and, occasionally, from Ms. Skinner).

Ms. Skinner collected baseline data and found that Lucy's desk-tipping occurred only about three times per day during the nine-day baseline phase. Three times a day was judged often enough to warrant a behavioral intervention. Ms. Skinner decided to adopt positive practice and overcorrection, since she had heard that other EMR teachers had successfully used them to reduce various misbehaviors. She especially liked the idea that the student would practice an alternate, incompatible behavior.

On the first day of the behavioral intervention, Ms. Skinner explained to Lucy that if she overturned her desk (or anyone else's) she would have to right the desk, pick up any materials that may have fallen from it, dust the desk, and wax it. After

---

*See Unit 4 for a complete discussion of why academics should not be used as punishment.

overcorrecting her misbehavior, she would then be required to repeatedly sit down at her desk then get up without ever tipping the desk over (positive practice). The first time Lucy tipped her desk over, Ms. Skinner told her to right it, dust and wax it, which she did. However, Lucy refused to complete the exercise of repeatedly sitting at her desk. This noncompliance required Ms. Skinner to use *manual guidance* with Lucy. (Manual guidance involved Ms. Skinner guiding Lucy physically, so that Lucy would complete the positive practice component. In other words, Ms. Skinner helped Lucy sit down, then get up again, insuring that the desk was never tipped over.)

By the end of the first day of treatment, Lucy had tipped her desk over three times and had to be manually guided (during positive practice) all three times. On the second day, she tipped her desk twice and had to be manually guided once. After the third day, Lucy did not turn her desk over for three weeks. On this occasion, she voluntarily initiated and carried out the overcorrection and positive practice and continued to do so on the infrequent occasions when she overturned her desk.

Overcorrection and positive practice are two more alternatives for teachers when confronting problems of misbehavior. Neither is especially difficult to implement (although they can be time-consuming) and both have been found effective in a variety of cases.

Selecting Overcorrection and/or Positive Practice

Educators intending to use overcorrection and positive practice to reduce misbehavior should first examine several issues. Among the issues to be considered are the advantages and disadvantages of both procedures and the factors which influence whether or not the procedures will be effective. After weighing these issues, you should be able to decide if one or both of the procedures are applicable to the particular situation and how to implement your selection to achieve optimum results.

Advantages and Disadvantages

There are several advantages to overcorrection and positive practice that other, more aversive procedures do not enjoy. First, even though the procedures are technically forms of punishment, their use does not, as yet, involve the legal restrictions punishment usually entails. Second, neither procedure typically evokes the severe behavioral side-effects which are often associated with punishment and other aversive procedures. Third, studies concerned with the procedures indicate that they effect a quick, long-lasting behavioral reduction. Additionally, some researchers (Azrin and Foxx, 1971; Epstein *et al.*, 1974) have found that overcorrecting one target misbehavior is frequently associated with a reduction in other, different inappropriate behaviors. Also, these procedures are useful for a wide range of misbehaviors. The final advantage of the procedures is the most important one and has been discussed earlier. Overcorrection and positive practice are unique among the aversive techniques because they often teach the misbehaver appropriate forms of behavior (this is especially true of positive practice).

The disadvantages of overcorrection and positive practice are not as serious as those of the other aversive procedures, but still must be carefully considered and evaluated before one can decide to use the procedures. Because overcorrection is a form of punishment, undesirable side-effects, while rare, have been encountered. Doleys, Wells, Hobbs, Roberts, and Cartelli (1976) caution that "the use of manual guidance may set the occasion for aggressive responding by the subject" (p. 471).

An important disadvantage of either procedure (particularly positive practice) is that the time demands placed on the teacher, as well as the energy required when manual guidance is necessary, may be prohibitive. If the teacher is either unable to consistently consequate the misbehavior or cannot implement the procedure fully because of other time demands, then an alternative procedure should be selected.

The final issue to discuss in this section is not so much a

disadvantage of the procedures but more of a caution concerning them. Compared to the other behavior reduction procedures, there have been relatively few research studies that have investigated overcorrection or positive practice. The majority of studies that have used the procedures were not done in school or home settings (most were done in institutions). Also, in the majority of cases, individuals who were not typical (e.g., they were retarded, emotionally disturbed, etc.) were studied rather than average, school students.

Beyond this general cautionary note, there is at least one study available that broadly criticizes many of the claims made by proponents of the procedures. Rollings, Baumeister, and Baumeister (1971) conducted a series of experiments designed to investigate (a) if effects produced by the procedures generalized to settings other than where the training occurred (e.g., to the home) and/or other misbehaviors; (b) the effectiveness of the procedures; and (c) the durability of the reductions achieved. Their findings indicate that the procedures were *not* more effective than other procedures in reducing misbehaviors; reductions that were achieved were specific to the training area (lack of generalization) and inappropriate behaviors other than those targeted *increased* rather than decreased; and that reductions in target misbehaviors were not durable.

The results of one study are not a sound enough basis to decide whether or not to use a procedure. Until further findings are presented which either substantiate or refute the claims made for the procedures, remember that the effectiveness of the procedures are not, at this time, conclusively established. Still, until the final word is in, you can utilize the procedures in your classroom and judge for yourself whether the procedures work and are worth the effort required to implement them. If you do want to use the procedures, you must evaluate various factors which can influence how well they will work.

The Effectiveness of
Overcorrection and Positive Practice

Beyond the advantages and disadvantages of the two procedures, a teacher should be familiar with several factors which
determine the effectiveness of either an overcorrection or positive
practice contingency. These factors influence how quickly and
effectively target misbehaviors can be reduced. First, before using
the procedure, explain it thoroughly to administrators, parents,
and the misbehaver. This should be done to alleviate their possible
fears about the requirements of the procedures. (The procedures
are *not* based on fairness; they do not let the "punishment fit the
crime." Rather, they are intended to rapidly decrease a target
misbehavior's occurrence while both teaching the individual an
acceptable behavior and having the students experience the effort
usually required of others to repair the effects of the misbehavior.)
Most importantly, however, explanations help the procedures to
more quickly take effect.

Second, you should initiate the procedure for each transgression
as soon as the misbehavior occurs, and you should have the child
do the restitutional and/or positive practice activities continually
from start to finish (e.g., no breaks). You should not praise the
misbehaver for the activity during the sessions as this may act as
reinforcement for the misbehavior (this is especially true if you
must use manual guidance).

The final factor that can influence the effectiveness of the
procedures is whether you differentially reinforce behaviors that
are incompatible with the target misbehavior (DRI, Unit 11). As
we have discussed in previous Units, DRI, when used in combination with other procedures, can decrease the misbehavior faster
than when the procedures are used by themselves. Also, the
reductions are generally more permanent when such combinations
are used.

Using Overcorrection and/or Positive Practice

The final decision to use overcorrection and/or positive practice can be difficult. You must consider the advantages and determine if they offset each procedure's disadvantages. You must determine if you have the time required by each, and you must evaluate the factors which will affect the performance of either procedure. Once you have made the decision to use one or both of the techniques, there are a series of steps you should follow to properly implement the procedure. As in all the Units, some of the steps are the same for every procedure and they were discussed in Units 1-3. The steps specific to the proper implementation of overcorrection and/or positive practice have been discussed in this Unit. Table 8.2 lists the steps you should follow.

TABLE 8.2: STEPS TO FOLLOW TO IMPLEMENT
OVERCORRECTION AND/OR POSITIVE PRACTICE

1. Specify and define target misbehavior(s).
2. Choose measure for target misbehavior(s).
3. Collect baseline data.
4. Choose design to evaluate effectiveness.
5. Determine which procedure (or both) is applicable to the target misbehavior(s).
6. Select relevant restitutional and/or positive practice activities.
7. Explain system to concerned administrators, parents, and students.
8. Consequate each misbehavior (use manual guidance if necessary).
9. Combine with DRI.
10. Follow design—evaluate data.
11. Continue program or try another procedure.

Conclusions

The procedures discussed in this Unit were satiation, overcorrection, and positive practice (the reverse of the Premack principle was also explained, as an often used procedure commonly confused with positive practice). Satiation, at its basic level, is a form of saturation. People behave because either the behavior itself is reinforcing or the behavior results in the person being reinforced. Satiation occurs when a behavior decreases because the individual either has received so much reinforcement that the reinforcers have temporarily lost their reinforcing properties or when the individual has been required to do a reinforcing behavior so often that the activity is no longer, by itself, reinforcing.

Overcorrection and positive practice are both forms of mild punishment that do not have the many drawbacks usually associated with punishment. The overcorrection process requires that the misbehaver restore the environment so that it is better than it was before the misbehavior. If a child colors on the wall, overcorrection (sometimes called restitutional overcorrection) would specify that the child not only clean the place where he colored, but the entire wall, as well (and, depending on the size of the room, perhaps the other walls in the room).

Positive practice can be used by itself or along with (after) overcorrection. Positive practice mandates that the misbehaver repeatedly practice an appropriate form of the misbehavior. If a student slams a door shut (if the door does not break, no environmental damage has occurred, so overcorrection is not indicated), you may require that student to open and close the door 200 times. If the student refuses, then you could manually guide the child in the practice (which requires extensive time and possibly energy). An alternative to positive practice, the reverse Premack principle, was also mentioned. Where positive practice has the student repeatedly do a behavior that is an appropriate form of the misbehavior (and is, therefore, relevant to the misbehavior), the reverse Premack principle only has the student repeatedly do a low probability behavior (for example, running 50 laps around the gym) because the student emitted a high probability behavior (the target misbehavior).

These three procedures (and the one alternative) most often require students to participate in some activity when they have done a misbehavior. That is why we have included them in the same Unit. In many cases of misbehavior, you could use any of the procedures effectively. For example, if your target misbehavior was paper-throwing, you could employ:

1. Satiation—student throws paper for one-half an hour.
2. Overcorrection—student cleans up the entire room.
3. Positive Practice—student repeatedly practices walking to basket from desk and placing paper in can.
4. Reverse Premack Principle—student writes, "I will not throw paper" 300 times.

In another case, if your target misbehavior was hitting others, you could employ:

1. Satiation—student hits another 200 times (not really an alternative is it?).
2. Overcorrection—student rubs and soothes place on other where hit.
3. Positive Practice—student practices appropriate physical contact (such as touching).
4. Reverse Premack Principle—student runs 100 laps.

From this second set of examples, it is obvious that not every one of these procedures is useful for every problem. Still, they do give you several more selections for your growing repertoire of behavior reduction skills. It is important to remember that there is little applied research on any of these procedures. So, while they appear to be quite suitable to certain educational settings and populations, we can say very little definitely about many of the ramifications of these procedures. To be sure of your use of any of these procedures, collect careful data and evaluate your own results.

SUGGESTED PROJECTS

1. Select a misbehavior that currently occurs in your classroom and operationally define the misbehavior.
2. Explain why satiation would or would not be an appropriate procedure to use in reducing the misbehavior.

3. If satiation is appropriate, use the procedure to reduce the misbehavior.
4. How long did it take before the misbehavior was eliminated? Did the student(s) exhibit any side-effects? If so, what were they? If you were to do it over, explain what you would do differently.
5. Select three misbehaviors (one appropriate to overcorrection, one appropriate to positive practice, and one for the reverse Premack principle).
6. Apply the various procedures to their appropriate target misbehavior.
7. Did overcorrection plus positive practice work faster than just positive practice or reverse Premack principle? Explain why you think it did or did not.
8. Were the time requirements for overcorrection or positive practice excessive? What could you do differently, if anything, so that implementation would not require so much time?
9. Did any side-effects occur? Explain what they were and how severe they were.

REFERENCES

Ayllon, T. Intensive treatment of psychotic behavior by stimulus satiation and food reinforcement. *Behaviour Research and Therapy,* 1963, *1,* 53-61.

Azrin, N.H., and Foxx, R.M. A rapid method of toilet training the institutionalized retarded. *Journal of Applied Behavior Analysis,* 1971, *4,* 89-99.

Azrin, N.H., and Wesolowski, M.D. Theft reversal: An overcorrection procedure for eliminating stealing by retarded persons. *Journal of Applied Behavior Analysis,* 1974, *7,* 577-581.

Barton, E.J., and Osborn, J.G. The development of physical sharing by a classroom teacher through the use of positive practice. Paper presented at the meeting of the Midwestern Association of Behavior Analysis, Chicago, May, 1977.

Deitz, S.M. Some alternatives for the "yeller." *BeMod*, 1973, *1*(3), 2-4.

Doleys, D.M., Wells, K.C., Hobbs, S.A., Roberts, M.W., and Cartelli, L.M. The effects of social punishment on noncompliance: A comparison with timeout and positive practice. *Journal of Applied Behavior Analysis*, 1976, *9*, 471-482.

Dreikurs, R. *Maintaining Sanity in the Classroom.* New York: Harper and Row, 1971.

Epstein, L.H., Doke, C.A., Sajwaj, T.E., Sorrell, S., and Rimmer, B. Generality and side-effects of overcorrection. *Journal of Applied Behavior Analysis*, 1974, *7*, 385-390.

Foxx, R.M., and Azrin, N.H. The elimination of Autistic self-stimulatory behavior by overcorrection. *Journal of Applied Behavior Analysis*, 1973, *6*, 1-14.

Long, J.D., and Frye, V.H. *Making It Till Friday.* Princeton, N.J.: Princeton Book Co., Publishers, 1977.

Reese, E.P., with Howard, J., and Reese, T.W. *Human Behavior: Analysis and Application*, 2nd. ed. Dubuque, Iowa: Wm. C. Brown Co., 1978.

Rollings, J.P., Baumeister, A.A., and Baumeister, A.A. The use of overcorrection procedures to eliminate the stereotyped behaviors of retarded individuals. *Behavior Modification*, 1971, *1*, 29-46.

Sulzer, B., and Mayer, G.R. *Behavior Modification Procedures for School Personnel.* Hinsdale, Illinois: The Dryden Press, Inc., 1972.

Sulzer-Azaroff, B., and Mayer, G.R. *Applying Behavior-Analysis Procedures with Children and Youth.* New York: Holt, Rinehart, and Winston, 1977.

Unit Nine

REINFORCING OTHER BEHAVIOR

Study Questions

1. Explain the difference between emission and omission of behavior. When is each a problem?
2. Define and develop an educational example for DRO.
3. What is the "other" behavior? What is the main intent of DRO?
4. How are time intervals used with DRO? When do you reset the interval (two answers)?
5. Explain the advantages and disadvantages of DRO. For what types of misbehavior is DRO most useful? What is superstitious behavior? How is it established through DRO and how can it be avoided?
6. List the factors which influence the effectiveness of DRO. What needs to be considered when increasing the size of the DRO interval? Why would a teacher want to increase it?
7. How can you combine DRO with other behavior reduction procedures?
8. List the steps one should follow to implement DRO.

We have mentioned how there are many types of misbehavior and that these types are spread across the misbehavior continuum from "usual" to "serious" (see Unit 1). Most misbehaviors are problems of action (emission); students are actually doing some behavior which has been judged to be inappropriate. These problems of action include such behaviors as talking-out, hitting, and running around the room.

Some misbehaviors, however, are problems of inaction; these are problems which arise when students do not do something they are supposed to do. A problem of inaction is called a problem of *omission.* In other words, when a child fails to behave, we say a behavior has been omitted. Omission misbehaviors are such events as not completing an assignment, not asking questions, not interacting socially with other children (isolation), and not attending class.

Emission or omission of behavior is not always a problem. It is desirable for a child to emit an appropriate behavior or omit a misbehavior. Obviously, it is not inappropriate when a child answers all the math problems correctly, or when she shares her games with the other children. These behavioral emissions are examples of desired classroom action. When a child does not get angry after losing a sports contest, or does not hit his neighbor, or does not talk-out during social studies, we are pleased with that student's inaction. An appropriate objective for a teacher to specify when changing a student's social behavior could target an appropriate emission or omission.

The procedure explained in this Unit is designed to teach children to stop doing misbehaviors they are currently emitting. In other words, an emission of a misbehavior is changed to the omission of that misbehavior. Through this procedure a student learns *not* to do a specific misbehavior. The teacher, in fact, reinforces the student when the target misbehavior has not occurred for some period of time. So, this procedure is quite important for two reasons. First, the teacher is changing an emission of misbehavior to the omission of misbehavior. Second, this is the first of the three procedures we discuss which is nonaversive in its reduction of misbehavior; most importantly, this procedure specifies the use of positive reinforcement in the classroom.

Definition and Explanation

Reinforcing other behavior is our shorthand name for what is generally known as the *differential reinforcement* of *other* behavior or *DRO*. Since using these initials to describe as well as label the procedure is common, and probably easier to remember, we will refer to this procedure of reinforcing other behavior as simply DRO. DRO is defined as a procedure through which reinforcement is delivered at the end of a specified interval of time if the target misbehavior did *not* occur during the interval. So, through DRO, the student is reinforced when he does not emit (omits) a target misbehavior for certain periods of time.

The name of this procedure sometimes is confusing when it is compared to its contingencies. If reinforcement is delivered after a 10 minute period during which Johnny did not talk-out, for example, what is the "other behavior"? The expression, other behavior, comes from the fact that Johnny was doing *something* when the 10 minute period ended and he was reinforced. Whatever that "something" was, received reinforcement. So, in a sense, by accident, some other behavior that Johnny was doing was reinforced. Because people are never totally inactive, they are behaving in some way when reinforcement is delivered with DRO. Since reinforcement for that other behavior is unplanned, usually occurs after different other behaviors each time, and is somewhat irrelevant to our intent of reinforcing for omission, we just say that some "other behavior" was reinforced.

It is the intent of the DRO procedure, however, to strengthen (reinforce) the omission of a misbehavior; we are trying to insure that a student does not misbehave. Because reinforcement is given after periods of time in which no misbehavior occurs, we could say we are reinforcing the *absence* of misbehavior. Since that is our intent, to strengthen the absence of misbehavior, it will probably be easier to understand DRO if you consider it as a procedure through which the absence of misbehavior is reinforced.

Traditionally, DRO is used by dividing the class period into time intervals of equal length. If by the end of an interval, the target misbehavior has not occurred, the student is immediately reinforced and you start a new interval. If the target misbehavior does occur during an interval, that interval is immediately terminated and a new one is begun. The process of starting a new interval contingent upon the occurrence (emission) of a misbehavior delays the student's opportunity for reinforcement and makes the procedure more effective. If you stayed in the same interval, even though the student had lost the chance for reinforcement, the student could do several more misbehaviors before the next interval in which reinforcement was available began.

Deciding the length of the intervals is one of the last issues to cover before an explanation of DRO is complete. Basically, the length of the intervals is decided by examining the baseline level of misbehavior. The length of an interval should not be much longer than the average number of minutes during which one misbehavior occurred in baseline. For example, if Ralph was throwing rocks during recess about 10 times and recess lasted 30 minutes, he threw one rock on the average of every three minutes. So, the interval size should start at about three minutes. After the three minute intervals are working (rock throwing is not occurring when reinforcement is delivered at the end of each interval) you can gradually increase the interval. Eventually, in this case, the interval could be the whole length of recess, or 30 minutes. For more on this issue see The Effectiveness of DRO, a later section in this Unit.

Perhaps an example will further clarify DRO. Mrs. Tompkins was a bus driver for Parkston Elementary School. State law required that students be seated with their arms, heads, or other parts of their bodies remaining inside the bus (instead of sticking them out the window). This is a good law because the chance of being severely hurt should an accident occur is substantially diminished if one is seated properly rather than leaning out the window. Still, it is often a very hard restriction to enforce with young children, especially when there are an average of 30 children on the bus at any given time and only the driver and an aide to enforce the regulation.

The children that rode Mrs. Tompkins' bus, like most children, viewed the bus ride to and from school as a social event. It was a time to visit with friends and to play. Consequently, many of the students were consistently out of their seats, standing up, or walking around. Mrs. Tompkins instructed her aide to "keep them in their seats," which often resulted in the aide yelling at students and even, on occasion, physically shaking some of them.

After several weeks of such aversive tactics, Mrs. Tompkins noticed that their attitudes towards the bus ride, Mrs. Tompkins, and the aide seemed to be suffering. In Mrs. Tompkins' words, they were exhibiting an "I don't like you" air which Mrs. Tompkins, in turn, did not like.

Mrs. Tompkins felt she was in quite a problematic situation. She could not have the children out of their seats, but she also did not want to continue with the somewhat ineffective and aversive tactics presently being used. Fortunately for Mrs. Tompkins (and the children on the bus), Parkston's guidance counselor was familiar with several behavior reduction procedures.

After having the problem explained to her, the counselor decided that DRO was appropriate to the situation because, (a) it was positive and (b) the circumstances were such that the driver wanted the children to cease or omit certain misbehaviors. After having the DRO procedure thoroughly explained to her, Mrs. Tompkins was ready to try DRO.

Because she was busy driving the bus, Mrs. Tompkins had her aide collect the data. Duration recording was chosen as the method of measuring the target misbehavior. After the students were told to sit down and the bus began the journey, whenever any of the children got out of their seat the aide started a stopwatch. The stopwatch was stopped only when *all* children were again seated correctly. The total duration of time children were not in their seats would be expressed as a percent of the total amount of time of the bus ride. Mrs. Tompkins calculated the percent of time students were not in their seats by dividing the total of the number of minutes students were out of their seats by the total number of minutes students were on the bus. That figure multiplied by 100 gave the percent of time at least one student was improperly seated.

During Phase I (baseline), students were out of their seats an average of 80.7% of the time. The aide had noticed that the longest period that everyone had remained seated was three minutes (though this had occurred only a few times). Based on this, however, the initial DRO interval was set at three minutes. Before intervention began with DRO, it was explained to the children that they could talk and partially turn around in their seats, but they were not to get out of their seats. If three minutes elapsed without anyone getting up, a kitchen timer would buzz and the students would earn a point. If anyone got up during the interval, the timer would be reset to three minutes and restarted after the student(s) had sat down in their own seat.

The maximum number of points that could be earned in a day was 13, and that number was only available if all the students always stayed in their seats (the average trip to pick up and drop the children off was 20 minutes each way for a total of 40 minutes per day spent on the bus). The students could exchange, as a group, their points for a piece of sugarless bubble gum that they could chew while on the bus (10 points per piece of gum). This was a powerful reinforcer since the children were normally not allowed to chew gum on the bus because of the mess typically associated with such a privilege.

During the first intervention, the average percent of time spent out-of-seat dropped to 36.5%, which was a dramatic decrease, but still too high. To further reduce the target misbehavior, Mrs. Tompkins increased the DRO interval from three to five minutes in Phase III. This resulted in the students being out of their seats an average of 8.2% of the time, which Mrs. Tompkins deemed satisfactory. When she increased the DRO interval, she also decreased the number of points required to earn the sugarless gum. Under a three minute interval the exchange rate for gum was 10 points; with a five minute interval, however, the maximum

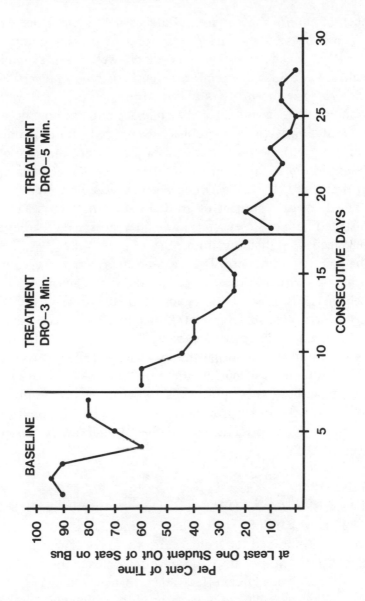

FIGURE 9.1. The percent of time the children were out of their seats on Mrs. Tompkins' bus each school day is shown. After baseline, gum was available through a DRO procedure with 3-minute intervals. The last phase shows the effect of DRO when intervals were increased to 5 minutes.

number of points the children could earn was eight per day, so Mrs. Tompkins set the exchange rate for gum at seven points.

The DRO schedule worked exceedingly well in this example for several reasons. First, the reinforcer (gum) was very powerful since the children were normally not allowed to chew gum and were still only allowed to chew it when they had accumulated the necessary number of points (once these were exchanged, the accumulation period restarted). Second, there was a lot of peer pressure placed on transgressors to conform to the demands made of them by the DRO procedure. If the DRO contingency was met, everyone was reinforced. When a student or group of students caused a point to be delayed (timer reset and new interval started), the other students censured that student.

This example shows how DRO can be an effective procedure for reducing a misbehavior by reinforcing the absence of that misbehavior. To use DRO you need to specify the target misbehavior, collect baseline data, calculate the interval size, use a timer to measure intervals, and reset the timer if (1) the student emits the misbehavior during the interval, or (2) after an interval elapsed with no misbehavior and you have delivered reinforcement. This whole DRO process is somewhat more cumbersome than many of the other procedures explained in this book. Still, it is an attractive and effective alternative to the aversive procedures mentioned earlier.

Selecting DRO

The decision to use DRO should not be hastily made merely because it is a reinforcement-based procedure. You must still weigh the combined advantages of the procedure against its disadvantages. Additionally, you have to evaluate the factors that influence the procedure's effectiveness. Once you decide to use DRO, you must implement the procedure following this book's guidelines as closely as possibly.

Advantages and Disadvantages

When implemented correctly, DRO has several advantages which recommend its use. First, and very importantly, DRO is a positive approach to behavior reduction since it does not depend on aversive, or even possibly aversive, contingencies to effect the behavioral reduction. Because it depends only on reinforcement, DRO is not associated with either the legal sanctions some procedures may entail, or the unpleasant emotional side-effects that often accompany the use of the procedures we have discussed up to this point (Units 4-8).

The remaining advantages of DRO all relate to various aspects of the procedure's effectiveness. In general, DRO has been found to be quite effective for reducing a wide range of misbehaviors of a variety of types of individuals. Initially, the effectiveness of DRO was established in the laboratory. Several studies demonstrated that DRO, while sometimes taking longer to reduce behavior, was as effective as either mild punishment (Unit 4) or extinction (Unit 7). DRO was also shown to establish a more lasting reduction than either of those procedures (Nevin, 1968; Uhl and Sherman, 1971; Zeiler, 1971).

In applied settings such as schools and institutions, studies investigating the effectiveness of DRO are somewhat contradictory. Some researchers (Corte, Wolf, and Locke, 1971; Foxx and Azrin, 1973) reported that the DRO procedure, by itself, was not as effective as other procedures such as timeout (Unit 6) or overcorrection (Unit 8). Other researchers have achieved excellent success when DRO was used by itself (Deitz, Repp, and Deitz, 1976; Repp, Deitz, and Deitz, 1976; Hummel, Deitz, Sundrup, Wagner, and Silavent, 1977), or when DRO was combined with other procedures (Repp and Deitz, 1974; Repp, Deitz, and Speir, 1974). It is difficult to determine exactly why these differences have been found but, currently, the greatest amount of evidence seems to support the conclusion that DRO is an effective procedure.

The final issue relating to the effectiveness of DRO concerns the types of misbehavior with which DRO is optimally effective. There is no question that DRO, even when used by itself, is effective for misbehaviors from the middle to the "usual" end of the misbehavior continuum (Unit 1). The conflict over the effectiveness of DRO mentioned above concerns misbehaviors toward the "serious" end of the continuum. When used properly, DRO is probably effective for almost any type of misbehavior. Still, for some serious misbehaviors, it may need to be combined with one of the other behavior reduction procedures.

The disadvantages of DRO are less numerous and less serious than those discussed for the procedures explained in Units 4-8. Still, teachers planning to use DRO will be more able to effectively employ the procedure if they are aware of potential problems sometimes associated with the technique. For example, there is a good chance that use of the procedure in many instances would not produce a behavioral reduction. The reason for this is that the first disadvantage of DRO is that it will not work unless you select a reinforcer that is *stronger* than the one currently maintaining the misbehavior.

To illustrate, suppose a child was stealing money from the desks of other children and you decided to use DRO (you wanted to reinforce the child each time stealing did not occur for a certain amount of time). If you contingently provided one minute of free time each time the individual omitted the behavior during the DRO interval, it is doubtful that the free time, by itself, would be a strong enough reinforcer to reduce the child's stealing (money is *probably* a stronger reinforcer than free time). Of course, as we explained in Unit 7, it is not always possible to identify the reinforcer maintaining a particular misbehavior. In such cases you must try the reinforcer you (with input from the child) have selected, and if it is not effective, adopt a new, hopefully more powerful, one.

The second disadvantage of DRO is that it requires some time to implement properly. The teacher must use a timing device*

---

*In our research, we have found ordinary kitchen timers to be satisfactory.

which must be reset (a) when the DRO interval has elapsed or (b) when the child emits the misbehavior. Additionally, because of the second factor listed above, the teacher must constantly observe the child in order to determine *if* the misbehavior does occur, and such sustained observation can be very demanding of the teacher.

Because sustained observation can be a burden, many teachers, instead of using the procedure for the entire day, will opt for one of the following alternatives. Teachers may only observe what the child is doing at the moment the timer buzzes. This, in effect, only requires the omission of the misbehavior at the sound of the buzzer. In other words, the students could be reinforced if the misbehavior occurred during the interval but not when the timer buzzed (Sulzer-Azaroff and Mayer, 1977). Such a schedule of observation is similar to the time-sampling technique we discussed in Unit 3 and involves similar difficulties. Consequently, we do *not* recommend this variation of DRO (neither do Sulzer-Azaroff and Mayer).

The second alternative requires that the procedure be used only during a specific time period during the day instead of the whole day. If this option is adopted, you should use the procedure during the time period in which the misbehavior usually occurs at its greatest rate. For example, if Terry frequently disturbs the property of neighbors, and, via preliminary observations, you have discovered that the disturbing occurs most frequently during the period after recess in the morning and before classes end in the afternoon, you might apply DRO only during those two periods instead of during the entire day. We have found this alternative to be quite useful.

Another disadvantage of DRO is that it can produce "superstitious behavior" since reinforcement is delivered for the absence of a particular misbehavior for a specific length of time. Whatever the student is doing at the moment the reinforcer is presented (the "other" behavior) is, by definition, reinforced even though the reinforcement was *not* intended to strengthen that behavior (such accidental reinforcement is called "adventitious" reinforcement).

If the student is looking around the room when the reinforcer is presented, then the student's looking around has been accidentally reinforced as well as the absence of the misbehavior. In that case looking around might be accidentally strengthened by the delivery of reinforcement.

The adventitious reinforcement of behaviors that occur at low rates is usually not a problem because the probability of any one behavior being frequently correlated with the presentation of reinforcement is minimal. However, behavior that occurs at moderate or high rates stands a good chance of being associated with the delivery of the reinforcer and, thus, increased in frequency due to adventitious reinforcement. Again, such increases in the frequency of these moderate to high rate behaviors are superstitious, since no real relationship exists between the *behavior* and the *reinforcement.* There is really little problem with behaviors being increased in such a manner unless, of course, the behavior being adventitiously strengthened is a misbehavior. Also, superstitious behaviors produced by accidental reinforcement tend to disappear in a short time, anyway.

There is a way of avoiding the adventitious reinforcement of inappropriate behaviors. The method to accomplish this does not conform to the exact definition of DRO, but can be considered a variation of the procedure. In this variation, the student still earns the reinforcement by not emitting the target misbehavior during the specified interval. However, instead of presenting the reinforcer to the student automatically at the end of the interval, you wait until the student is doing something you wish to see increased before you present the reinforcer. Essentially, you are still reinforcing "other" behavior, but the other behavior would be appropriate rather than neutral or possibly even inappropriate. If such a variation is used, the buzzer on the timer should be removed as it becomes a signal to the student that reinforcement has been earned. If not removed, when the buzzer sounds, whatever the student is doing is adventitiously reinforced.

After having evaluated the advantages and disadvantages of

DRO, the teacher is in a more secure position to make the decision to use or to not use the procedure. The advantages of DRO show that DRO, by itself, is both effective and lasting with normal to moderate misbehaviors and is very effective with even serious misbehaviors but might need to be used in combination with other reductive procedures.

The Effectiveness of DRO

In addition to the procedure's advantages and disadvantages, teachers should also be familiar with the factors that influence DRO's effectiveness. These factors influence how quickly an inappropriate behavior can be reduced or eliminated by DRO. The factors which contribute to the effectiveness of DRO include the strength of the reinforcer, the size of the DRO interval, explaining the procedure to the student, consistency, and combining DRO with other behavior reduction procedures.

As was previously mentioned, a strong, durable reinforcer is necessary for DRO to be effective. Social, activity, consumable, material, or exchangeable reinforcers can be used. The critical point is that the reinforcer must be strong enough to insure that the absence of misbehavior is strengthened. Remember, you can increase the strength of the reinforcer by insuring that reinforcement delivery is immediate and that the reinforcer is individualized (review Unit 2).

The second major factor influencing the effectiveness of DRO relates to the DRO interval. Remember that the initial DRO interval should not be too much longer than the average of the baseline level of the misbehavior. This allows the student to experience success early so there is a better chance the procedure will work. Increasing the length of the interval after this initial success is also quite important, however, and we have not yet discussed this issue in much detail.

A teacher is interested in further increasing the DRO interval for two reasons. First, the longer the interval, the greater the chances the misbehavior will entirely disappear. Second, much less effort is required by the teacher when longer DRO intervals are being used. Both of these reasons relate to a long-term goal of eventually phasing out use of the procedure, entirely. Increasing the length of the DRO interval is a step toward reaching that goal.

The question of when and by how much to increase the size of the DRO interval presents different problems than initially setting the interval. Once the misbehavior is not occurring in most of the initial, small intervals, your first increases should be slight. If your initial DRO interval is small (as when you are working with a high rate misbehavior), your increase should be small, preferably less than twice your initial interval. For example, if you started with 3 minute intervals to reduce talk-outs, your first change might increase the interval to 5 minutes. If your initial interval is longer, say 15 minutes, your increase could be larger while staying under the "do not double" rule. After success with a 15 minute interval, you could increase the interval to 20 or 25 minutes.

After several such small increments, the student should have adapted to increases, and future increases in the interval size can be progressively greater. The important point is that students should remain at near the same level of success. If you increase the interval and the student does not earn approximately the same amount of reinforcement, you have either increased the interval too soon or increased it by too much. At that point, you should lower it again so that students can be successful.

A good rule-of-thumb concerning *when* to increase the interval is to make sure the student has earned reinforcement a majority of the time, and that reinforcement was earned at least 70% of the time during the session before you raise the interval. Additionally, when and how much to increase the interval is related to how much reinforcement the student is able to earn. While you are initially increasing the interval, it is a good idea to insure that the student is able to earn the same amount of reinforcement. For example, in the illustration involving Mrs. Tompkins, the exchange rate for gum was originally 10 points (the maximum number of points the children could earn under DRO with 3 minute intervals was 13 per day). When the DRO interval was raised to five minutes, the maximum number of points the students could earn was 8 per day, so Mrs. Tompkins reduced the exchange rate. Of course, later in the intervention program, instead of increasing the time interval, you can increase the exchange rate to facilitate phasing out the procedure.

The third factor that will influence how quickly the behavior will be reduced by DRO is whether you explain the procedure to the misbehaver. DRO will work even if the students are not verbal (for example, if they are profoundly retarded) and the procedure is not explained. Still, if you explain (especially if the child is of normal intelligence) the requirements, it should decrease the amount of time required to bring the misbehavior under the control of the schedule. Suppose you had two very similar students, Joe and Jim, who were both exhibiting the same misbehavior at approximately the same rate. If you started Joe on DRO *with* instructions and Jim on the same schedule *without* first explaining the procedure, Joe's misbehavior would most likely decrease faster than would Jim's. You can also increase the effectiveness of the procedure by commenting to the children when reinforcement is delivered or the timer is reset. Comments such as, "I'm glad you didn't talk-out during this period," or "I have to start the time over again because you talked," can be very useful.

The fourth factor influencing DRO's effectiveness relates to consistency. This factor has been identified and discussed by Sulzer and Mayer (1972). As we mentioned earlier, DRO places heavy demands on the teacher's time, and it is not unusual for a teacher to use the procedure for only specific times or sessions during each day (instead of the entire day). In situations where the contingency is not maintained throughout the day, "it becomes very important to insure that the behavior does receive reinforcement at other times. If a particular behavior is placed on DRO under some conditions, it is possible that the undesirable response rate, while decreasing under the condition paired with DRO, might increase under the other condition" (Sulzer and Mayer, 1972, p. 208). When a behavior decreases under certain conditions and increases under different conditions, the behavioral result is referred to as *behavioral contrast.** If a behavioral contrast occurs, you will probably also have to implement DRO in the situation(s) where the misbehavior is increasing.

The final issue for using DRO effectively concerns combining it with other behavior reduction procedures. As we mentioned previously, for most types of misbehavior this is usually unnecessary. For serious forms of misbehavior, it might be necessary to combine DRO with some other procedure. Effecting such a combination is relatively easy. The other procedure would be used if a misbehavior occurred in an interval. If, for example, you combined response cost (Unit 5) with DRO, reinforcement would be immediately earned for an interval in which no misbehavior occurred. If a target misbehavior did occur, however, the student would immediately lose a specific amount of that reinforcement (response cost) *and* the interval would be reset. The same general policy would occur for combining DRO with most of the other procedures in this book.

If DRO is properly implemented, it is an excellent choice for behavioral reduction. While it is somewhat cumbersome, it is quick, effective, and lasting. Controlling those factors which influence the effectiveness of DRO is critical, but, once accomplished, you have added an excellent alternative for reducing misbehavior to your classroom.

Using DRO

The final decision to use DRO is, of course, in your hands. You must, on a case-by-case basis, weigh the advantages against the disadvantages, and evaluate how the factors that influence the effectiveness of DRO will affect the procedure in any particular situation. Once the decision is made to use DRO, you should

*See Units 4 and 6 for a more complete discussion of behavioral contrast.

follow the steps listed in Table 9.1 to insure that you implement the procedure properly.

TABLE 9.1: STEPS TO FOLLOW TO IMPLEMENT DRO

1. Specify and define target misbehavior(s).
2. Choose measure for target misbehavior(s).
3. Collect baseline data.
4. Choose design to evaluate effectiveness.
5. If target misbehavior is "serious," determine the procedure with which DRO should be combined.
6. Decide on initial length of DRO interval (based on baseline data).
7. Select reinforcer (student input is suggested).
8. Explain procedure to concerned student(s).
9. Be consistent.
10. Follow design—evaluate data.
11. A. If not working, select new/additional reinforcer(s) or new procedure(s).
    B. If working, continue program—gradually increase interval size.

Conclusions

Hopefully, the use of DRO has been shown to be an important skill for teachers to master. The advantages of DRO outweigh the disadvantages. The procedure is somewhat cumbersome but, with practice, a teacher should be able to effectively implement DRO. Since DRO is the first of the three reinforcement procedures we will discuss, we recommend its use above any procedure we have presented up to this point. Adding DRO to your list of skills for reducing misbehavior can produce a more pleasant classroom and one in which more academic success can be achieved by the students.

SUGGESTED PROJECTS

1. Choose a misbehavior that you believe may be appropriate to DRO. Operationally define the misbehavior.
2. Collect baseline information. Determine, from your baseline, the times of the day in which the misbehavior occurs most frequently.
3. From your baseline, calculate the initial DRO interval. Explain the program to the student(s) and implement in the period(s) selected from #2 above.
4. Is the reinforcer you selected "strong" enough? Is the interval too long, too short, or about right? If the interval is too long or too short, (a) how did you determine this and (b) what did you do about it?
5. Did the student(s) complain about the procedure? Did you observe any side-effects such as "superstitious" behavior?
6. When you increased the interval, did the students have any difficulty adjusting to the new length? What could you tell them to assure them of the "fairness" of such increases?

REFERENCES

Corte, H.E., Wolf, M.M., and Locke, B.J. A comparison of procedures for eliminating self-injurious behavior of retarded adolescents. *Journal of Applied Behavior Analysis*, 1971, *4*, 201-203.

Deitz, S.M., Repp, A.C., and Deitz, D.E.D. Reducing inappropriate classroom behavior of retarded students through three procedures of differential reinforcement. *Journal of Mental Deficiency Research*, 1976, *20*, 155-169.

Foxx, R.M., and Azrin, N.H. The elimination of autistic self-stimulatory behavior by overcorrection. *Journal of Applied Behavior Analysis*, 1973, *6*, 1-14.

Hummel, J.H., Deitz, S.M., Sundrup, D., Wagner, M., and Silavent,

L. Misbehavior in the classroom: A comparison of two reinforcement-based behavior-reducing procedures (DRO and DRL). Paper presented at the meeting of the American Educational Research Association, New York, April, 1977.

Nevin, J.A. Differential reinforcement and stimulus control of not responding. *Journal of the Experimental Analysis of Behavior,* 1968, *11,* 715-726.

Repp, A.C., and Deitz, S.M. Reducing aggressive and self-injurious behavior of institutionalized retarded children through reinforcement of other behavior. *Journal of Applied Behavior Analysis,* 1974, 7, 313-325.

Repp, A.C., Deitz, S.M., and Deitz, D.E.D. Reducing inappropriate behaviors in classrooms and in individual sessions through DRO schedules of reinforcement. *Mental Retardation,* 1976, *14,* 11-15.

Repp, A.C., Deitz, S.M., and Speir, N.C. Reducing stereotypic responding of retarded persons by the differential reinforcement of other behavior. *American Journal of Mental Deficiency,* 1974, *79,* 279-284.

Sulzer-Azaroff, B., and Mayer, G.R. *Applying Behavior-Analysis Procedures with Children and Youth.* New York: Holt, Rinehart, and Winston, 1977.

Sulzer, B., and Mayer, G.R. *Behavior Modification Procedures for School Personnel.* Hinsdale, Illinois: The Dryden Press, 1972.

Uhl, C.N., and Sherman, W.O. Comparison of combinations of omission, punishment, and elimination methods in response elimination in rats. *Journal of Comparative and Physiological Psychology,* 1971, *74,* 59-65.

Zeiler, M.D. Eliminating behavior with reinforcement. *Journal of the Experimental Analysis of Behavior,* 1971, *16,* 401-405.

Unit Ten

REINFORCING LOW RATES
OF BEHAVIOR

Study Questions
1. Why would a teacher want to only lower levels of misbehavior rather than eliminate it entirely?
2. What does DRL stand for?
3. List three ways teachers can program DRL.
4. Explain Spaced Responding DRL. What is meant by the time between behaviors? When is reinforcement delivered? What happens if the criteria for reinforcement are not met? How do you reduce misbehavior further than originally planned? Give an example of a teacher using Spaced Responding DRL.
5. Explain Interval DRL. How do you determine an interval? When is reinforcement delivered? What happens on the second behavior within an interval? How do you further decrease misbehavior? Give an example of Interval DRL.
6. Explain Full Session DRL. What is the DRL Limit? How is it set? When is reinforcement delivered? What happens if the DRL Limit is exceeded? How is Full Session DRL easier than the other two types of DRL? Give an example of a teacher using Full Session DRL.
7. Explain the five advantages of DRL. Why is reduction rather than elimination appropriate? How could elimination be achieved by starting with DRL? Why is it advantageous to use positive reinforcement to reduce misbehavior? How is DRL effective? Compare the three types of DRL in terms of ease of implementation.

8. List and explain the three disadvantages of DRL.
9. What are the important components of a reinforcement system? How do they influence the effectiveness of DRL?
10. How does the decision concerning the initial size of the reduction influence the effectiveness of DRL? What about the size of subsequent reductions?
11. Explain the remaining two factors which influence the effectiveness of DRL.
12. List and give examples for the steps you would follow to implement each of the three DRL procedures.

Quite often, when teachers become especially frustrated with classroom misbehavior, they think the best policy would be to initiate plans to completely eliminate all instances of all misbehavior. They dream of classes where all students are always well-behaved. They contemplate how nice it would be if their students spent all their time joyfully working on their academic subjects or respectfully listening to the teacher's explanations. A tranquil, productive classroom would seem to be a secret wish of all teachers, at least sometimes.

As most teachers know, however, that wish will probably never come true. In fact, in many cases, especially with young children, it is an unreasonable, as well as unrealistic, expectation. Children get excited and interested as well as hurt or angry. At those times, and probably others, misbehavior might occur and it might even be justifiable. So, the problem is not always the presence or absence of misbehavior. In fact in many classrooms, the problem is only the *level* of misbehavior. If misbehavior were occurring at a low level, the teacher would not find a problem of misbehavior and would probably not be at all upset. In these cases, a teacher's goal would be to control the level (or rate) of misbehavior rather than to eliminate it.

This Unit presents methods for bringing the level of misbehavior in a classroom within reasonable limits. Collectively, the three procedures presented here are all ways for teachers to convert high levels of misbehavior to low levels of misbehavior. One pleasant way to reach that goal is by using reinforcement, and the procedures explained in this Unit are reinforcement procedures. By using these procedures, teachers not only reduce levels of misbehavior, but also they use positive reinforcement to do it. The combination of reduction and reinforcement makes these procedures for lowering levels of misbehavior quite attractive for use in the classroom. When a teacher's goal is to reduce, rather than eliminate, misbehavior, these procedures for reinforcing low rates of behavior are excellent choices.

Definitions and Explanations

The procedures to be described which reinforce low rates of behavior are technically referred to by applied behavior analysts as variations of a reinforcement schedule called the differential reinforcement of low rates, or *DRL* for short (Ferster and Skinner, 1957). DRL schedules have been investigated in laboratory settings for quite some time but only recently have they been examined in applied settings. Through this recent research, DRL has been found to be effective in a variety of applied settings and with many types of misbehavior.

There are three different ways through which teachers can reinforce low rates of behavior. In other words, there are three different ways teachers can program DRL in their classrooms (Deitz, 1977). These ways have been labeled Spaced Responding DRL, Interval DRL, and Full Session DRL. Any of these types of DRL produces lowered levels of misbehavior through the use of positive reinforcement. They differ only in how they are implemented. Since each of the types of DRL is implemented in a different way, they are defined and explained separately.

1. Spaced Responding DRL
Spaced Responding DRL is the most commonly used type of

DRL in the laboratory. It is also the most difficult to understand and the most cumbersome to implement in applied settings. For some goals and types of misbehavior, however, it is the most useful. Spaced Responding DRL is defined as a procedure through which a target behavior is reinforced if it has been separated from the previous occurrence of that target behavior by at least a minimum amount of time. In other words, a teacher would reinforce a behavior if the student had not done that behavior for at least a prespecified amount of time.

The goal of the Spaced Responding DRL procedure is to increase the amount of time *between* consecutive instances of the behavior. By increasing the amount of time between behaviors, the overall rate or level of that behavior will decrease. For example, if Billy talks out about once every five minutes, he will talk out 12 times in an hour, an average class period. If the teacher reinforces a talk-out, for example by acknowledging it, only if a talk-out has not occurred for at least 10 minutes, that could decrease the overall number, or rate, of talk-outs to around 6 in an hour. The decrease would of course only occur if the reinforcement worked to strengthen the behavior in regard to the time factor. This way to decrease behavior also serves to make the behavior occur at regular, long intervals. There is "space" between behaviors (which explains the name for this type of DRL); they occur, but not in bursts or very often. So increasing the time between behaviors not only lowers the overall rate but also creates a "spaced" pattern of behavior.

Spaced Responding DRL is cumbersome in that a teacher must not only identify, operationally define, and count the target behavior, but the teacher must also measure the amount of time which elapses between each instance of the target behavior. For each instance of the target behavior, the teacher must then compare the actual elapsed time to the prespecified minimum. If the minimum is met or exceeded, reinforcement is delivered; if the minimum has not been met, reinforcement is not delivered and the timer is started over again. For one student and one target behavior, or if the whole class is used as a group (any instance of the behavior from any student must meet the minimum), the procedure can be fairly easily done with a stopwatch. More than one project at a time, however, becomes quite difficult.

A study reported by Deitz (1977) might help clarify Spaced Responding DRL. In that study, a teacher was having trouble with three students who were repeatedly asking the same type of questions to which the teacher was certain they knew the answers. After measuring the rate of the misbehavior for each student (baseline), she implemented the Spaced Responding DRL procedure. The teacher determined the size of the required amount of time between the specific type of questions by closely examining baseline data. She looked at the average amount of time between questions for each subject (a rate of 2 behaviors per minute means an average time between behaviors of 30 seconds, for example). For the procedure she decided to double that average for each student. So, for student one, the required time between questions was set at 3 minutes; for student two, it was 4 minutes; and for student three, it was 6 minutes.

When, for example, student one first asked a target question, the teacher would answer it and start a stopwatch. The second time student one asked the same type of question, the teacher would look at the stopwatch. If at least 3 minutes had passed, the teacher would answer the question and comment that she was pleased that the student had not asked that type of question for such a long time. If 3 minutes had not yet passed, she would not answer the question, tell the student it was too soon since the last question of that type, and start the stopwatch over again. The same process with different required times between questions was used for the other two students. It was unwieldy in that the teacher had to use three stopwatches, but also quite successful. By the end of the study, each student was asking inappropriate questions at least seven times less often than before the Spaced Responding DRL treatment began.

Once the misbehavior is occurring at a steady, low rate, the teacher can decrease that rate even further by increasing the minimum required time between misbehaviors. If Spaced Responding DRL were being used to decrease the out-of-seat misbehavior of a group, the teacher might start with a 10 minute interval. Any time a student was the first to get out of his or her seat, she would start her stopwatch. If at least 10 minutes had passed when another student got out-of-seat, the teacher would put a mark on the chalkboard. If 10 minutes had not yet passed, no mark would go on the board. The students had previously been informed that each mark earned them one minute of extra recess. If the procedure worked, and students were out-of-seat only about once every 10 minutes, the teacher might then want to reduce the level of that misbehavior even further; at that point, she could increase the required time between out-of-seats to 15 minutes with all other rules remaining the same. Of course, any or all of the teacher's decisions could be made in conjunction with the students. They might enjoy that participation and the procedure might be more effective.

By reinforcing a behavior only if it has been separated from a previous instance of that behavior by a fixed amount of time, a teacher can lower the overall rate of that behavior and also space it out so that no occurrences of the behavior are in rapid succession. Further reductions can also be accomplished by increases in the required minimum time between behaviors. Spaced Responding DRL can be effective especially for certain types of misbehavior (see Advantages and Disadvantages) but can be, at times, unwieldy. While laboratory research on the procedure is plentiful (for a review see Kramer and Rilling, 1970), applied research is limited. Even though there is a lack of supporting data and Spaced Responding DRL can be difficult to use, the procedure is an excellent solution for some problems in certain situations.

2. Interval DRL

A second method of programming DRL is called Interval DRL. It is similar to Spaced Responding DRL in that both procedures separate behaviors by some amount of time. In Interval DRL, however, the amount of time is not as specific. Interval DRL is defined as a procedure through which reinforcement is delivered at the end of an interval if fewer than two target misbehaviors occur within that interval. In other words, a teacher divides a class period into several intervals of equal length. If during any given interval, only one target misbehavior is exhibited, the teacher reinforces the student, at the end of the interval. If a second misbehavior occurs within the interval, the teacher simply starts that interval over again. Since a misbehavior can occur at any time during the interval, the time between behaviors is not important.

A study reported by Deitz (1977) demonstrates how Interval DRL can be used in a classroom. In that study the teacher identified and defined talk-outs of a six-year-old girl as the target misbehavior. The teacher counted the talk-outs during a 30 minute study session before lunch. After a six day baseline phase where the student was talking out almost 10 times during each of those six 30 minute sessions, the Interval DRL procedure was introduced.

The student was told that for every 5 minute interval in which she talked out fewer than two times she would receive a piece of chocolate caramel (consumable reinforcers were therefore used). If within any 5 minute interval she talked a second time, the whole interval started over again, postponing her opportunity to earn the candy. During the days this procedure was in effect, talking out steadily declined from a high of 5 talk-outs on the first day to zero talk-outs by the sixth day. Since an ABAB design was being used, the treatment was then removed and talking increased to its original, high level. When the treatment was reintroduced in the final phase, talk-outs fell to an average of 1.5 for the final six days of the study.

Interval DRL is a relatively new procedure and therefore has not been studied extensively. In fact, the Deitz (1977) study was the first to explain and illustrate the procedure. Deitz, Slack, Schwarzmueller, Wilander, Weatherly, and Hilliard (1978) presented two other studies which investigated Interval DRL. In one of the studies, a variety of inappropriate behaviors of one learning disabled male was reduced when stars, exchangeable for free time, were made contingent on short intervals in which fewer than two misbehaviors occurred. In the other study, talk-outs of a group of 14 preschool children were reduced by making minutes of access to a sand table available after intervals in which fewer than two target misbehaviors occurred.

Deciding the length of the interval and figuring out how to use the procedure can be a problem with Interval DRL. The length of the interval is determined by examining the baseline level of responding. If a child is throwing paper 10 times in a 30 minute class period, it is happening on the average of once every 3 minutes. To decrease paper-throwing, the teacher might start therefore with a 5 minute interval (less than twice the average baseline interval). To implement the procedure with the 5 minute interval, when class started, the teacher would start a timer (a kitchen timer is handy because it sounds a bell when the time is over). When the timer showed 5 minutes had passed and the student had thrown paper a maximum of once, she would reinforce the child with praise or tokens or whatever type of reinforcer she had originally chosen. If before the timer expired the student threw a second wad of paper, she would immediately start the interval over again (another good reason to use a kitchen timer, because it can easily be reset). Resetting the timer makes the opportunity for reinforcement delayed and adds to the effectiveness of Interval DRL.

Since paper-throwing once every 5 minutes may still be too much, once misbehavior is under control, it can be further reduced by increasing the length of the interval in which fewer than two behaviors are allowed. For example, in the study reported by Deitz (1977), examining the misbehaviors of the learning disabled boy, the interval used in the first treatment phase was 2 minutes. In the second treatment phase, that interval was extended to 3 minutes. Obviously, over a 30 minute class, 15 misbehaviors could be done in 30 minutes and still earn all the possible reinforcement. Only 10 misbehaviors could be done with 3 minute intervals, however. With our example of paper-throwing, the teacher could increase the interval to 8 minutes, then 10 minutes, and eventually to 30 minutes or more. She would have to carefully observe that the misbehavior remained under control, however, and not make changes too quickly or abruptly.

Interval DRL is less unwieldy than Spaced Responding DRL in that the measurement of intervals is not as difficult as measuring the time between two instances of the same behavior. Still, it is not as simple as only counting misbehaviors with no worry about timing. Through Interval DRL, you are using reinforcement to decrease the overall frequency of a misbehavior and you are insuring that misbehaviors do not occur in "bursts." Since the procedure requires that only one (or zero) misbehavior occurs within each interval, very little reinforcement can be earned if several misbehaviors occur together. So, while Interval DRL is somewhat difficult to use, it has been shown to produce excellent results. For certain problems, it is among the best procedures to use and in any case is a good skill for a teacher to have mastered.

3. Full Session DRL

The last type of DRL is called Full Session DRL. It is the easiest of the three DRL procedures to use in a classroom and also has been investigated in applied settings the most frequently. Full Session DRL is defined as a procedure through which reinforcement is delivered at the end of a session if fewer than a prespecified number of misbehaviors occurred during the session. The session is usually the whole class period in schools so there is no need to time between behaviors or measure intervals. The prespecified number of misbehaviors is the maximum number of misbehaviors the students are allowed while still earning reinforcement. That number is called the DRL Limit. So reinforcement is delivered at the end of a class period if the students do not exceed the DRL Limit.

To use Full Session DRL the teacher needs to, first, choose, specify, and define the target behavior. Then baseline data should be collected. From the baseline data, the DRL Limit is derived (try not to set it too low at first). Finally, the teacher (and the children) select a reinforcer to be earned on days when the limit is not exceeded. For example, let's say that Mr. Norton has specified Billy's teasing as the target misbehavior. During baseline, Billy teased someone about eight times each morning. Mr. Norton sets the DRL Limit at four and tells Billy that if he teases only four or fewer times during a morning he will get to sit by Mr. Norton at lunch (usually a reinforcer for young children). After the explanation, he begins the system, counting as usual, and informs Billy of the results at the end of each morning. If four or fewer "teases" occur, Billy sits next to Mr. Norton. If more than four occur, he sits away from Mr. Norton. By making a lunchroom privilege contingent on a low level of misbehavior during the morning (session), Mr. Norton has effectively been using Full Session DRL.

In Full Session DRL, the goal is only to reduce the overall number of misbehaviors occurring during a session or period of time. There is no attempt to insure that bursts of misbehaviors do not occur. While Spaced Responding DRL separates misbehaviors by reinforcing only those misbehaviors which occur a certain length of time after a previous misbehavior, and Interval DRL separates misbehaviors by allowing a maximum of one per interval, Full Session DRL incorporates no contingency for spacing out misbehaviors. No matter how they occur during the session, all at the beginning or end, or throughout the session, if the DRL Limit is not exceeded, reinforcement is delivered at the end of the session.

Deitz (1977) used Full Session DRL to reduce the talk-outs of a 15-year-old Educable Mentally Retarded male. During the baseline phase the student averaged over 32 talk-outs during every 55 minute class period (session). The Full Session DRL procedure used in the second phase of this ABAB design specified that if three or fewer talk-outs occurred during the 55 minutes, the student would earn 15 minutes alone with the teacher to work on the state driver's manual. During the first seven days, reinforcement was not earned but for six of the next seven days it was earned. The overall average of talk-outs over the 14 day treatment phase was only 2.3 talk-outs per class. During the reversal the behavior increased again and when the Full Session DRL treatment was reintroduced the average fell to only 1.5 per class period.

Full Session DRL has also been proven to be effective with many other types of target misbehaviors and many other types of students, both individually and in groups. Deitz and Repp (1973) used Full Session DRL to reduce talking of an individual retarded student and of a group of retarded students. Off-task talking and out-of-seats have been reduced through Full Session DRL with normal elementary and high school students (Deitz and Repp, 1973, 1974). The procedure has been shown to be effective for reducing the time between classes, called transition time, in an elementary class (Deitz, Hummel, Sundrup, and Hughes, 1977), for reducing self-stimulatory behaviors of an autistic child (Sundrup and Deitz, 1977), and for a variety of disruptive behaviors of individuals and groups of other special populations (Deitz, Repp, and Deitz, 1976). Variations of the procedure have been used to reduce classroom noise (Schmidt and Ulrich, 1969; Wilson and Hopkins, 1973). The reinforcements used in these studies have included many types of social, activity, exchangeable, and consumable reinforcers. Interestingly, it was Full Session DRL that was shown to be more effective than "talks" with children about the reduction of their misbehavior (see Unit 1) (Deitz, Hummel, Sundrup, Meeks, and Butler, 1977). There is no question that Full Session DRL is an effective procedure for reducing misbehavior.

As with the other types of DRL, misbehavior can be reduced further once the misbehavior is under control. As soon as the level of misbehavior is reliably at or below the DRL Limit, that limit can be reduced to lower the level of misbehavior. One excellent way to reduce the misbehavior is to lower the limit in a series of steps rather than through an initial, large decrease. When Deitz and Repp (1973) decreased off-task talking by the group of high school girls in the Business Education class, the initial limit was six misbehaviors within 50 minutes. Over the next several weeks the DRL Limit was lowered to 3, then 1, and finally to zero. (NOTE: Technically a DRL Limit of zero is a change to a DRO contingency, which is explained in Unit 9, since the absence of misbehavior rather than a low level of misbehavior is being reinforced.) Successive reductions of the DRL Limit are usually more effective than immediately setting your limit too low. In the study previously explained, concerning the Educable Mentally Retarded boy who did not earn reinforcement until the eighth day (Deitz, 1977), an initially higher limit would probably have allowed him to earn reinforcement sooner thus increasing his success when interacting with the procedure. Later the limit could have been reduced to three.

An important variation of Full Session DRL has been explained by Barrish, Saunders, and Wolf (1969) and investigated further by Medland and Stachnik (1972) and Wilson and Hopkins (1973). That variation has been called *The Good Behavior Game*. The Good Behavior Game is a group contingency where students are divided into teams, rules posted, and misbehaviors of each team noted by the teachers on the chalkboard. Certain reinforcers are made available to the team with the fewest misbehaviors. In the game, the DRL Limit is flexible and is in fact set by the losing team. For example, if Team 1 misbehaves eight times, Team 2 can win by staying below that limit. Usually a second DRL Limit is also employed. This second limit is specified so that if both, or all, teams stay below a certain number of misbehaviors, both teams win, thus earning reinforcement. The Good Behavior Game has proved an excellent variation of the DRL procedure in that it is not only effective but also fun for the participants.

Full Session DRL in all its varieties is relatively easy to use and has been found to be quite effective. The teacher only needs to identify the target misbehaviors, decide how they will be counted, select an initial limit, and decide on the reinforcement plan. Except for observing the end of the class period, no timing is required. If the DRL Limit is not exceeded, reinforcement is delivered; if the limit is exceeded, reinforcement is not delivered. Full Session DRL is really a simple, but elegant, procedure which should be a part of any teacher's behavior reduction skills.

Selecting DRL

When making the decision concerning whether or not to select one of the DRL procedures for use in your classroom, several factors should be considered. Although the advantages of any of the types of DRL far outweigh the disadvantages, there are some problems for which the disadvantages are more important. Before a teacher selects DRL to use, these advantages and disadvantages must be carefully considered. The teacher must also be familar with the factors which influence the effectiveness of DRL. Unless the procedure can be properly implemented so that it is effective, some other procedure should be used. The following sections should provide sufficient information to allow you to make a wise choice concerning the selection of DRL for your particular problem.

Advantages and Disadvantages

The advantages and disadvantages of DRL are not as clearly distinguished as they are for some of the other procedures. Primarily, this is because there are three types of DRL procedures. In some cases, for example, what is an advantage for Full Session DRL might be a disadvantage for Spaced Responding DRL. Still, because so many of the advantages and disadvantages are common across all types of DRL, we have decided to treat them jointly, rather than become redundant. Where differences occur, we will be as specific as possible in pointing them out. Careful examination of all the following issues should help clarify your selection of one of the DRL procedures.

A primary advantage of DRL is that it is intended to reduce, rather than eliminate, misbehavior. For many, possibly most, common types of misbehavior, all parties involved in the classroom can be entirely satisfied with a reduction of misbehavior to a level which is not counterproductive to the classroom environment. Any of the DRL procedures are especially fair for young children, for they are not required to be "perfect." Clear limits are delineated and children are taught to improve. Also, improvement can be accomplished in a series of steps so that too much is not expected of children too soon. In this regard, the teacher, when using DRL, is required to treat misbehavior like academic behavior. When learning an academic skill, children are not expected to master that skill immediately and with perfection. By specifying a step-by-step reduction of misbehavior as the teacher's goal, DRL requires that a plan which is reasonable and soundly based on the principles of learning is being employed.

So, when the teacher's goal is to reduce misbehavior, DRL is advantageous, for it is the one procedure specifically designed for that purpose. Other aspects of that goal need to be examined, however, before a teacher can decide which type of DRL is the most useful for the particular problem. In some situations, behaviors are inappropriate only because of their high frequency.

> . . . for example, adding to classroom discussion is appropriate but dominating that discussion is not. In this case, one would want to decrease the (behavior), probably space it out, but surely maintain it in some strength. Spaced Responding DRL would be most appropriate. If a (behavior) is annoying, troublesome, or a hindrance to other students, even though it is not dangerous, the (behavior) need not be kept at any strength. In fact reinforcing the (behavior) at all . . . might be disadvantageous. In that case, Interval DRL or Full Session DRL would be more appropriate. (Deitz, 1977, p. 109)

Since behaviors are directly reinforced only in Spaced Responding DRL (reinforcement occurs for a behavior if the required amount of time has passed since the last behavior), it is the only DRL procedure which insures that a behavior remains in at least some strength. In Interval DRL, reinforcement occurs at the end of an interval in which fewer than two behaviors occurred; and in Full Session DRL, reinforcement is delivered at the end of the session in which fewer misbehaviors than were specified by the DRL Limit occurred. Thus, there could be no misbehavior occurring, and reinforcement would still be earned.

Another advantage, related to the teacher's goals for a specific problem, of using DRL concerns planned eventual elimination.

> If the final goal is to eliminate the behavior, one may still start with DRL. Using Full Session DRL, the DRL Limit could be gradually decreased with the schedule eventually converting to DRO (zero responses per session). With Interval DRL, the length of the intervals could be extended, thus greatly reducing the (behavior), and then it too could be converted to a DRO schedule by reinforcing only intervals in which no (behavior) occurred (Deitz, 1977, p. 109).

Misbehavior can eventually be entirely eliminated by starting with two of the types of DRL, increasing the requirements, and converting those requirements to DRO. DRO is explained in Unit 9, and you might want to read that explanation and definition if you are unclear about some of this discussion.

What should be clear, however, is that this first advantage of DRL is complex. Since DRL is a procedure intended to reduce, rather than eliminate, misbehavior, it is advantageous in that it is fair, helps the teacher set reasonable expectations, and reduces misbehavior in the same style with which a teacher establishes academic behavior. The manner through which each type of DRL reaches that goal causes the confusion. Spaced Responding DRL is best for behaviors which should remain at some strength. Interval DRL and Full Session DRL do not ensure the existence of a behavior, so are better for other types of misbehavior. These last two types are also better when the teacher's eventual goal is to eliminate the misbehavior entirely. So the relative value of each type of DRL depends on the particular behavior, not just the general goal of only reduction. Still, all three illustrate their usefulness and overall value because of their orientation to reduction.

A second, less complicated advantage is that positive reinforcement is being used to reduce misbehavior. In general, it is always a good idea to find ways to incorporate more positive reinforcement in the classroom. It is more pleasant for the children and they can be actively working to earn something pleasant for their improvement rather than behaving to avoid some aversive consequence. Positive reinforcement used within a DRL contingency can also make the classroom more fun, especially when the reduction of misbehavior is accomplished through using a game (like the Good Behavior Game for groups or Full Session DRL with the whole class or an individual). Using positive reinforcement should be more pleasant for the teacher, as well. It is nicer spending time praising or rewarding students than criticizing or punishing them. Since schools should be pleasant places where much positive reinforcement is found, using one of the DRL procedures moves toward the realization of that goal.

A third advantage of DRL is that it is effective. Full Session DRL has repeatedly been proven effective across a wide range of types of misbehaviors. Interval DRL has been investigated less frequently and Spaced Responding DRL has only been used once in an applied setting. Still, in every case so far, the use of any DRL procedure has reliably and rapidly reduced the level of the misbehavior under study. A related issue is that DRL is effective with groups as well as individuals. Since it is often easier and more efficient to work with a group, especially when a large percentage of the group is exhibiting the same misbehavior, it is advantageous that DRL has been shown effective with groups.

Fourth, there are several issues concerning the ease of implementation of DRL in the classroom. Primarily, Full Session DRL is quite easy to use in the classroom. Only counting, comparing the count to the DRL Limit, and reinforcing are required. For Full Session DRL this is an obvious advantage. Interval DRL, where some timing is required, is not as easy as Full Session DRL but not that difficult to say it is disadvantageous. Spaced Responding DRL is not very easy to implement because it requires timing between behaviors. In the case of this type of DRL, the difficulty of implementation is a disadvantage. One has to weigh the many other advantageous aspects of Spaced Responding DRL against this disadvantage when deciding on its use.

The last advantage of DRL is that it is easy to combine other behavior reduction procedures with any of the types of DRL. Since several procedures used jointly can be more effective than one procedure used alone, this is a decided advantage. For example, if you combined Response Cost (see Unit 5) with DRL, you could employ the following procedures. In Full Session DRL, one minute of free time could be removed for every misbehavior *above* the DRL Limit (while extra free time would be earned if misbehavior stayed below the limit). The same type of reinforcement could be used with Interval DRL; with that procedure, the second misbehavior in an interval would lose time while a successful interval would earn the time. With Spaced Responding DRL, free time would be earned when the required time had passed between misbehaviors, and lost when it had not. Of course, the best procedure to combine with DRL (or any of the procedures in this book) would be DRI (see Unit 11), since only DRI actually teaches appropriate social behavior to replace the inappropriate social behavior.

While these five advantages of DRL make the selection of any of the types of DRL quite attractive, several disadvantages must be examined before the selection is made. First, none of the types of DRL are useful for serious or dangerous misbehaviors. Since DRL is designed to only reduce misbehavior, its use is not suitable for those types of misbehaviors. This disadvantage is especially relevant for Spaced Responding DRL, since it ensures the maintenance of a misbehavior by directly reinforcing it.

A second disadvantage of DRL is that some types are cumbersome. Spaced Responding DRL is difficult to use in the classroom, and Interval DRL is moderately difficult to use. Full Session DRL, however, is not at all difficult. Each requires the arrangement and implementation of some form of reinforcement system, but that burden should be one that teachers would enjoy carrying. No deleterious side-effects have yet been reported from the use of DRL, a disadvantage common to those procedures which do not use reinforcement, so the implementation of a reinforcement system should be a valued task.

The last disadvantage of the three types of DRL is that none are arranged to teach appropriate behavior. They are directed at behavioral reduction, and thus can orient the student toward misbehavior rather than appropriate behavior. With DRL this is a less serious disadvantage than it is with many of the other procedures presented in this book (except for DRI, for which this is not a disadvantage at all—see Unit 11). Since DRL teaches students to control their level of misbehavior, they are learning an appropriate social skill. As far as we are concerned, the advantages of DRL far outweigh the disadvantages. For misbehaviors which are neither serious nor dangerous, we recommend DRL above every procedure other than DRI.

The Effectiveness of DRL

Once a teacher has decided to reduce a misbehavior by using a type of DRL, he or she must be able to implement it so as to maximize the chances of success. Understanding the following four factors which influence the effectiveness of any of the types of DRL is essential for achieving that success. Of course, before the system is begun, the teacher should have adequately prepared by properly specifying and counting the misbehavior. Once those steps are completed, the teacher must consider (1) the reinforcement system, (2) the initial amount of reduction and the size of subsequent reductions, (3) instructions to the students, and (4) the combination of the type of DRL with other behavior reduction procedures.

The first factor to consider is the reinforcement system. There are several important components of that system which need examination. The major component concerns the selection of the reinforcers. Teachers should choose from among the five types of secondary reinforcers which were discussed in Unit 2. The choice should be made initially on two grounds. First, the probable effectiveness and durability for the individual or group involved should be considered. If students seem to prefer free time or games, activity reinforcers should be selected. If students seem to prefer a wide range of types of reinforcers, you might consider an exchange system. In any case, your data will eventually inform you of the effectiveness of the reinforcer you have chosen. The second ground on which the selection of a reinforcer should be made involves the difficulty for the teacher to implement the system. In general, you should use the least cumbersome system which is still effective. The major aspect of this component, however, is that without the availability of effective reinforcers, the DRL system cannot work.

The second component of the reinforcement system concerns how those reinforcers are made available. In other words, you should be sure to follow the rules for using reinforcement which were presented in Unit 2. Briefly, we mentioned that reinforcement should be immediate, individual, and consistent, and that the teacher should comment on the particular behavior being reinforced. These rules are important for using DRL effectively because the different types of DRL all rely on the proper implementation of a reinforcement system.

An interesting potential problem arises in the area of immediacy. With Spaced Responding DRL, reinforcement is immediately delivered for a behavior which meets the time requirement. For Interval DRL, reinforcement is delivered at the end of short intervals in which fewer than two behaviors occurred. Reinforcement is not delivered until the end of a whole session, however, in Full Session DRL. Because of these successively increasing delays in reinforcement delivery, control might be easier to establish through the first two types of DRL than through Full Session DRL.

But students receive other forms of feedback besides reinforcement which also help to control the misbehavior. Students can be told that the correct amount of time has not passed between

behaviors while the teacher is resetting the timer in Spaced
Responding DRL. That type of information (feedback) can be
provided in Interval DRL as well. In Full Session DRL, feedback
may or may not be given for each misbehavior in the class period.

> In most studies of Full Session DRL, the subject has not been
> informed of his moment-to-moment accumulation of re-
> sponses . . . Harris and Sherman (1973) found that during the
> "Good Behavior Game," feedback on cumulative misbehaviors
> made very little difference. They reported that students usually
> made the maximum number of responses with both teams still
> winning. They speculated that were the group treated as a whole
> no feedback would be the best alternative (Deitz, 1977, p. 110).

With Full Session DRL, similar misbehavior patterns would
probably occur. With information about their moment-to-moment
accumulation of target misbehaviors, they would probably misbehave to the limit. If they exceeded the limit, a large amount of
misbehavior might occur, since they would know that reinforcement was no longer available. Most likely they would stay below
the limit without feedback. So with Full Session DRL it might be
best to avoid feedback until the very end of the session.

To be sure, then, that the whole reinforcement system supports
the effectiveness of any DRL procedure, several areas must be
examined. The reinforcers must be effective. The manner in which
they are made available should follow the four rules of reinforcement. The type of informational feedback to be provided in
addition to reinforcement must be carefully planned. With proper
implementation of these factors, you have gone most of the way
toward insuring the effectiveness of your use of DRL.

The second major factor to consider which influences the
effectiveness of DRL concerns the size and rate of both initial and
subsequent reductions. In other words, first, you need to be
careful in initially setting the level of misbehavior at which
reinforcement can be earned. The important point is not to aim
toward too much of an initial reduction. For example, if Sarah is
talking out during baseline about 20 times every 30 minutes, you
might want to set your initial DRL Limit (assuming you're using
Full Session DRL) at 10. Requiring more than a 50% reduction

would make your procedure too difficult for the student to be successful. Second, you should not further lower the limit until behavior is under control; for the further reduction, the amount of reduction should not be too drastic, either. The same principles hold for Spaced Responding DRL and Interval DRL. Your initial requirement of time between behaviors or interval size should not require too much of a change from baseline rates. Your successive reductions would also be in relatively small steps. By requiring reductions to be small and gradual, the student will be successful and the reinforcement will work to strengthen low, rather than high, levels of misbehavior.

Communicating instructions to the students is the third factor through which you can increase the chances of the effectiveness of DRL. You should explain the target behaviors to those involved so you are sure they know exactly what they should not do. You should also explain the "rules" of the procedure. Tell the students how they can earn their reinforcement, what happens when they misbehave, and what happens when they do not misbehave. Instructions cannot replace the contingencies but they do help the students to be successful so they can earn reinforcement.

The last factor influencing the effectiveness of DRL is combining it with other procedures. As was mentioned earlier, whenever two procedures are used, the chances of reduction are greater than when there is only one. Many procedures can be used with any of the types of DRL, but we recommend DRI (Unit 11) the most highly. Through DRI you are teaching an appropriate behavior which can replace an inappropriate behavior. Other procedures, such as timeout (Unit 6), response cost (Unit 5), and even punishment (Unit 4), can be combined with DRL. For example, with Spaced Responding DRL, a behavior which occurred too closely to the previous behavior could earn response cost. The second behavior in an interval could be punished when using Interval DRL. Through Full Session DRL, timeout could be used each time the DRL Limit was exceeded. As you more thoroughly master all the procedures in this book, you will find ways to combine them so that you are maximally effective as well as comfortable with your selections.

Any type of DRL can be extremely effective when done properly. In your preparation for implementing a procedure, you must consider the various aspects of your reinforcement system. You must also plan your initial reduction requirement as well as future reductions. Decide exactly how you will inform your students of the rules. Finally, decide if you will try DRL alone or in combination with other procedures. When those preparations are completed, you will almost always be successful in meeting your goal of reducing a target misbehavior through one of the three types of DRL.

Using DRL

Deciding to use DRL is not as difficult as deciding to use some of the other procedures. The procedures are nonaversive and even use positive reinforcement to achieve behavioral reduction. Many legal and ethical issues are avoided and children often find the procedures to be fair as well as fun. Implementing DRL, however, can present some problems. Spaced Responding DRL and Interval DRL are somewhat cumbersome, all require careful preparation, and all require the implementation of a reinforcement system. Once you have decided to use DRL, though, we are sure the benefits to you and your class will far outweigh the burdens. Table 10.1 should help you in planning and implementing an effective DRL procedure.

Conclusions

DRL presents teachers with an excellent option for reducing misbehavior. It is a positive procedure which has been found effective in a wide range of settings and with many types of misbehaviors. It uses positive reinforcement to teach students that there are acceptable limits; students are not required to try to be "perfect." By now it should be quite clear that we believe the advantages of DRL far outweigh its disadvantages. In fact, DRL is one of our favorite procedures (but we guess that is also clear).

TABLE 10.1: STEPS TO FOLLOW TO IMPLEMENT DRL

1. Specify and define target misbehavior.
2. Choose measure for target misbehavior.
3. Collect baseline data.
4. Choose design to evaluate effectiveness.
5. Plan reinforcement system.

Spaced Responding DRL	Interval DRL	Full Session DRL
6. Determine time between behaviors.	Determine interval size.	Determine limit.
7. Explain procedure.	Explain procedure.	Explain procedure.
8. Implement.	Implement.	Implement.
9. Increase time between behaviors.	Increase interval size.	Decrease limit.

10. Combine with other procedures.
11. Evaluate your data (effectiveness, further reduction).
12. Make necessary changes.

Spaced Responding DRL and Interval DRL can be considered "specialty" procedures in that they are most useful for problems which require a large amount of feedback (disturbed or retarded children, for example) or misbehaviors which should be spaced out over time (dominating discussion vs. appropriate participation). Full Session DRL is not only the easiest of the three types of DRL, it is also the most widely useful. With usual to moderate misbehaviors and with individuals or groups, Full Session DRL is an excellent choice for a teacher to make. We hope that teachers spend the time to master at least Full Session DRL, for we believe that, over time, they will find it one of the two most useful and successful misbehavior-reduction procedures they can employ in their classrooms.

SUGGESTED PROJECTS

1. List four misbehaviors occurring in your classroom for which you think reduction rather than elimination would be most appropriate.
2. For each misbehavior, plan how you would use one of the types of DRL. Be sure your planning covers all aspects of implementing the procedure. Try to plan how you would use each of the types of DRL for one of your misbehaviors.
3. Choose one problem, and follow the steps in Table 10.1. Evaluate your data to determine the effectiveness of your use of the procedure.
4. Are you satisfied with reduction? Do you want further reduction? Do you want to eliminate the misbehavior?

REFERENCES

Barrish, H.H., Saunders, H., and Wolf, M.M. Good behavior game: Effects of individual contingencies for group consequences on disruptive behavior in a classroom. *Journal of Applied Behavior Analysis*, 1969, *2*, 119-124.

Deitz, S.M. An analysis of programming DRL schedules in educational settings. *Behavior Research and Therapy*, 1977, *15*, 103-111.

Deitz, S.M., Hummel, J.H., Sundrup, D.J., and Hughes, L. Combining DRL schedules to reduce transition time in an elementary classroom. Paper presented at the meeting of the Southeastern Psychological Association, Hollywood, Florida, May, 1977.

Deitz, S.M., Hummel, J.H., Sundrup, D.J., Meeks, C.M., and Butler, S.C. The effectiveness of talking to children about the reduction of their misbehavior. Paper presented at the meeting of the American Educational Research Association, New York, April, 1977.

Deitz, S.M., and Repp, A.C. Decreasing classroom misbehavior through the use of DRL schedules of reinforcement. *Journal of Applied Behavior Analysis*, 1973, *6*, 457-463.

Deitz, S.M., and Repp, A.C. Differentially reinforcing low rates with normal elementary school children. *Journal of Applied Behavior Analysis*, 1974, *7*, 622.

Deitz, S.M., Repp, A.C., and Deitz, D.E.D. Reducing inappropriate classroom behavior of retarded students through three procedures of differential reinforcement. *Journal of Mental Deficiency Research*, 1976, *20*, 155-169.

Deitz, S.M., Slack, D.J., Schwarzmueller, E.B., Wilander, A.P., Weatherly, T.J., and Hilliard, G. Reducing inappropriate behavior in special classrooms by reinforcing average interresponse times: Interval DRL. *Behavior Therapy*, 1978, *9*, 37-46.

Ferster, C.B., and Skinner, B.F. *Schedules of Reinforcement.* New York: Appleton-Century-Crofts, 1957.

Harris, V.M., and Sherman, J.A. Use and analysis of the "good behavior game" to reduce disruptive classroom behavior. *Journal of Applied Behavior Analysis*, 1973, *6*, 405-417.

Kramer, I.J., and Rilling, M. The differential reinforcement of low rates: A selective critique. *Psychological Bulletin*, 1970, *74*, 225-254.

Medland, M.B., and Stachnik, T.J. Good behavior game: A replication and systematic analysis. *Journal of Behavior Analysis*, 1972, *5*, 45-51.

Schmidt, G.W., and Ulrich, R.E. Effects of group-contingent events upon classroom noise. *Journal of Applied Behavior Analysis*, 1969, *2*, 171-179.

Sundrup, D.J., and Deitz, S.M. Reducing self-stimulatory behaviors through the application of DRL. Paper presented at the meeting of the Southeastern Psychological Association, Hollywood, Florida, May, 1977.

Wilson, C.W., and Hopkins, B.L. The effects of contingent music on the intensity of noise in a junior high school economics class. *Journal of Applied Behavior Analysis*, 1973, *6*, 269-275.

Unit Eleven

REINFORCING INCOMPATIBLE BEHAVIOR

Study Questions

1. Define DRI and develop an educational example that illustrates the procedure.
2. Explain how DRI works to reduce a misbehavior. What is an incompatible behavior?
3. How did Mr. Burrhus reduce aggressive behavior in his classroom? Explain his procedure in detail.
4. List the advantages and disadvantages of DRI.
5. How does DRI increase appropriate teacher behavior? What type of teacher behavior does it increase?
6. List and explain the factors which influence the effectiveness of DRI. Explain the necessary components of the reinforcement system. When might you need to combine DRI with other behavior reduction procedures?
7. List the steps one should follow to implement DRI.
8. Defend the statement that every teacher should use DRI in the classroom.

Many teachers do not appreciate having to spend much of their time reducing misbehavior. They would prefer having all their time available for establishing or strengthening academic, or appropriate social, behavior. In other words, teachers prefer teaching, not

233

disciplining. Teachers are sure that they quite adequately could oversee the learning segment of their job if only they could avoid the time-consuming tasks of the reduction of problem behavior.

The problems of misbehavior often occur because so many students just do not know very many appropriate ways to interact in classrooms. Therefore, a teacher would approach these problems somewhat differently from what we have advocated for other procedures. Teachers could specify appropriate academic or social behaviors that students need to know and teach those behaviors. If the teacher strengthened (reinforced) these appropriate behaviors, students would be engaged in those behaviors instead of the misbehaviors. The teacher would be teaching, students would be learning, and misbehavior would be reduced.

This Unit explains that process. In this Unit are ways to *replace* misbehavior with appropriate social or academic behavior. This process is really an explanation of teaching; but, here, the teacher must teach specific types of social or academic behavior, rather than just any academic behavior. Approaching the reduction of misbehavior as the process of replacing an inappropriate action with an appropriate action is, in many cases, the most advantageous of the behavior reduction procedures.

Definition and Explanation

The process of replacing a misbehavior with an appropriate behavior is called reinforcing incompatible behavior. Technically, however, it is the differential reinforcement of incompatible behavior, or *DRI*. DRI is defined as a procedure through which reinforcement is delivered for an appropriate target behavior which cannot be done by the student at the same time as a target misbehavior.

The appropriate behavior is labeled, incompatible, because it is one that the student cannot engage in while doing the misbehavior. In other words, the student cannot behave appropriately and misbehave at the same time. Therefore, the appropriate behavior is incompatible with the misbehavior. When attempting to reduce a misbehavior with DRI, the teacher must be certain of that incompatibility.

While this process of replacing a misbehavior with an appropriate behavior is relatively easy to understand, there are aspects of DRI which add some difficulty to the correct implementation of the procedure. First, DRI requires the specification of *two* target behaviors. You must specify the misbehavior you want to reduce, and you must carefully select and specify the appropriate, incompatible behavior. For example, if you want to reduce out-of-seats (the target misbehavior), you might choose to reinforce completed math worksheets (the target incompatible behavior), and require that action to be done while in-seat.

This example points out the potential difficulty in selecting an appropriate, incompatible behavior to reinforce. You must be sure that the two behaviors cannot be done simultaneously. Talk-outs, for example, can be done while the student is working at the desk. Also, you must insure that you are reinforcing an action rather than an inaction. Reinforcing a student for not talking is reinforcing an inaction and, in that case, you would really be using a procedure called DRO (Unit 9). While reinforcing the absence of a misbehavior (DRO) is an excellent procedure, DRI is intended to teach an appropriate behavior, and DRO does not accomplish that task (for a more complete explanation of correctly choosing the incompatible behavior, see the section on "The Effectiveness of DRI" later in this Unit).

The second aspect of DRI which can cause some difficulty in implementing this procedure is that you must measure both target behaviors in order to evaluate the change produced by DRI. From the earlier example, you would have to count both out-of-seats and math worksheets completed. You could also graph each target behavior; but you must graph the misbehavior, since that is your primary goal. While these tasks are not really too difficult, they are quite important for evaluating your effectiveness (see Unit 3).

The last aspect of DRI is that a teacher needs to establish a reinforcement system so that the incompatible behavior is strengthened. This system must be effective to insure that the incompatible behavior is strengthened. By increasing the incompatible behavior, it eventually replaces the misbehavior. The teacher must, therefore, follow the reinforcement rules outlined in Unit 2, and take care that the measurement system assesses the effectiveness of the reinforcer. (This aspect, too, is more fully explained in the "Effectiveness" section of this Unit.)

To illustrate the use of DRI, including coverage of these three important aspects, let's say that Mr. Burrhus, a fifth grade teacher, was troubled by the amount of "aggressive" behavior (defined as hitting, kicking, pushing, or shoving) being emitted by his students. The problem was especially difficult because it seemed that a majority of the students in the class engaged in such behaviors on a fairly regular basis. Mr. Burrhus had previously been involved with several minor behavioral studies. Also, he had a functioning token economy in his classroom (see Unit 6 for a discussion on how to set up a token economy) which could be used to reinforce appropriate behavior. Mr. Burrhus chose to use DRI because he was generally opposed to using aversive procedures to reduce levels of misbehavior.

The target incompatible behaviors selected by Mr. Burrhus for reinforcement were collectively labeled as "appropriate work behavior"; these behaviors required the students to be sitting at their desks and working on academic tasks. Mr. Burrhus chose this class of incompatible behavior for several reasons. First, the students did not have to be taught the behaviors (e.g., they already knew how to sit and work on assignments) and, second, these behaviors were already occurring in the classroom.

Mr. Burrhus' casual observations supported his contention that the aggressive behavior was not limited to specific individuals, or to any certain period of the day. Accordingly, he planned to collect data during the whole class day (excluding recess and lunch). Since he did not have the time to count every instance of the misbehavior, or the incompatible behavior, he decided to use time-sampling (Unit 3). He divided each class hour into 2 minute intervals. At the end of each interval, he noted whether an aggressive misbehavior was occurring. He also noted whether an appropriate work behavior was occurring. Either action by at least one student counted as an occurrence; therefore, he was doing a group project.

Each hour Mr. Burrhus tabulated his results. He divided the number of intervals in which he observed a target misbehavior by the total number of times he observed (usually 30, but sometimes he forgot to check at the end of one or two intervals). After dividing, he multiplied by 100, and obtained the percent of intervals in which aggressive behavior occurred. He made the same calculations for the appropriate, incompatible behavior. Therefore, Mr. Burrhus now had data showing the percent of aggressive behavior per hour and the percent of academic behavior per hour.

Because he was mainly concerned about decreasing aggressive behavior, Mr. Burrhus graphed only the percent of aggressive behavior per hour. He noted the percent of academic behavior in a table, so he could see if it increased when reinforcement began. From seven days of baseline data, Mr. Burrhus saw that aggressive behavior occurred during an average of 11.4% of the intervals. This data confirmed his opinion that too much aggressive behavior was occurring.

On the next class day, Mr. Burrhus began the DRI treatment. During that phase, Mr. Burrhus dispensed tokens to students who, at the end of an interval, were engaged in the appropriate, incompatible academic behaviors. For example, if Mary, Jack, and Susan were sitting at their desks working on math assignments when the interval ended, they received one token. If an aggressive behavior occurred, Mr. Burrhus immediately focused his attention on one of the students who was behaving appropriately. He remarked on what that student was doing ("Bill, I am glad to see that you are working on your assignment."). He also reinforced that student with a token. This tactic not only reinforced Bill's appropriate behavior but also used Bill as a model for the rest of the class. It informed the other students that they, too, could earn attention and reinforcement by engaging in the appropriate, incompatible behaviors.

Under this DRI treatment, aggressive behavior declined to where it was occurring an average of only 9.2% of the intervals. The decline was steady; in the last day of this phase, in fact, the misbehavior occurred in only 6% of the intervals. Mr. Burrhus was not satisfied, however. The decline was too slow and the aggressive misbehavior still occurred too often. To solve these problems, Mr. Burrhus added a response cost (Unit 5) procedure in his third phase. Now, students could still earn points for appropriate behavior, but they would *lose* 2 points each time they engaged in an aggressive act (the response cost). As you can see in Figure 11.1, aggressive behaviors immediately declined to less than 1% of the intervals.

Once that level of misbehavior was achieved, Mr. Burrhus removed the response cost procedure, but maintained the use of DRI. Now, DRI, by itself, was able to keep the aggressive behavior at a very low level.

This study makes some interesting points about DRI. First, while the procedure is effective, it can also be somewhat slow. Second, it is easy to combine DRI with other behavior reduction procedures. Since DRI requires the use of positive reinforcement to establish appropriate behavior, it is important that teachers become familiar with this procedure. As we will see, DRI can be one of a teacher's most useful skills.

Selecting DRI

All teachers should use DRI in the teaching process. This is a very broad endorsement, but once you are familiar with the procedure's advantages and disadvantages, and have had an opportunity to evaluate the factors that influence its effectiveness, it should be clear that DRI constitutes sound teaching practice. DRI is quite advantageous, relatively easy to implement, and contributes toward making classrooms more pleasant, productive environments.

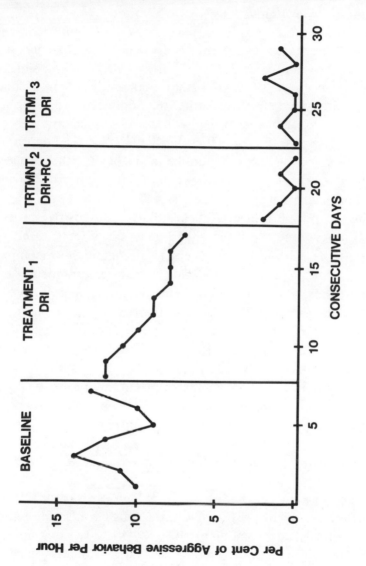

FIGURE 11.1. Mr. Burrhus reduced the aggressive behavior in his classroom. After baseline, DRI was used. Because of the slow decline, he combined response cost with DRI, achieved a satisfactory reduction, then removed the response cost procedure, returning to the use of DRI, by itself, as in Phase 2.

Advantages and Disadvantages

DRI has several advantages, many of which are interrelated. All of these advantages support our endorsement that teachers should use this procedure, above the others, whenever possible. The primary advantage of DRI is that you are teaching a child an appropriate way to behave. Rather than only decreasing misbehavior, you are also increasing a beneficial academic or social behavior. Because you are focusing your efforts on appropriate, incompatible behavior, DRI, unlike many of the other procedures we have discussed, draws the child's attention to appropriate behavior, not misbehavior.

The second advantage of DRI is that it is a positive procedure which does not occasion undesirable side-effects. Since DRI specifies the use of reinforcement to strengthen an incompatible behavior, the problems from using aversive environmental events do not occur. The increase in the incompatible behavior produces the decrease in the misbehavior, so there is no requirement to add aversive events with DRI.

The third advantage of DRI is that its effects are durable. The reasons for this durability are quite evident. You are not just decreasing a misbehavior; you are replacing that misbehavior. The appropriate, incompatible behavior with which you replace the misbehavior cannot be emitted at the same time as the misbehavior. Once a child learns this new way to behave, which earns reinforcement, that child will tend to continue to behave in the new manner.

Fourth, DRI can be easily combined with other behavior reduction procedures. This is advantageous because the reductive effects of DRI are sometimes slow. By initially combining DRI with another procedure, you can more quickly produce a reduction (as Mr. Burrhus did). After the reduction has been achieved, you can remove the second procedure. At that point DRI, alone, will effectively maintain the reduction. However, this process is not always necessary since DRI, in many cases, is useful without combinations.

The last advantage of DRI is not directly related to how well the procedure reduces misbehavior. Rather, it specifies an issue critical to appropriate *teacher* behavior. In Unit 9, we discussed how the omission of behavior is sometimes a problem of students (Sarah does *not* turn in her homework). Teachers, too, sometimes fail to behave appropriately in certain situations. When teachers do not act when they should, these acts of omission may be creating their problems of student misbehavior. As Clarizio (1976) notes:

> How often do you pay attention to: the talkative child when he is quiet, the hyperactive child when he is in his seat, or the irresponsible student when he turns in a good assignment? How often do you phone or jot the parent a note when the disorderly child has had a good day? Do you ever send the child to the office so that the principal can reinforce the student's acceptable behavior? How often do you put the child's name on the board when he is good? (pp. 18-19)

If you are not doing many, or any, of these appropriate teacher actions, your omission of these important behaviors may be one of the most crucial causes for the misbehavior currently occurring in your classroom.

The use of DRI trains teachers (and gives them practice) to pay attention to the "good" behaviors of students rather than the "bad." We mentioned in Unit 1 that reducing misbehavior in young children may prevent more serious misbehaviors from developing. We believe this to be especially true when teachers use DRI. In fact, if parents and teachers used DRI with all children, the other procedures we have discussed would probably never become necessary. As Ayllon and Roberts (1974), who have successfully used this procedure to reduce classroom misbehavior, mentioned, "teach them better and they may sit still" is a better and more pleasant approach than the traditional, "make them sit still so they will learn" (p. 75).

The disadvantages of DRI are not numerous and, in most instances, are not serious. First, DRI, by itself, is similar to extinction (Unit 7) in that it usually takes time to effect a behavioral reduction. Because of this disadvantage, consideration must be given to the type of misbehavior for which DRI is being planned. By itself, DRI is best suited for behaviors on the "usual" end of the continuum discussed in Unit 1. A slow decline could create serious difficulties when attempting to change misbehaviors such as fighting, playing with matches, or stealing. However, in situations where the target misbehavior is serious, you can combine DRI with a second procedure to quickly produce a reduction. Then you can use DRI by itself to maintain the reduction (as Mr. Burrhus did in the earlier example).

The only other disadvantage of DRI is that it is slightly difficult to implement. DRI requires the specification and measurement of two target behaviors. You need to specify and measure the target misbehavior in order to insure that it is decreasing. You need to complete the same tasks for the appropriate, incompatible behavior to be sure it is increasing, as well as to demonstrate that your reinforcer is effective.

Neither disadvantage is critical. You can easily overcome the first by combining DRI with another procedure. The many beneficial advantages of DRI show the small inconvenience of DRI to be of minor concern. Having a procedure such as DRI available should make teachers quite pleased, for they can accomplish many of their classroom objectives as well as reduce misbehavior, simultaneously.

The Effectiveness of DRI

Educators need to be familiar with the factors which influence the effectiveness of DRI in order to correctly implement the procedure. Probably the most important factor to consider is the selection of the incompatible behavior, itself. As mentioned earlier, a target incompatible behavior must be chosen with care. You must be sure that it cannot be done while the student is simultaneously doing the target misbehavior. Additionally, DRI specifies that the child should learn to do something constructive. Therefore, you must be careful that you are reinforcing a behavior emitted by the student and not the absence of the misbehavior (which would be DRO, Unit 9). Finally, the incompatible behavior should be an appropriate behavior which the students already can do. That way, you do not slow the effect of the procedure by having to establish an entirely new behavior.

The second factor influencing the effectiveness of DRI is the reinforcement system. You should try to choose reinforcers (social, activity, consumable, material, or exchangeable) which are powerful and durable (their effectiveness does not diminish over time). Having the students join you in the selection of reinforcers is often quite helpful. Also, you should be sure to follow the four reinforcement rules (Unit 2) when reinforcing the incompatible behavior. Briefly, the four rules are: (a) reinforcement should be *immediate;* (b) reinforcement should be *individual* (since what Jimmy finds reinforcing may be different than what is reinforcing for Sheri); (c) reinforcement should be *consistent*, especially when you are trying to increase a target behavior; and (d) one should *comment on the behavior* being reinforced. Telling children *why* they are receiving reinforcement can clarify a possibly ambiguous situation, and your comments also present a model for other students.

This last rule of reinforcement is similar to the third factor which can influence the effectiveness of DRI. You should inform the students of what you are doing. Explain the target misbehaviors and the target incompatible behaviors. This use of explanations often helps the procedure become effective quickly. The students do not have to "figure out" what you are doing, and you have helped the atmosphere of your classroom by sharing your decisions with your students.

Finally, you may need to combine DRI with other procedures. While that process is not always necessary, such a combination can often result in a quick reduction, rather than a slow one. As we previously mentioned, combining other procedures with DRI is more often necessary with "serious" than "usual" misbehaviors.

From these factors, you can see that careful planning is one essential ingredient for effectively using DRI. You need to plan the choice of the incompatible behavior, the reinforcement system, the communication of the plans to the student, and possibly the combination of DRI with another procedure. Of course, careful implementation of these plans is equally important.

Using DRI

To implement DRI as effectively as possible requires that certain steps be followed. As in the previous Units, the beginning steps are common to all the behavior reduction procedures and were explained in Units 1-3. The remaining steps were discussed in this Unit. Table 11.1 presents the ordered list of steps you should follow to properly use DRI in your classroom.

TABLE 11.1: STEPS TO FOLLOW TO IMPLEMENT DRI

1. Specify and define target misbehavior(s) and incompatible behavior(s).
2. Choose measure for target misbehavior(s) and incompatible behavior(s).
3. Collect baseline data.
4. Choose design to evaluate effectiveness.
5. If target misbehavior is "serious," determine the procedure with which DRI might need to be combined.
6. Select reinforcer(s) for incompatible behavior(s) (student input and use of a token economy is suggested).
7. Explain procedure to student(s).
8. Use models and verbalize what behavior you are reinforcing.
9. Be consistent.
10. Follow design—evaluate data.
11. If not working, modify program (usually reinforcer) or adopt a new procedure.
12. If combination of procedures is used (see 5), phase out additional procedure once target misbehavior is at an acceptable level.
13. Continue.

Conclusions

This Unit has explained the differential reinforcement of incompatible behavior or, as we have referred to it, DRI. DRI specifies that one reinforce appropriate behavior that cannot be emitted at the same time as the target misbehavior. Knowing how to use DRI is important for all teachers because DRI does not draw attention to the misbehavior, teaches the child something appropriate, does not evoke any unfavorable behavioral side-effects, and works well in combination with all other behavior reduction procedures. Additionally, DRI trains the teacher to focus on what the students are doing right rather than what they are doing wrong.

At the risk of being redundant or committing what could be called a type of "overkill," let us stress again the importance of DRI. It is the only procedure in this book which requires teaching an appropriate behavior. For that reason, alone, we recommend its use above all others. Only DRI allows teachers to reduce misbehavior and establish appropriate behavior. While we reluctantly admit that you will probably find several of the other procedures necessary, for certain problems, we hope that you will try DRI first, or at least use DRI in combination with other procedures.

SUGGESTED PROJECTS

1. Choose two misbehaviors (one serious and one usual) to be reduced using DRI. Operationally define each.
2. Select an incompatible behavior for each target misbehavior and operationally define each.
3. Collect baseline data.
   A. For the serious misbehavior, determine which procedure you should combine with DRI.
   B. Explain your programs to the interested student(s).
4. Is the reinforcer you have selected for the incompatible

behavior "strong" enough? How do you know? What can you do to more fully insure that the reinforcer will be strong enough?

5. If the students commented on the programs, were the comments favorable? Did you notice any unfavorable side-effects?

6. Did the combination program effect a reduction faster than the DRI (only) program? If so, explain why you think it did (or did not if that was the case).

REFERENCES

Ayllon, T., and Roberts, M. Eliminating discipline problems by strengthening academic performance. *Journal of Applied Behavior Analysis*, 1974, *1*, 71-76.

Clarizio, H.F. *Towards Positive Classroom Discipline*, 2nd ed. New York: John Wiley and Sons, Inc., 1976.

Section Three

MISBEHAVIOR AND THE
TOTAL CLASSROOM ENVIRONMENT

Unit Twelve

MISBEHAVIOR AND THE
TOTAL CLASSROOM ENVIRONMENT

No matter how serious your problems of misbehavior, it is essential to remember that eliminating those problems should only consume a small portion of your day. Teaching academic skills and appropriate social behavior should be your highest priorities. The procedures presented through this book will allow you to become skillful at behavioral reduction so that you can concentrate on the more pleasant and important tasks of teaching.

Assuming that you have read the Units of this book, there are a few other issues we can now discuss to help make the behavioral reduction task even easier. First, the decision concerning which procedure to select for a particular problem or child can be made according to some specific guidelines. Second, a procedure you select can be tailored to fit your particular teaching style. Third, combining several procedures to solve a particular problem of misbehavior, while not always essential, can increase your effectiveness. Finally, structuring your classroom along some specific dimensions can decrease your chances of encountering misbehavior problems in the first place. Each of these issues is covered to help you make your total classroom environment a pleasant place for children to learn and for you to teach.

Selecting Procedures

Any behavior reduction procedure can be rated by referring to three specific dimensions. When making a selection, you should ask: (1) How *effective* is the procedure? (2) How *ethical* is the procedure? (3) How *efficient* is the procedure? The order of importance of the questions is your first decision. For each problem, you will set your priorities for these three dimensions and choose a procedure which fits your priorities. In the following discussion, we provide some guidelines, but the final decision must be yours.

The *effectiveness* of a procedure can be partly judged by referring to the research on the procedure. We have referenced articles for each procedure, and all procedures have been found effective for the problems with which they have been used. Still, the effectiveness of a procedure *for you* may be a different matter. You must remember to collect data and to evaluate your data. The issues discussed in Unit 3 are essential if you want to insure that what you are doing is effective.

Whether or not a procedure is *ethical* is much more difficult to determine. Ethics usually are concerned with moral issues but can also be considered as issues relating to professional conduct. While there are few clearcut guidelines for deciding if a procedure is ethical, some factors can be examined. First, you can closely examine the disadvantages of a procedure and weigh them against the advantages. Second, you can consider the level of "aversiveness" of a procedure. Will you be using unpleasant environmental events to reduce a misbehavior? How unpleasant are those events? Also, what are the chances of producing undesirable behavioral or emotional side-effects? Third, are there local or national professional sanctions against using a procedure? Fourth, are you being coercive, unnecessarily rude, or unfair by using a procedure? While it is difficult to measure how ethical a procedure is, you must carefully decide on your own personal grounds. One way to make the decision is to ask yourself whether you would want to be treated that way by someone, or whether you would want your own child's teacher to use that particular procedure.

The *efficiency* of a procedure is somewhat easier to determine. Since reducing misbehavior should consume only a small part of your daily activities, the procedures you choose should not detract a great deal of time from your teaching. A procedure which requires one hour per day to properly implement is less efficient than one which requires one-half hour. One way to help judge the efficiency of a procedure is to closely examine the implementation of a procedure, concentrating on the factors which influence its effectiveness. Remember, however, that the more practice you have with a procedure, the more efficient you will become.

But efficiency, effectiveness, and ethics cannot be looked at separately. None of the procedures ranks "Number 1" in all three dimensions. At each decision point you must place priorities on one or two of the dimensions while accepting problems with the other. For example, punishment is easily one of the most effective procedures and also among the most efficient. But it is also probably the least ethical procedure. Maybe the misbehavior is so serious that you must use punishment. Maybe another procedure, such as DRO, could be used instead, since it too has been found effective with serious misbehaviors. DRO would be much more ethical but much less efficient. We wish the decisions were simple but because these three dimensions are so often contradictory, they are not.

To try to help you, we have constructed the following Tables. Table 12.1 ranks each procedure according to each of the three dimensions. Table 12.2 ranks each procedure along the misbehavior continuum presented in Unit 1. We must stress that a great deal of personal opinion, based on our own experience, is incorporated into our rankings. There is no research supporting the order of the procedures in our lists. They can serve only as guides. Each final decision as to the selection of a procedure is yours, and your experience and opinions will, at times, disagree with ours. As long as you are carefully weighing each dimension and know how you are setting your priorities, you will make a defensible selection. As long as you let your data instruct you as to your effectiveness and watch for unexpected side-effects, your decision will be accurate.

Discipline in the Schools

TABLE 12.1: RANK ORDERS
OF PROCEDURES ALONG THREE DIMENSIONS

Ethics	Effectiveness	Efficiency
MOST		MOST
1. DRI	1. Punishment	1. Extinction
2. Full Session DRL	2. Response Cost	2. Punishment
3. Interval DRL	3. Extinction	3. Full Session DRL
4. Spaced Respond- ing DRL	4. Timeout	4. Response Cost
5. DRO	5. Full Session DRL	5. DRI
6. Positive Practice	6. DRI	6. Satiation
7. Extinction	7. DRO	7. Positive Practice
8. Satiation	8. Interval DRL	8. Timeout
9. Overcorrection	9. Spaced Respond- ing DRL	9. Overcorrection
10. Timeout	10. Overcorrection	10. DRO
11. Response Cost	11. Positive Practice	11. Interval DRL
12. Punishment	12. Satiation	12. Spaced Respond- ing DRL
LEAST		LEAST

It is important to remember when reading these tables that being on the bottom of a list does not mean the procedure is totally unethical, ineffective, or inefficient. There are circumstances within particular problems which can change the order entirely. For example, using punishment to stop "headbanging" may be the most ethical decision. Also, when properly used, any procedure can be effective; satiation of paper-throwing may be the most effective procedure for a certain child. Finally, Spaced Responding DRL may work very easily for you when you use it in your own way. You must also remember that the differences among procedures along the three dimensions are usually slight. Never decide on a procedure *only* because we have ranked it number six if you feel more confident than if you used one we ranked five. Studying the various sections of a Unit and knowing your students and your style are better criteria upon which to choose than a small difference in our ranking.

TABLE 12.2: RANK ORDERS OF
PROCEDURES ALONG MISBEHAVIOR CONTINUUM

	Usual	Serious
MOST RECOMMENDED	1. DRI	1. DRO
	2. Full Session DRL	2. Punishment
		3. Response Cost
	3. Extinction	4. Timeout
	4. Interval DRL	5. Overcorrection
	5. DRO	6. DRI
	6. Satiation	7. Interval DRL
	7. Spaced Responding DRL	8. Full Session DRL
	8. Overcorrection	9. Positive Practice
	9. Positive Practice	10. Extinction
	10. Timeout	11. Satiation
	11. Response Cost	12. Spaced Responding DRL
LEAST RECOMMENDED	12. Punishment	

Individualizing Procedures

Like all other aspects of teaching, one excellent way to insure the success of a behavior reduction procedure is to incorporate individualization. When individualizing a misbehavior program, however, we recommend tailoring procedures to the teacher's style as well as to individual children. Your specific planning should include not only choosing a procedure with which you are comfortable but also varying that procedure, if necessary, so that it "fits" your style. Planning also includes a close examination of the misbehaving student so that you pick a procedure you think will be successful for the particular child.

Since all teachers are different, no one procedure is best for every classroom. Some teachers are quite strict, while others are lenient. A strict teacher might always specify the elimination of all types of misbehavior, so any of the DRL procedures would be avoided. The lenient teacher might always rely on DRL but never punish. Most teachers are neither too strict nor too lenient, however, and they should find at least two or three of the procedures that fit them comfortably.

Also, do not hesitate to make variations of the procedures and to experiment. You can try different types of response cost or satiation, try to turn any of the procedures into games like the Good Behavior Game, or work opportunity for academics into your reinforcement programs. Variations you invent might work best for you; you are limited only by your own imagination once you have mastered the basics presented in this book. When you come up with an exciting, useful variation, let us know about it; we will be happy to communicate with any readers whose imagination provides a procedure which we have overlooked or just not considered.

When individualizing, do not forget to consider the specific child or the group of children with whom you are working. Some children respond better to a firm hand, so a procedure such as response cost or timeout might be appropriate. Some children will be better off with reinforcement for improvement (DRL). All children will at times need to learn appropriate social actions to replace their misbehavior, so DRI is useful, at times, with any type child. Try to be fair and considerate. Ask the children which procedures they prefer, what the rules should be, and what they might earn for good behavior. Be sure to include a data collection system to see if their decisions are effective.

When you select procedures that fit both your style and the individual child who is misbehaving, your chances of success are greatest. Invent variations. Include children in decisions. Evaluate your effectiveness. Through these steps you can make reducing misbehavior a normal part of your classroom, one through which children learn to behave appropriately, and one which makes your job as a teacher a little bit easier.

Combining Procedures

We have mentioned in each of the Units on the procedures that you might be more successful by combining several procedures into one behavior reduction program. This is usually quite true but let us stress that any of the procedures, if correctly selected and properly implemented, can work very effectively alone. Each procedure has been demonstrated to reduce misbehavior without combining it with any other procedures. In fact, you will probably increase the efficiency dimension by using procedures by themselves.

Still, we have recommended the combination of procedures for two reasons. First, as has already been mentioned, you can increase the effectiveness of your program. Second, if you select an aversive procedure, we believe your overall classroom environment will be more beneficial for the students if you combine it with one of the reinforcement procedures. In a sense, we recommend the possible loss of efficiency because it will result in an increase in the ethical dimension as well as a probable increase in effectiveness.

Most combinations, by necessity, require using an aversive procedure with a nonaversive one. When using DRO or any of the types of DRL, it is easy to add punishment, response cost, timeout, overcorrection, positive practice, or satiation. You couldn't combine DRO and DRL because of their different requirements for the consequences of a misbehavior. The exceptions to most of the above are extinction and DRI. You can always try to stop the critical reinforcer for the misbehavior. Thus, you can combine extinction with any procedure *if* you can identify and control the reinforcer. DRI can be used with all the other procedures because it teaches a new, appropriate behavior to replace the misbehavior. You can use any procedure to reduce the misbehavior while you are also trying to teach the new behavior.

Since combinations of reduction procedures are usually more effective, can be arranged to be more ethical, but are usually less efficient, we recommend their use. Any time you have selected an aversive procedure, one which is low on the ethical dimension, you should always combine it with a nonaversive procedure, one high on the ethical dimension. If you have chosen a nonaversive procedure, especially DRO, DRL, or DRI, we recommend you combine it with other procedures only when it is not effective by itself. Again, by using the important dimensions of ethical, effective, and efficient, you can make decisions about combinations in much the same way you make decisions about initial selection.

Teaching: The Rest of the Day

While this book does not directly cover issues concerned with aspects of a teacher's job beyond the elimination of misbehavior, we would like to conclude by commenting on a few of those aspects. There are some concepts presented in this book which suggest excellent ways for teachers to approach several of these other tasks of teaching. Specifically, the acquisition of academic behavior can be enhanced by referring to many of the variables discussed in the early Units of this book.

Teaching academic behavior requires, among other things, thorough preparation, careful assessment, and individualized feedback. Each of these areas has been discussed in terms of misbehavior but much of what was discussed also relates to academic behavior. While insufficient space is available to demonstrate these similarities in much depth, we would like to briefly cover some of the more important ones.

One important aspect of teaching is thorough preparation. Much of that can be accomplished through what we have called specification. When you write instructional objectives for academic skills, you usually include a specific "terminal behavior." A terminal behavior is a target behavior. A target behavior could as easily be "reading" as "talk-outs." If you approach your preparation of teaching academic behavior in the same ways Unit 1 presented an approach to misbehavior, you have the advantage of having specified the exact behaviors you want the child to acquire. You know where you're going and the student knows where he or she should be going. Dealing with specific, definable, academic target behaviors helps you structure your teaching time to insure that all students reach the mastery of important skills.

Excellent instruction also requires the careful assessment of acquired skills. Unit 3 presented an approach to assessment that is quite useful to the teacher. Once you have a specified academic target behavior, regularly measuring it is quite important. Counting academic behavior (frequency, rate, percentage correct) allows you to carefully assess whether or not skills are being acquired. *Frequent* assessment allows you to quickly identify small problems for remediation. Using a single-subject research design (for academics usually a Multiple baseline design) allows you to assess the effectiveness of your teaching procedures. The incorporation of those concepts presented in Unit 3 into your academic repertoire can greatly enhance your ability to help children learn their skills.

Probably the most important principles which can improve your teaching were presented in Unit 2. These reinforcement principles present methods for individualizing the types of feedback you give your students. Since reinforcement strengthens behavior, it should be obvious that its use is essential to the classroom. No goal should be more important to a teacher than strengthening a child's academic behavior.

Using positive reinforcement for academic behavior requires some effort. The four rules must be followed—immediate, consistent, individual, and comment on the action you are reinforcing. Since academic behavior is acquired in small steps over a period of time, the reinforcement must also be frequent. Frequent reinforcement not only strengthens academics, it also makes the classroom a happier, more pleasant place for children. Social, activity, consumable, material, or exchangeable reinforcers, when correctly used in the classroom, make learning easier and more fun. Being reinforced for math behavior, for example, increases competence but also makes math more enjoyable. Try reinforcing more often than you already do; practice applying it correctly; try to reinforce ten times for each critical comment you make. The payoff for you and your students will be well worth the effort.

It would be wonderful if schools were full of busy, happy children, who were mastering the academic subjects and learning appropriate, productive social skills. While no instructional system can promise that result for all children, the principles of applied behavior analysis, when systematically applied to all aspects of the classroom, can go a long way. Individualized instruction, as much positive reinforcement as possible, preparation for success, systematic and frequent assessment, remediation—all of these factors will improve schools and might just make this book obsolete.

GLOSSARY

ACCIDENTAL CONSEQUENCE: A consequence which occurs after a behavior which was neither planned nor a normal result of the behavior.

ADVENTITIOUS REINFORCEMENT: The accidental delivery of positive reinforcement that still increases the future probability of the behavior.

APPLIED BEHAVIOR ANALYSIS: That branch of psychology which views behavior as a function of past and present, external, environmental events.

ARBITRARY COSTS: Costs or consequences that are not logically related to a behavior. For example, requiring a child to do 50 pushups for cursing is classified as an arbitrary cost since there is no relationship between the behavior and the cost (see Logical Costs).

AVERSIVE (EVENTS): Either unpleasant environmental events or behavioral procedures which can produce undesirable behavioral side-effects (Units 4-8).

AVOIDANCE BEHAVIOR: Behavior that prevents an individual from coming in contact with aversive environmental events.

BACK-UP REINFORCERS: Items or events for which students can exchange tokens. Generally, the cost (in tokens) for each back-up reinforcer is specified in a "reinforcement menu."

BASELINE: Behavioral data that shows the level of behavior before any procedure is systematically applied. Also called operant level.

BEHAVIOR: Any action by an organism that is measurable and observable. A response.

BEHAVIORAL CONTRAST: Occurs when a misbehavior being reduced in one setting increases in another setting where the misbehavior is not being reduced.

BEHAVIORAL INFLEXIBILITY: The inability to emit a behavior in an appropriate setting because the behavior was reduced or eliminated in a different setting.

CONDITIONED REINFORCER: See Secondary Reinforcer.

CONSEQUENCES: Environmental events which occur after a behavior.

CONTINGENCY: An "if-then" relationship between a behavior and its environmental consequence (if the behavior occurs, then the consequence follows).

CONTINGENCY ANALYSIS: The process used to identify the reinforcers that are maintaining a behavior. The process involves observing and recording what events occur immediately after the target behavior.

CONTINGENT OBSERVATION: This variation of timeout specifies that the misbehaver not be allowed to participate in an activity for a specified amount of time (opposed to having no access to the reinforcing situation at all as in timeout).

CONTINUOUS REINFORCEMENT SCHEDULE (CRF): The schedule of reinforcement which specifies that every instance of the target behavior is reinforced.

DIFFERENTIAL REINFORCEMENT OF INCOMPATIBLE BEHAVIOR (DRI): Reinforcement is delivered contingent on the emission of an appropriate target behavior that cannot be emitted at the same time as the target misbehavior.

DIFFERENTIAL REINFORCEMENT OF LOW RATES (DRL): Reinforcing misbehavior if it occurs at or below a specified level. See Interval DRL, Spaced Responding DRL, and Full Session DRL.

DIFFERENTIAL REINFORCEMENT OF OTHER BEHAVIOR (DRO): Specifies that positive reinforcement be delivered at the end of a preset time interval if the target misbehavior has not occurred during the interval. If the target misbehavior does occur, the interval is reset and reinforcement is delayed.

DISCRETE: In behavioral terms, a behavior is discrete when there is a clear beginning and end to each episode of the behavior.

DURATION: Duration recording involves timing how long a behavioral episode lasts.

ENVIRONMENTAL EVENTS: External events which occur in the environment and affect behavior.

ESCAPE BEHAVIOR: Behavior that removes an individual from contact with aversive environmental events.

EVALUATION: The process which enables one to determine if changes in the level of a behavior are due to planned manipulations or to chance.

EXTINCTION: The process of no longer reinforcing a previously reinforced behavior.

FREQUENCY: A recording procedure through which you count the number of discrete episodes of a behavior.

FULL SESSION DRL: Reinforcement is delivered at the end of a session (class period, day, etc.) if the target behavior occurs at or below a prespecified minimum.

FUNCTIONAL DEFINITION: A definition, usually of a process, that indicates the direction of change that a consequence has on behavior (increases or decreases the probability of the behavior reoccurring).

GOOD BEHAVIOR GAME: A variation of Full Session DRL used with the misbehavior of two or more groups. At the end of the session, the group with fewer number of target behaviors receives reinforcement. If all groups stay at or below a prespecified minimum, all earn reinforcement.

GRAPH: A pictorial representation of data. Typically, the vertical axis reflects the frequency, rate, or duration of a behavior and the horizontal axis represents the particular observation session.

INTERMITTENT SCHEDULE OF REINFORCEMENT: Any schedule of reinforcement in which some, but not all, instances of a target behavior are reinforced.

INTERVAL DRL: Reinforcement is delivered at the end of a pre-set interval if one or no target behaviors occur during that interval.

LOGICAL COSTS: A cost or consequence of a behavior that rationally relates to the behavior. For example, the athlete that refuses to attend practice is not permitted to play in the game (see Arbitrary Costs).

MEASUREMENT: The process of determining the level (frequency, rate, duration) of behavior which is occurring at any given time.

MULTIPLE BASELINE DESIGN: An experimental design that evaluates the effectiveness of a treatment across (a) subject, (b) behaviors, or (c) settings.

NEGATIVE REINFORCEMENT: The removal of an environmental event, contingent on a behavior occurring, that increases the probability of the behavior reoccurring.

OBSERVATIONAL RECORDING: Ways of empirically measuring the level of a behavior by observing the behavior while it is occurring. Includes frequency, rate, duration, and time-sampling.

OPERANT LEVEL: See Baseline.

OPERATIONAL DEFINITION: Defining or specifying the characteristics of a target behavior in terms that are measurable and observable.

OVERCORRECTION: See Restitutional Overcorrection.

POSITIVE PRACTICE: A variation of mild punishment that requires the misbehaver to repeatedly practice an appropriate behavior that is relevant to the misbehavior.

PREMACK PRINCIPLE: Increasing a low frequency behavior by making access to a high frequency behavior contingent upon the emission of the lower frequency behavior.

PRIMARY REINFORCERS: Environmental events that satisfy physiological needs.

PUNISHMENT: The presentation of an environmental event, contingent on a behavior, that decreases the probability of the behavior reoccurring.

RATE: Rate is the frequency of a behavior divided by the length of the observation period.

REINFORCEMENT: A behavioral process that indicates that a behavior has been strengthened in that the probability of its occurrence in the future has been increased.

REINFORCEMENT RESERVE: Generally, it is a build-up or "cushion" of positive reinforcers that helps to insure that students are successful. Such reserves are frequently associated with token economies and response cost contingencies.

REINFORCING INCOMPATIBLE BEHAVIOR: See Differential Reinforcement of Incompatible Behavior.

REINFORCING LOW RATES: See Differential Reinforcement of Low Rates.

REINFORCING OTHER BEHAVIOR: See Differential Reinforcement of Other Behavior.

RESPONSE: A synonym for behavior.

RESPONSE COST: The removal of specified amounts of positive reinforcers contingent on a behavior.

RESTITUTIONAL OVERCORRECTION: A variation of mild punishment that requires the misbehaver to restore the environment to a condition that is better than it was before the misbehavior occurred (e.g., the misbehaver must *over*correct any effect the misbehavior had on the environment).

REVERSAL DESIGN: The reversal or ABAB design requires one to systematically collect data during the baseline ("A") phases and during the treatment ("B") phases. Such a system enables one to determine the level of a behavior before, during, and after a treatment; one can then evaluate whether the treatment was responsible for behavior changes that occurred during the "B" phases.

REVERSE PREMACK PRINCIPLE: A procedure requiring one to emit a low probability behavior (often repeatedly) contingent on the emission of a high probability behavior (a misbehavior).

SATIATION: The process through which a target behavior is decreased by presenting an oversupply of the reinforcer(s) that maintains the target behavior. (If the behavior itself is the reinforcer, satiation would require the misbehaver to repeatedly emit the misbehavior.)

SCHEDULE OF REINFORCEMENT: These are specifications relating to which instances of a behavior are likely to be reinforced (see Continuous Reinforcement Schedule and Intermittent Reinforcement).

SECONDARY REINFORCERS: Environmental events that increase the probability of a behavior reoccurring when presented contingently. Secondary reinforcers are learned or conditioned reinforcers. They acquire their reinforcing properties by being paired with either primary reinforcers or other, very powerful, secondary reinforcers (like money). There are five types of secondary reinforcers: social, activity, material, consumable, and exchangeable.

SPACED RESPONDING DRL: A target behavior is reinforced if a minimum amount of time has elapsed since the last occurrence of the target behavior.

SUPERSTITIOUS BEHAVIOR: Behavior that is learned or strengthened through accidental consequences (usually via adventitious reinforcement).

SYSTEMATIC EXCLUSION: A variation of timeout that involves sending the misbehaver home for the remainder of the school day contingent on a misbehavior.

TARGET BEHAVIOR: The exact behavior you will work with during a behavior analysis project. It should be operationally defined so it is observable and measurable.

TOKEN ECONOMY: A reinforcement system that is similar to a monetary system. Students are able to earn tokens (which are exchangeable for back-up reinforcers) for doing certain appropriate behaviors and can lose (usually under a response cost contingency) tokens for doing certain targeted misbehavior.

TIMEOUT: Technically known as "timeout from positive reinforcement," timeout is the contingent removal from access to all positive reinforcers for a specified period of time.

TIME-SAMPLING: A method of recording behavior where the observational period is divided into equal-length intervals. At the end of each interval, it is noted whether the behavior is occurring or not.

INDEX